Using

MICROSOFT®

PowerPoint® 97

Contents at a Glance

Table of Contents

III | Adding Visual Elements to the Presentation

VI | Advanced PowerPoint Topics

Appendixes

Credits

PRESIDENT
Roland Elgey

SENIOR VICE PRESIDENT/PUBLISHING
Don Fowley

PUBLISHER
Joseph B. Wikert

PUBLISHING DIRECTOR
Karen Reinisch

MANAGER OF PUBLISHING OPERATIONS
Linda H. Buehler

GENERAL MANAGER
Joe Muldoon

DIRECTOR OF EDITORIAL SERVICES
Carla Hall

MANAGING EDITOR
Thomas F. Hayes

DIRECTOR OF ACQUISITIONS
Cheryl D. Willoughby

ACQUISITIONS EDITOR
Lisa Swayne

SENIOR PRODUCT DIRECTOR
Lisa D. Wagner

PRODUCT DIRECTOR
John Gosney

PRODUCTION EDITOR
Julie A. McNamee

EDITORS
Geneil Breeze
Gina Brown
Thomas Hayes
Jean Jameson
Kathy Simpson

PRODUCT MARKETING MANAGER
Kourtnaye Sturgeon

ASSISTANT PRODUCT MARKETING MANAGER
Gretchen Schlesinger

TECHNICAL EDITOR
Coletta Witherspoon

MEDIA DEVELOPMENT SPECIALIST
David Garratt

ACQUISITIONS COORDINATOR
Michelle Newcomb

SOFTWARE RELATIONS COORDINATOR
Susan D. Gallagher

EDITORIAL ASSISTANT
Virginia Stoller

BOOK DESIGNERS
Ruth Harvey
Kim Scott

COVER DESIGNER
Sandra Schroeder

PRODUCTION TEAM
Maribeth Echard
Julie Geeting
Laura A. Knox
Staci Somers

INDEXER
Tim Tate

Composed in *Century Old Style* and *ITC Franklin Gothic* by Que Corporation.

Acknowledgments

To the comic book industry, which is reaching new creative heights at the same time that it's suffering badly financially. Do yourself a favor and stop by a good comic book store! You'll find comics for kids, comics for adults, and even comics for the little kid that dwells within the adult. For people who are designing presentations, comics make an excellent example of visual communication of information. There's more to comics than you think!

About the Authors

In addition to writing seven previous Que books, from *Computers Illustrated* to *The Complete Idiot's Guide to PowerPoint 97*, **Nat Gertler** has worked as a software programmer, program tester, trainer, support technician, and Web-site designer. He's also written many comic books—including Adventures of The Flintstones, Speed Racer, and Power Rangers—as well as original concepts such as "The Factor" (in *Negative Burn*) and "Mister U.S." (in *Big Bang Comics*). Other writing credits include a column in *Hogan's Alley* magazine, prose fiction for books and magazines, nonfiction articles, one TV episode, and several crossword puzzles. For more information on Nat, check out **http://www.gertler.com** on the World Wide Web.

Nancy Stevenson is a freelance writer, teacher and consultant. Her most recently completed book, *Using Word for Windows*, was published by Que in the spring of 1995. Ms. Stevenson teaches technical writing at Purdue University in Indianapolis. Prior to going freelance, she was a Publishing Manager at Que, and before that worked as a trainer, consultant, and product manager at Symantec Corporation in California.

Brian Reilly is a partner in Singer and Reilly Enterprise in New York City, which is a company that designs custom applications in corporate communication management. His background in consumer products management has convinced him of the need to be able to suppress unwanted information and graphically show only actionable information with instantly understandable graphics. Brian holds a B.A. in Communications from Fordham University, and an M.B.A. from Columbia University. An avid sailor in the Northeastern waters, he appreciates the difference between a datasheet and a spinnaker sheet. Brian can be reached on CompuServe at **75663,3456**.

We'd Like to Hear from You!

Que Corporation has a long-standing reputation for high-quality books and products. To ensure your continued satisfaction, we also understand the importance of customer service and support.

Tech Support

If you need assistance with the information in this book or with a CD/disk accompanying the book, please access Macmillan Computer Publishing's online Knowledge Base at **http://www.superlibrary.com/general/support**. If you do not find the answer to your questions on our Web site, you may contact Macmillan Technical Support by phone at **317/581-3833** or via e-mail at **support@mcp.com**.

Also be sure to visit Que's Web resource center for all the latest information, enhancements, errata, downloads, and more. It's located at **http://www.quecorp.com/**.

Orders, Catalogs, and Customer Service

To order other Que or Macmillan Computer Publishing books, catalogs, or products, please contact our Customer Service Department at **800/428-5331** or fax us at **800/835-3202** (International Fax: 317/228-4400). Or visit our online bookstore at **http://www.mcp.com/**.

Comments and Suggestions

We want you to let us know what you like or dislike most about this book or other Que products. Your comments will help us to continue publishing the best books available on computer topics in today's market.

John Gosney
Product Director
Que Corporation
201 West 103rd Street, 4B
Indianapolis, Indiana 46290 USA
Fax: 317/581-4663 E-mail: *jgosney@que.mcp.com*

Please be sure to include the book's title and author as well as your name and phone or fax number. We will carefully review your comments and share them with the author. Please note that due to the high volume of mail we receive, we may not be able to reply to every message.

Thank you for choosing Que!

Welcome to *Using Microsoft PowerPoint 97*

Using *Microsoft PowerPoint 97* is your guide to making the most of Microsoft PowerPoint. This book is specifically designed around the revision known as PowerPoint 97, which works under Microsoft Windows 95 and Windows NT operating systems. This book is designed to be used either as a tutorial or as a reference, so that you can learn to use all of PowerPoint's features quickly, or you can look up how to use individual features as you need them. ■

Who This Book Is For

This book is intended for intermediate computer users. You don't have to be a computer expert to understand anything you'll find in this book. If you're already comfortable using any other Windows program—a word processor, a spreadsheet, a Web browser, or anything else—you should have no trouble understanding this book.

What This Book Will Do for You

This book teaches you to use Microsoft's PowerPoint 97 presentation software program. By the time you've worked your way through this book, you'll be able to create printed presentations with graphs, charts, and text. You'll be able to create slides for projecting with slide projectors. You'll know everything that you need to make presentations filled with moving pictures and sound, and you'll be able to show those presentations to a group of people by using a projecting computer display. You'll be able to deliver interactive presentations that people can interact with on their own computers and to put your presentations on the Web, where anyone can see them.

How This Book Is Organized

This book is designed so that you don't have to sit down and read the entire thing. You can read the early portions and get a basic understanding of how PowerPoint works and what its basic functions are. Then, when you need to use a specific feature of PowerPoint, you can just read that portion. If, for example, you never need to use numerical graphs, you don't need to read the chapter on that topic. You won't have any problems understanding later portions because you didn't read that chapter.

The book is organized in six major parts, each made up of several chapters:

■ Part I, "Getting Started with PowerPoint 97," gives you all the tools you need to get up and running with PowerPoint. You learn to start the program, work the buttons and menus, and create a simple presentation. You learn to create new parts of your presentation, which are called *slides* (whether you're working with slides, a printed presentation, or an on-screen presentation). Adding text and pictures to a slide and then formatting them are also covered in this part. In short, this part contains the information that you most need to know. You should absolutely read these ten chapters of the book completely.

■ Part II, "Emphasizing Your Points with Organization Charts, Tables, and Graphs," deals (unsurprisingly) with organization charts, tables, and graphs. Chapter 11, "Adding Organization Charts," teaches you how to create organizational charts that show who works for whom in a company or department. Chapter 12, "Creating and Customizing Charts and Graphs," explains how to use the wide range of graphs that PowerPoint can create, including pie charts, bar graphs, and line graphs. Chapter 13, "Working with Tables," focuses on *tables*, which are spreadsheet-like grids of words and numbers. You don't have to read any of these chapters until the first time you use the feature that that chapter covers.

■ Part III, "Adding Visual Elements to the Presentation," covers how to give your presentation a strong appearance. Chapter 14, "Creating and Editing PowerPoint Templates," tells you how to create a look that runs throughout your entire presentation by using design templates, choosing fonts and designs for your presentation. Chapter 15, "Drawing Graphic Objects," tells you how to add lines, shapes, and fancy logos to your presentation. Chapter 16, "Inserting Predesigned Artwork," shows you how to use artwork that Microsoft provides for you. Again, these chapters are read-'em-as-you-need-'em chapters, although you should consider skimming them to get a sense of what PowerPoint can do.

■ Part IV, "Using the Internet," is designed specifically for presentations that are to be shown on the screen of your computer. You learn to add moving pictures, animation, and sounds to your presentations. You even see how your presentation can use music right from audio CDs. If your presentations are just going to be printed, put on overhead transparencies, or put on projection slides, however, you won't be able to use these interactive and multimedia features. If you're showing the presentation over a network, you can use only a few of these features.

■ Part V, "Delivering the Slide Show," shows you many ways of showing your finished presentation. Chapter 19, "Playing to a Live Audience," covers showing the presentation to an audience that is in the room with you. The chapter also covers sending the slide show to people on disk or via e-mail, as well as leaving the presentation running on a kiosk, allowing people to stop by and look at it without your help. Chapter 20, "Collaborating via a Local Network, Intranet, or the Internet," shows you how to run a slide show over a local area network or over the Internet, so that people in other parts of your organization can watch the presentation, mark it up, and comment on it while you're displaying it. Chapter 21, "Putting Your Slide Show on the Internet," tells you how to publish your presentation on the Internet so that anyone can look at it whenever they want.

■ Part VI, "Advanced PowerPoint Topics," can turn you into a real PowerPoint power user. Don't even try reading this part until you've grown comfortable with PowerPoint, unless you're already comfortable with other Microsoft Office programs. This part covers how to customize PowerPoint (Chapter 22, "Customizing PowerPoint"), how to get PowerPoint working with Microsoft Word, Excel, and other programs (Chapter 23, "Integrating PowerPoint with Other Programs"), and using macros to add custom commands and special features to PowerPoint (Chapter 24, "Automating Your Work with Macros"). Finally, Chapter 25, "Building Your Own Custom Presentation," shows you how to put together all that you've learned.

This book also has both a table of contents and an index to help you find the topic that you're looking for and an appendix on how to install PowerPoint. You'll also find an appendix listing valuable resources and a glossary.

Conventions Used in This Book

Anything that you're supposed to type appears in bold. For example "Type the Heading, First Quarter at the Top."

You may hold down any of three keys on the keyboard while pressing another key. These keys are marked Alt, Shift, and Ctrl. If you need to hold down one of these keys while pressing another key, you'll see the name of the key to hold down, followed by the plus sign and then by the name of the key to press. Ctrl+B, for example, means to hold down the Ctrl key and press the B key.

Any text that you read from the computer screen or typing appears like this. Any new words that are being defined appear in *italic,* with the definition appearing in that sentence or the next.

If you see the name of a button or menu item, and one of the letters is underlined, you can choose that item by holding down the Alt key and pressing that letter. You can choose the Delete Picture button, for example, by pressing Alt+E.

For commands to be chosen from the menu, the menu name and command are listed together, separated by a comma. If the book says "Choose File, Send To, Mail Recipient," for example, you should pull down the File menu, choose the Send To submenu, and choose the Mail Recipient command from that menu.

When the book says to *click* something, it means to move the mouse until the mouse pointer points to that item and then press the left mouse button. (If your mouse is set up for left-handed use, you press the right mouse button instead.) To *double-click* something, point to it and then press the mouse button twice, rapidly. To *right-click* something, point to it and then click the right mouse button (unless you have a left-handed mouse, in which case you click the left button).

To *drag* something, point to it; hold down the left mouse button (the right button, for lefties); and, with the button held down, move the mouse pointer (and the item, which follows) to where you want it. Then release the mouse button.

 Some places in the book you'll see a tip, note, or caution separated from the main text. Tips and notes provide additional information and shortcuts that can make your life easier.

What's New in PowerPoint 97

If you've used earlier versions of PowerPoint, you have a good sense of what the new version does and how to work with it. Many new features and enhancements have been added to this new version, however, so a lot of stuff is worth learning. Some of the new features and capabilities in PowerPoint 97 include:

- *Interactively link your presentation with Web addresses,* allowing viewers to see Web sites by clicking something in your presentation.

- *The ability to save your presentation in HTML format for publishing on the Web.* You can also embed a presentation in a Web page in such a way that anyone who has the proper viewing software can see your presentation over the Web.

- *Run a simultaneous conference with many people* over your local area network, an intranet, or the Internet.

- *Set up idiot-proof kiosk presentations,* so that people can view your presentations with no risk that they will mess up your computer.

- *Record a narration track to go with your slide show,* so that people can hear you give your presentation even when you're not available.

- *Use greatly improved drawing tools* called Office Art that are part of all the Microsoft Office programs, allowing you to build fancy shapes and logos with 3-D effects to enhance your presentation, and to reuse those items in Excel and Word.

- *Make better graphs* with a wider array of graphs and graphing features in the new Graph 97 module, including the ability to animate graphs.

- *Define and arrange animations on your slide more easily* with new animation commands.

- *Play movies directly from within PowerPoint,* allowing better control.

- *Save PowerPoint slides as JPEG or GIF graphics,* in addition to other formats.

- *Organize your sounds, pictures, and movies* using the Clip Gallery to make what you're looking for easy to find.

- *Control your PowerPoint show from one computer while another displays the show.* Doing this allows you to see the controls without showing them to your audience.

- *Create a list of who is to do what after the meeting.* You can now have a Meeting Minder dialog box open while you're running the presentation. Meeting Minder can send those items to Microsoft Outlook to help you arrange the schedule.

- *Use ActiveX controls,* which allow your presentation to have advanced interactive features.

- *Turn an overcrowded slide into a series of slides quickly,* using the expand slide feature.

- *See spelling errors instantly.* Spelling is checked as you type, so you can fix errors immediately.

- *Undo several steps with one command,* to correct a mistake quickly.

Getting Started with PowerPoint 97

Getting Familiar with PowerPoint 97

Before trying to actually make a presentation, it's time to get to know the program, what it does, and how to work its controls. Most of what is covered in this chapter is standard for all Microsoft Office 97 programs (including Word and Excel), and much of it is standard for most Windows 95 programs. As such, much of this material may seem familiar. Nonetheless, you should read through this chapter to make sure we're using the same terminology you're used to. ■

Learn about PowerPoint

Find out exactly what this feature-rich program can do for you, and become familiar with some of the standard PowerPoint terminology being used in this book.

Start and exit PowerPoint

Start PowerPoint from the Windows 95 Start menu, and exit it when you're done.

Use the PowerPoint interface

Work with menus, buttons, scroll bars, dialog boxes, and other standard Windows 95 features used by PowerPoint.

Asking PowerPoint for help

Use PowerPoint's powerful built-in help features to help you figure out how to get the program to do what you want it to do.

Go to PowerPoint Central

Read Microsoft's regularly updated, computer-based magazine about PowerPoint for helpful ideas, new tips, and free art and sounds to use in your presentations.

What Is PowerPoint?

PowerPoint is a *presentation software* application. That means it is designed to help you convey information to others. PowerPoint can help you create the following types of presentations:

- Printed versions of your information
- Transparencies and slides, for projecting your information on a screen where an audience can see it
- Computer screen presentations that you can show to others or send to them via disk or e-mail
- Presentations to run on a kiosk, an unattended, tamper-proof display
- Network presentations, where you can share and discuss your presentation with people over a computer network
- Web sites, so that anyone connected to the World Wide Web can see what you have to say

PowerPoint lets you combine text, pictures, charts, graphs, sounds, and movies as part of your presentation. Of course, some of these features are available only on certain types of presentations; it's impossible to put sound into a printed handout or a movie onto an overhead transparency. PowerPoint also makes it easy to take one presentation and deliver it to different audiences in several formats.

A PowerPoint presentation is made up of *slides*, which is PowerPoint's term for a single display of information. A slide can be one slide-projector slide, one printed page, one overhead, one Web page, or one screen of information on a computer display. The presentation is a series of slides, which is why the presentation is sometimes called a *slide show*.

PowerPoint is most frequently purchased as part of Microsoft Office, a software suite whose full version includes Word (a word processor), Excel (a spreadsheet), Access (a database), Outlook (a scheduling program), and Bookshelf Basics (reference works). PowerPoint is designed to work closely with these programs, so it's easy to move text from a Word document onto your slideshow or to take a graph from Excel to illustrate your slide.

Starting and Exiting PowerPoint

To start PowerPoint from the Windows taskbar, click the Start button and select Programs, Microsoft PowerPoint. PowerPoint will appear on your screen.

 TIP If you want to edit a slide show you've recently saved, click the Windows Start button, select Documents, and choose the name of the file from the list that appears. This will start PowerPoint and automatically open the selected file.

If this is the first time that PowerPoint 97 has been run on this machine, an animated character will appear on the screen with a list of tasks he can do for you. If this happens, click Start Using PowerPoint on this list, and the list will leave the screen.

As seen in Figure 1.1, PowerPoint displays a dialog box to get additional information from you. You'll learn more about dialog boxes shortly; just click Cancel to remove the dialog box from your screen.

Once the dialog box is removed, you're left with the main PowerPoint window. At the top is the *title bar*, which will say Microsoft PowerPoint at the left. At the far right of this bar is the *Close button*, which has an X in it. Click the Close button to exit PowerPoint. (If you've been working on a presentation and haven't saved your changes, PowerPoint will offer you a chance to save those changes before exiting the program.)

FIG. 1.1

The PowerPoint window has standard elements at the top and bottom, with the center used as a work area.

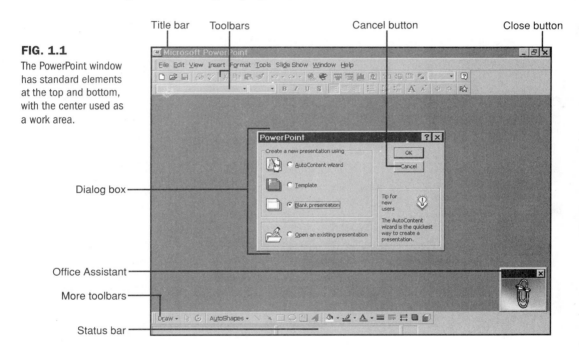

Working with Toolbars, the Status Bar, and Scroll Bars

Looking across the top of the PowerPoint screen, you'll see rows of little pictures. These rows are *toolbars*, groups of buttons with a related function. It's hard to see where one button ends and the next begins, but if you move the mouse pointer to a button, the edges of the button will appear. If you rest the pointer on a button, a description of what the button does (called a *ScreenTip*) will appear. To use a button, just click it. Some buttons will appear pressed-in while you're using their function; if you want to stop using their function, click the button again.

Some toolbars have white fields that contain text and a small down arrow at the end of the field. These fields are called drop-down lists. Click the down arrow, and a list will appear. You can select the value for that field from the list.

At the bottom of the window, below some other toolbars, is the *status bar*. The status bar gives you information about what you're currently looking at in the window; exactly what information it shows depends on what you're looking at. For example, if you're looking at one slide in a presentation, the status bar will show you how many slides are in the presentation, and which number slide this is.

When PowerPoint has something large to show you and only a small workspace to show it in, it will display *scroll bars*. Scroll bars allow you to select what portion of the larger item you are viewing. If the item is too wide for the workspace, a horizontal scroll bar (see Figure 1.2) will appear at the bottom of the workspace. The scroll box within the scroll bar shows you what horizontal portion (left, right, middle) of the item you are looking at. You can click the arrow at the left to see a portion more to the left or the arrow at the right to see more of the display to the right. To move quickly to a specific position on the item, just drag the scroll box to the appropriate place in the scroll bar.

FIG. 1.2

The width of this horizontal scroll bar represents the whole document, while the width of the scroll box in the bar represents the material currently displayed.

Similarly, if the item is too tall for the space, a vertical scroll bar will appear at the right of the work space. Use the up-arrow or the down-arrow button, or drag the scroll box, to navigate.

TIP The wheel on the Microsoft IntelliMouse can be used to move up and down through most displays that have a vertical scroll bar.

Using Menus and Dialog Boxes

Between the title bar and the toolbars is the *menu bar*, which contains such words as File, Edit, View, Insert, and so forth. Each word is the name for a list of commands, called a *menu*. Click one of these names, and the list will appear under it. Click a command name to execute that command.

If there's a right arrow at the end of the command name, this means that this command contains another level of menu items. Click the command to display the submenu. You can then select the desired command from the sub-menu.

If a command name is followed by . . . (an *ellipsis*), you need to provide more information before the program can execute the command. Selecting one of these commands will cause a dialog box to appear.

There are two types of shortcuts related to menus. Each menu name and command has a single letter underlined in it. Hold down the Alt key and press the underlined key, and it will work the same as clicking that name or command. For example, to select the Edit menu and to pick the Cut command from it, press Alt and press E and then T.

Additionally, some menu commands have a key combination displayed next to them, such as Ctrl+X next to the Cut command. This shortcut key combination enables you to execute the Cut command at any time just by pressing Ctrl+X, without having to go to the menu at all.

When the computer needs information from you to complete a command, it will display a dialog box, such as the one seen in Figure 1.3. A dialog box is a simple on-screen form that you complete by clicking items and typing text into fields. Some dialog boxes are very simple, with just a single button to click to let the computer know that you've received the information it was giving you. Others have pages of fields that you can fill out. The types of fields sometimes included are as follows:

- *Check boxes* are small white squares used for yes-or-no questions. Click one of these boxes to make a check mark appear in it, indicating "yes" for whatever is written next to it. To remove a check mark from the check box, click it again.
- *Option buttons* are small circles used to select one, and only one, of a set of options. Click the option button next to the option you want, and a dot will appear in the circle to show it's selected.
- *Text fields* are white rectangles where you can type information, such as a "name" or "title." Click the field to put the text insertion point there and then type your entry. (When you're finished typing, don't press the enter key, because the computer will take that to mean that you're finished with the entire form.)
- *Numerical fields* are used for entering numbers. They look like short text fields with up- and down-arrow buttons at the right end of them. You can type the number in as if it were a text field, or you can use the arrows to increase or decrease the number.
- *Drop-down menus* are used when you have to choose one option from a list of possibilities. They look like text fields with a down-arrow at the right end. To use a drop-down menu, click the down arrow. A list of possible entries will appear. Click the one you want. (Some drop-down menus also work as text fields, allowing you to type a new entry instead of selecting an existing one from the menu.)
- *Tabs* appear at the top of the dialog box and look like file folders. When tabs are present, it means there are several pages to the dialog box. Each tab has a name describing the material on its page. To move to that page, click the tab.
- *Buttons* are raised areas with text on them. The most common buttons you'll find in a dialog box are OK, which you click to indicate that you're done with the dialog box, and Cancel, which you click to indicate that you want to close the dialog box without carrying out the selected command.

FIG. 1.3

This dialog box has examples of most of the standard dialog box features.

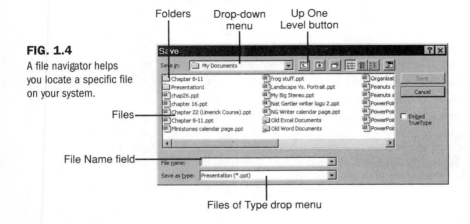

Drop-down menu

Option buttons

Numeric field

Text field

Check boxes

Buttons

 TIP To find out what a field in the dialog box is for, click the ? button near the upper-right corner of the dialog box and click the field. A ScreenTip appears, describing the field. It will disappear the next time you click anything.

You can move from field to field in a dialog box using the Tab key. Using the keyboard, you can toggle check boxes, select option buttons, and push buttons by tabbing to them and pressing the space bar.

File Navigation

Whenever you're retrieving an existing presentation, saving a new presentation, importing a picture into PowerPoint, or doing anything else that requires creating or finding a file, you'll have to be able to specify the location of that file. In order to do this, you will use a special dialog box called a *file navigator*, like the one seen in Figure 1.4.

Folders   Drop-down menu   Up One Level button

FIG. 1.4

A file navigator helps you locate a specific file on your system.

Files

File Name field

Files of Type drop menu

When PowerPoint displays a file navigator, it shows the contents of a disk folder that was recently used to store the type of file you're working with. If this is the folder you want to retrieve something from or replace a file in, then just double-click the name of that file. If you want to create a new file, then enter a name for that file in the File Name field and then click OK or Save.

If you want to find a different folder, follow these steps:

1. In the file navigator, click the drop-down menu at the top of the file navigator and select the disk drive (or network drive) that the folder is on.

2. A list of folders and files in the root folder of that drive will appear. To see the contents of a folder, double-click it.

3. Repeat step 2 until you find the folder you're looking for. If you've opened a wrong folder, click the Up One Level button (see Figure 1.4).

4. If you don't see the file you're looking for, it may be because the file navigator is displaying only files of a specific type. From the Files of Type or Save As Type drop-down list at the bottom of the navigator, select the type of file you're looking for (or the type you want to store). (You should always make sure that this has the right file type before saving a file.)

Sometimes the file navigator will have a preview area to the right of the list of files. Clicking a file will bring up a small picture of what the contents of that file look like, which makes it easy to verify that you're opening the correct file.

Asking for Help

Microsoft has plenty of helpful information to help PowerPoint users. Some of it is built right into PowerPoint. Other information is available on the World Wide Web. On the whole, the information is not that good at getting you started from the very beginning, nor does it go into the very specific detail that advanced users sometimes need. However, it is good at answering the questions that most users have, once they have a little experience.

The Office Assistant

One of the important new features of PowerPoint 97 is the Office Assistant, an animated character designed to help you with your PowerPoint problems. The Office Assistant tracks what you're doing and predicts what kind of help you're going to need.

The Office Assistant has its own window, which automatically stays out of the way of whatever you're working on. When you need help, just press F1. The Office Assistant will appear (if it wasn't already on-screen) and ask you what you want to know about. Type in your question.

The Assistant is not smart enough to actually understand your question. What it will do is scan your question for words that it recognizes and display a list of articles that deal with those topics. Click an article from the list, and specific help will be displayed.

If you leave the Office Assistant running, a light bulb will sometimes appear over its head. When this happens, click the Office Assistant and some helpful information about what you're doing will appear. This is a good way to learn a lot of tricks and shortcuts you can use with PowerPoint.

Right-click the Office Assistant to display a pop-up menu that lets you choose from a number of available modifications, including hiding the Assistant or changing him to a different animated character.

Help from the Web

Microsoft offers a lot of helpful information about PowerPoint on the World Wide Web. This is a good place to go if you have questions the Office Assistant can't answer. When the Office Assistant's files were written, Microsoft had to guess what help people would need. The files on the Web, however, are constantly updated so that they can solve the problems that people are actually calling about.

If you go to **http://www.microsoft.com/MSPowerPointSupport/**, you'll find the following services:

- KnowledgeBase, a catalog of informative reports created by Microsoft.
- Troubleshooting Wizards, which present you with a list of common problems. When you select one, you will be taken to a page explaining the problem and the solution.
- Frequently Asked Questions, which offers a single Web page with answers to the most common questions about PowerPoint.
- Submit a Question, which allows you to send a question to technical support. Technical Support will respond with an answer by e-mail.

In addition, Microsoft offers a newsgroup on PowerPoint where you can talk with other users about your problems and the solutions you've found. To read the newsgroup, tell your newsgroup reader to use the news server **msnews.microsoft.com** to get the **microsoft.public.powerpoint** newsgroup.

Visiting PowerPoint Central

There's another system of helpful information built into PowerPoint called PowerPoint Central. This built-in help is a PowerPoint-based magazine that is stored on your computer but which PowerPoint will update from the Web every three months. This way, you get fairly current information without having to connect to the Web every time you use it.

To start PowerPoint Central, choose Tools, PowerPoint Central. PowerPoint Central will load and start running (it's actually a PowerPoint presentation and a good example of what an accomplished PowerPoint user can create.) It will check to see if it's time for a new edition of PowerPoint Central. If it is, you'll be prompted for permission to download the update from the Web, then start running the downloaded version.

PowerPoint Central is not a full help system. Instead, it mainly points to PowerPoint features that you may not be familiar with. It also has articles on how to make better presentations and links that will help you get free art and sounds off the Web to use with your presentation. ●

Part
I

Ch
1

Creating a Presentation Quickly

With Microsoft PowerPoint 97, you can quickly and easily put together a good-looking, well-organized, straightforward presentation. In this chapter, you'll use the AutoContent Wizard to set up the framework of a proper presentation, which you can then change to suit your needs. There is still a lot more you need to learn to make the most of PowerPoint, but by the time you get through this chapter, you'll be able to put together and view a basic presentation and you'll have seen the fundamentals of what PowerPoint does. ■

Use the AutoContent Wizard

PowerPoint will put together the framework of a visually strong, well-organized presentation for you. Then you just have to adapt it to your needs.

Save the presentation

Put a copy of the presentation on disk so you can work on it or show it to someone later.

Add text to a slide

Do some simple customization of the text in the presentation.

Test the presentation

Run through the presentation as it would be seen in a computer slideshow.

Print the presentation

Put the presentation on paper so you can distribute it to other people.

Starting with the AutoContent Wizard

A *wizard* is a special Microsoft program designed to help you use one of their products. The *AutoContent Wizard* can help you build a presentation in PowerPoint. This wizard will offer you a list of predesigned presentations and, once you select one, customize it with information that you provide. It still won't be ready to use; after all, the wizard doesn't really know what it is that you have to say. However, it will put together a well-designed presentation outline with some guideline text that you can replace with the text you need.

To use the AutoContent Wizard, follow these steps:

1. Start PowerPoint by clicking the Windows Start button and choosing Programs, Microsoft PowerPoint.

2. If the Office Assistant appears on your screen to help you, click Start Using PowerPoint.

3. In the PowerPoint dialog box that appears, choose AutoContent Wizard and then click OK.

4. An AutoContent Wizard dialog box appears. Click Next.

5. A list of presentation types will appear at the right side of the dialog box, as seen in Figure 2.1. Click the type of presentation you want. (You can shorten the list of presentations to pick from by clicking one of the buttons with topics on them.) Then, click Next again.

Presentation categories

FIG. 2.1

Selecting one of the category buttons reduces the number of types displayed.

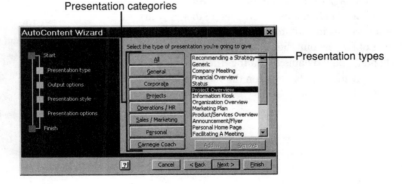

Presentation types

6. New fields appear in the dialog box. Select Presentations, Informal Meetings, Handouts and then click Next again.

7. Two sets of options appear. If you're designing an On-screen presentation, select Black And White Overheads, Color Overheads, or 35mm Slides from the first set of options. Then click Next once more.

8. Three text fields appear. Enter a title for the presentation, your name as you'd like it to appear on the first slide, and any additional information you want on the first slide.

9. Click Finish, and the wizard will generate your presentation.

The presentation is shown in *Outline view*, as seen in Figure 2.2. In this view of your presentation, there is a numbered list of the slides, with the primary text from each. There's also a small window showing you, in miniature, how the currently selected slide will look.

FIG. 2.2
The wizard-generated presentation suggests what text might appear in a presentation of the type you've chosen.

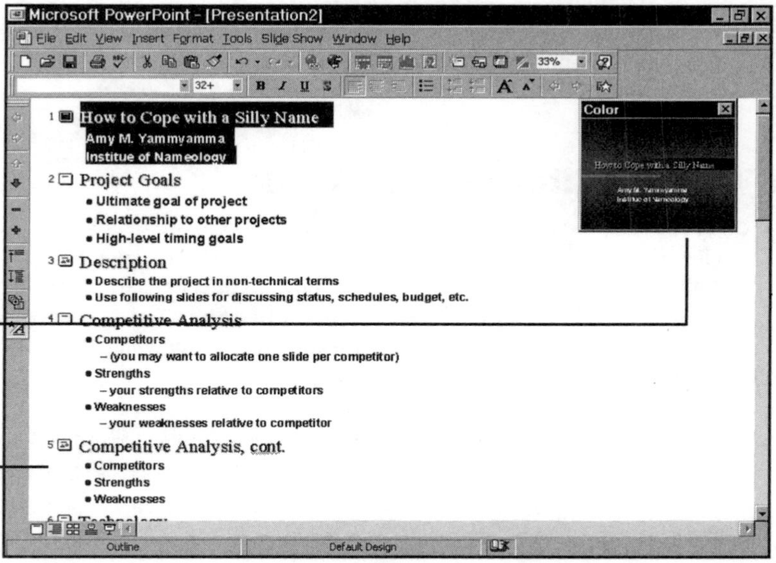

Miniature of current slide

Presentation text

Change Text on a Slide

To quickly customize the presentation, follow these steps:

1. Double-click any word in the presentation to highlight it.

2. Type a word to replace the highlighted word. Your new word will now appear in its place.

Now you have a custom presentation. You will learn more about adding and changing text in Chapter 3, "Adding and Editing Text in Your Presentation," and about adding and changing other parts of the presentation in later chapters. At this point, you have completed the basics of PowerPoint. Anything you learn from here may be more intricate and detailed, but the concept will remain the same—mixing elements that PowerPoint provides with your own words and customizing them to create an effective presentation.

Saving the Presentation

To store a copy of a new presentation on disk, so that you can work with it again later, follow these steps:

1. Press Ctrl+S or click the Save button.

2. A file navigator will appear. Navigate to the folder that you want to store the file in.

3. Type a name for the presentation in the File Name field and press Enter.

 If you've made changes to a presentation that you've already saved, just press Ctrl+S or click the Save button. The previously saved version will be replaced on the disk with the newly updated version. (If you don't want to replace the old version, choose File, Save As and a file navigator will appear. You can then select a new name to store it under or a different folder to store it in.)

Previewing the Presentation

To see what the presentation will look like as a computer screen slide show, choose Slide Show, View Show. Your entire screen will display the first slide of your show, as seen in Figure 2.3 (although with your specific slide). To move to the next slide, just click the mouse. If you want to exit the slide show, right-click and select End Show from the shortcut menu that appears. Otherwise, just keep clicking through your slides until you get to the end, at which point you'll be returned to the main PowerPoint window.

 N O T E There is also a button called Slide Show in the group of five buttons in the lower-left corner of your screen. This has the same effect as the command used above, except that it starts with the slide that you've most recently been working on rather than always starting at the beginning. ■

FIG. 2.3
In Slide Show view, the slides will fill your entire screen. (Your slides may differ.)

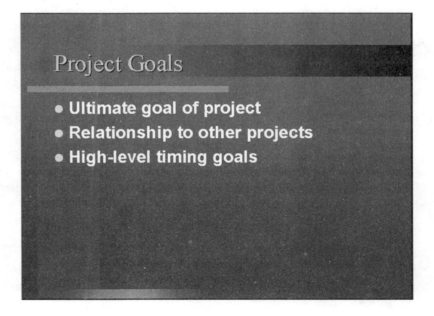

Printing the Presentation

 To print the presentation, just click the Print button. The presentation will print in the default format, one slide per page.

PowerPoint supports a wide range of printing options, including printing the outline, or printing several slides per page with spaces for notes. For more information on printing, see Chapter 10, "Printing Your Presentation."

Opening a Saved Presentation

Retrieving a file that has been stored on disk allows you to make further changes in that presentation or to use that presentation as a base for another presentation.

To open a saved presentation, follow these steps:

1. Pull open PowerPoint's File menu and check the last few lines of the menu.

   PowerPoint always keeps track of the last few presentations that you worked on and keeps them at the bottom of the list for easy reference. (You can set how many files are kept in this list by choosing Tools, Options and setting the number in the General tab.)

2. If the file that you want is in the list, click the file name, and the file is loaded into PowerPoint.

   If the file that you want is not in the list, click the Open command and choose the file that you want to open, using the file navigator that appears.

If you find that you've opened the wrong file, you can close it by clicking the Close (x) button at the right end of the menu bar. ●

CHAPTER 3

Adding and Editing Text in Your Presentation

Text communicates most of the information in a typical presentation. PowerPoint has a full array of tools to make inserting text easy and to help ensure that the text is clear and accurate. The AutoCorrect feature catches common typos and fixes them, and you can set it up to automatically expand abbreviations for terms that you use repeatedly. The Look Up feature allows you to call up computerized reference works from within PowerPoint, so you can check your facts and find interesting quotes. ■

Add and change text

Text is the core of most presentations. PowerPoint has a healthy array of editing features to allow you to build and rearrange your text.

Search and replace

Find specific text references. Quickly correct repeated mistakes or update outdated references.

Check and fix spelling errors

Have PowerPoint check for spelling errors as you write and suggest corrections. Set up PowerPoint to fix your most common errors and create your own typing shortcuts.

Adding Text

There are three primary ways to add text to your presentation. In this chapter, you learn to add text to the outline. This is the best way to add text to build your presentation, since you can see the text for the entire presentation at once.

The other two methods work only when you are viewing an individual slide. In one method, you create an area of standard text directly on the slide. Once you create it, you can work with it using the various commands described in this chapter.

▶ **See** "Creating a Text Object," **p. 56**

The other uses a PowerPoint feature called WordArt. This lets you create fancy, multi-colored, shaped logos and other text with a graphical appearance. The commands described in this chapter do not work with WordArt.

▶ **See** "Using WordArt," **p. 135**

Adding Text to a Slide in Outline View

To add text to an existing slide, move the mouse pointer to where you want to add text; then click. A vertical bar appears to show you where your text will appear. When you start typing, the text shows up there.

To start a new line of text, press Shift+Enter. (Just pressing Enter creates a new slide if the insertion line is in a line that is not indented.)

Adding slides and large amounts of text in Outline view can get tricky, particularly when you want to create varying levels of indentation.

▶ **See** "Promoting, Demoting, and Rearranging Text in Outline View," **p. 69**

You can also navigate the text by using the arrow keys and remove individual characters quickly by pressing Delete (for the character after the insertion point) or the Backspace key (for the character before the insertion point).

Selecting Text

You can make several types of changes in as much or as little text as you want. You can delete text; you can replace it; you can change the size and the appearance of the characters. To do these things, however, you need to know how to *select* text, which indicates to the computer what text you want to change.

The methods of selecting text are as follows:

- ■ To select a single word, double-click that word.
- ■ To select a series of words, point to the first word in the series and then drag the mouse pointer to the last word.

- To select an entire line of text, triple-click that line. (If that line has lines directly below it and indented more to the right, those lines are selected as well. PowerPoint considers that text to be a subtopic of what you selected.)
- To select an entire slide, click the little slide icon at the start of the first line of slide text.
- To select all the text in the entire presentation, press Ctrl+A.

Selected text shows up as inverted text (white letters on a black background).

Deleting or Replacing Text

To delete the selected text, just press the Delete key. Now may be a good time to learn about the Undo command, however.

 By clicking the Undo button on the Standard toolbar (or pressing Ctrl+Z, or choosing Edit, Undo), you can undo whatever mistake you just made. Clicking the down arrow next to the Undo button allows you to select how many steps you want to undo.

If you undo something and decide that you didn't want to undo it, click the Redo button on the Standard toolbar, or choose Edit, Redo, or press Ctrl+Y.

To replace the selected text with new text, just start typing. The selected text disappears, and your new text starts appearing in its place.

Part

I

Ch

3

Moving and Copying Text

A standard Windows feature is the *Clipboard*, an area of memory that can store one item at a time and allow you to put it somewhere. The Clipboard is handy to use in moving and copying text. The standard commands for working with the Clipboard are:

- The *Cut* command (Ctrl+X) removes the selected text from your document and puts it in the Clipboard.
- The *Copy* command (Ctrl+C) copies the selected text to the Clipboard without removing it from the document.
- The *Paste* command (Ctrl+V) copies whatever's currently in the Clipboard to the document. The Clipboard places the text where the insertion point is; if text is selected, the copied text replaces the selected text. Remembering that a copy of the pasted text is still in the Clipboard is important, so that you can paste the text repeatedly without having to recopy it every time.

 The same Cut, Copy, and Paste keyboard commands work with not only all of the Microsoft Office products, but with just about every Windows product that uses text. You can use these commands to copy text off of a Web page, for example, and paste it into your presentation. (The commands also work with many picture-oriented programs, but since you can't paste pictures into outline mode, that does no good here. We'll see how to paste pictures into your presentation later in the book.)

If you want to use the preceding commands to move text from one point to another, follow these steps:

1. Select the text that you want to move.
2. Press Ctrl+X to move that text from the document to the Clipboard.
3. Click the place where you want to move the text.

   The insertion point appears where you click.
4. Press Ctrl+V to paste the text in its new location.

Finding a Word or Phrase

To locate a specific word or phrase within your presentation, follow these steps:

1. Choose Edit, Find (or press Ctrl+F).

   The Find dialog box appears.
2. Type the word or phrase that you want to find into the Find What box.
3. Press Enter.

   PowerPoint searches the text, starting at the current insertion point and heading down through the presentation. If the program doesn't find the word or phrase, it starts again at the beginning of the presentation and searches up to the insertion point.

   When the word or phrase is found, PowerPoint selects it.
4. If you want to find another appearance of the selected word or phrase, click the Find Next button.
5. When you find exactly what you're looking for, click the Close button in the Find dialog box to make it disappear.

If you want to do work around the same phrase several places, click the PowerPoint menu bar after each time you find the phrase, do whatever you're doing to the phrase, and then click the Find Next button.

Replacing a Word or Phrase

Sometimes, you have to replace the same word or phrase with another one repeatedly in a document. You want to do this type of replacement if, for example, you discover that you've been repeatedly been calling a company Hard Drive Racing Co. instead of Hard Drive Racing, Inc., or if the August 1999 deadlines have been delayed to January 2000.

To replace all occurrences of a phrase in a document with another phrase, follow these steps:

1. Choose Edit, Replace (or press Ctrl+H).

   The Replace dialog box appears, as shown in Figure 3.1.

FIG. 3.1

The Replace dialog box includes check boxes that allow you to replace only whole words or only words that have the same capitalization as what you type.

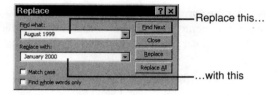

Replace this...

...with this

2. In the Find What box, type the word or phrase that you want to get rid of.

3. In the Replace With box, type the word or phrase that you want to use instead of the other word or phrase.

4. If you want to make the replacement everywhere that the word or phrase appears, click the Replace All button.

5. If you want to make the replacement only certain times that a phrase appears, click the Find button until one of those appearances is highlighted; then click the Replace button.

   Repeat this step until you find and replace all the occurrences of the phrase that you want.

6. When you're done replacing, click the Close button.

 TIP If you're looking for a short word, such as *any*, click the Find Whole Words Only check box, so that PowerPoint won't replace the word when the word shows up in other words, such as *miscellany* or *canyon*.

Checking Your Spelling

PowerPoint has a built-in spelling checker. Whenever you type a word, the spelling checker checks to see whether it knows that word. If not, the spelling checker puts a little red wiggly line below the word to tell you that it doesn't recognize the word, as seen in Figure 3.2.

FIG. 3.2

The spelling checker suggests alternatives that are spelled similarly or that sound similar.

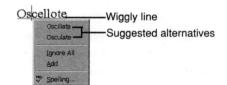

Wiggly line

Suggested alternatives

When one of these red lines shows up below one of your words, you have a choice of things to do:

■ If you recognize your mistake, you can go back and edit it out.

■ If you're not sure what the correct spelling is, right-click the word. A shortcut menu appears. At the top of the menu is a list of words that the computer thinks you may have meant. If you see the word that you want, choose it. The word that you choose replaces the erroneous word.

■ If the word is a genuine word that the program doesn't know, and a word that you'll be using only in this presentation, right-click it and choose Ignore All from the shortcut menu.

■ If the word is one that the computer really should know is correct because you're likely to use it at other times, right-click it and choose Add from the shortcut menu. PowerPoint adds the word to the dictionary that it shares with the rest of Microsoft Office.

> **CAUTION**
>
> The spell checker can tell you only when you typed something that isn't a word in its dictionary. If you meant to type **the mother ducks** and instead typed **them other ducks**, the spelling checker sees nothing wrong. Therefore, you should proofread your work carefully.

You can set options about how the spelling checker works by choosing Tools, Options and clicking the Spelling tab in the Options dialog box that appears.

Using AutoCorrect

AutoCorrect is an Office feature that can correct a specified word with another specified word or phrase as you type it. AutoCorrect is handy primarily for two purposes. One is fixing a typo that you regularly make (in fact, built into AutoCorrect are hundreds of fixes for common typos, such as typing **teh** for **the**). The other is allowing you to make a shortcut for complex things that you regularly have to type, such as using **hdri** as a shortcut for **Hard Drive Racing, Inc.**

To configure the AutoCorrect feature, follow these steps:

1. Choose Tools, AutoCorrect.

   The AutoCorrect dialog box appears as shown in Figure 3.3.

2. Check the list of types of corrections AutoCorrect handles, and make sure that a check appears in the check box for each correction that you want.

   Most of the options handle errors in capitalization.

3. To add a new correction that you want AutoCorrect to handle, enter the typo or shortcut in the Replace box, enter the correction or expansion in the With box, and click the Add button to add the correction to the list.

4. To stop a specific replacement, scroll the replacement list until you find the one that you want to stop; then click the replacement and then click the Delete button.

FIG. 3.3

Use AutoCorrect to create your own typing shorthand.

Errors and replacements

Checks for capitalization

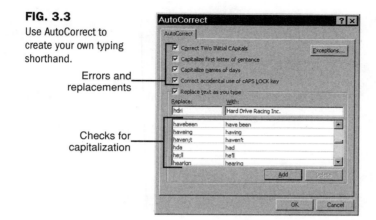

CHAPTER 4

Changing the Look of Text

The appearance of words can have as much impact as what the words themselves say. The bold largeness of a newspaper headline, the excitement of the emphasized type in an advertisement, and the sneakiness of the small print all suggest things by their presence. In this chapter, you learn how to create a look for your text and how to create the sort of special text needed for scientific and legal work. ∎

Change the size and style of text

Change the size of text to make it more visible or to fit more on a slide. Change the style for better readability and to give the work a mood.

Set text attributes

Create emphasis by italicizing, underlining, or making your text bold. Create subscripts and superscripts for footnotes and other uses.

Add symbols to your text

Use legal and mathematical symbols to communicate your ideas properly. Add dingbats for emphasis.

Add bullets to your list

Separate and highlight points in a list by putting an emphasizing bullet or symbol before each one.

Changing the Font and Size of Text

Windows comes with a variety of *fonts* (type styles), and literally thousands of additional fonts are available for purchase or downloading. Some fonts are businesslike; others are light-hearted. Some fonts are good only for headlines; others serve a multitude of purposes.

Like the other attributes covered in this chapter, you can set the font and size in two ways:

- ■ If you're about to type the text, set the attribute setting and then type, and what you type shows up in that setting.

- ■ If the text is already in the presentation, select the text and then issue the command to set the attribute. The change affects the selected text.

To set the font, pull down the Font drop-down list in the Formatting toolbar (see Figure 4.1) and choose the font that you want to use. The most recently used fonts are at the top of the list, and below them are all the usable fonts on the system, in alphabetical order. If you want to get to a specific font in a long list quickly, start typing the name of the font, and the list scrolls to that font.

FIG. 4.1
The Formatting toolbar is used to change the appearance of text in various ways.

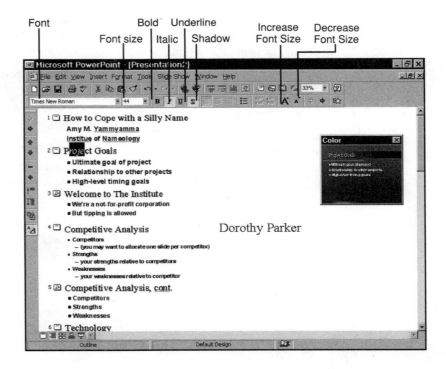

You can set a specific font size by choosing it from the Font Size drop-down list or by typing the size you want (measured in *points*, which are seventy-secondths of an inch). Realize that the size you are setting is how big it appears in the finished presentation; text is displayed much smaller in the Outline view in which you're working.

If you use the Font Size drop-down list, you set all the selected text the same size. If the selected text is different sizes, and you want to increase the size of all the text but still keep the size difference, click the Increase Font Size button. Similarly, to make all the selected text smaller, click the Decrease Font Size button.

To find out the font and size of a given piece of text, click it. The font and size appear in the Font and Font Size toolbar boxes.

Adding Text Attributes

In addition to size and style, you can set several other attributes, as listed in Table 4.1.

Table 4.1   Text Attributes

Button	Keyboard Shortcut	Description
B	Ctrl+B	Makes text **bold**.
I	Ctrl+I	Makes text *italic*.
<u>U</u>	Ctrl+U	<u>Underlines</u> the text.
S	Alt+O, F, Alt+A, Enter	Makes the text look as though it's casting a small shadow.
None	Alt+O, F, Alt+E, Enter	Makes the text appear embossed (raised from the slide). Can be selected only from the Font dialog box that appears when you choose F̲ormat, F̲ont.
None	Alt+O, F, Alt+R, Enter	Makes the text superscript (smaller and higher than the surrounding text). Can be selected only from the Font dialog box that appears when you choose F̲ormat, F̲ont.
None	Alt+O, F, Alt+B, Enter	Makes the text subscript (smaller and lower than the surrounding text). Can be selected only from the Font dialog box that appears when you choose F̲ormat, F̲ont.

Part
I

Ch
4

Using the Format Painter

The Format Painter is a handy tool that allows you to take the font, font size, and attributes of one piece of text and quickly apply them to other pieces of text. If you're using a variety of text styles in your presentation, using Format Painter can be much quicker than copying them by hand.

To copy the format of one piece of text to several others, follow these steps:

1. Click the text that has the format you want to copy, to place the insertion point there.

2. Click the Format Painter button.

   The mouse pointer turns into a paintbrush.

3. Select the text that you want to copy the format to.

   The format is copied to the selected text. The words of the text don't change—just the appearance.

To copy the format of one piece of text to another, follow these steps:

1. Click the text that has the format you want to copy, to place the insertion point there.

2. Double-click the Format Painter button.

   The mouse pointer turns into a paintbrush.

3. Select a piece of text that you want to copy the format to.

   Repeat this step for as many pieces of text as you want.

4. Click the Format Painter button again.

   The mouse pointer returns to normal.

Inserting Symbols

You may want to insert all sorts of special symbols into your text: foreign letters, legal symbols, zodiac symbols, playing-card suits, arrows, and other little icons. Many of these symbols are built into various fonts, but you do not have keys for them on your keyboard (which is just as well, as having them would make for one huge keyboard).

To insert one of these symbols into the text, follow these steps:

1. Choose Insert, Symbol.

   The Symbol dialog box appears, as shown in Figure 4.2.

2. Choose a font from the Font drop-down list.

   Only fonts that have symbols are listed. Different fonts have different symbols, so you may have to look through a few fonts before you find one that has the symbol you want.

3. Double-click the symbol you want to use.

FIG. 4.2
The Symbol dialog box
gives you access to an
array of useful and
decorative symbols.

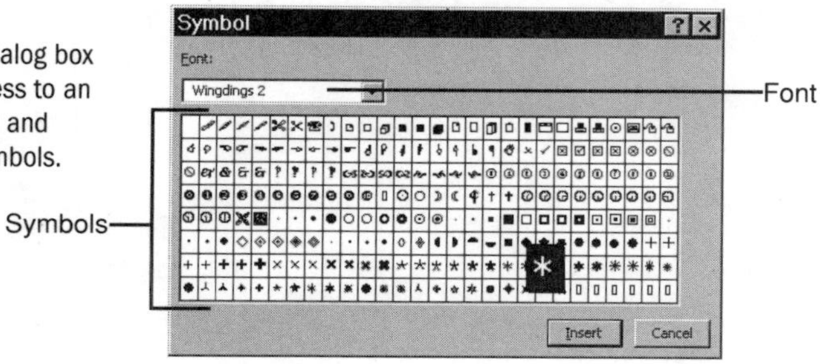

Symbols—

Font

4. If you want to add several symbols, repeat steps 2 and 3 for them.

5. Click the Close button after you insert all the symbols that you want to use.

Adding Bullets

Using *bullets* (dots or highlighting characters at the start of lines) is a good way to identify a series of points in a list. Numbering a list can be useful if the items are in a specific order or if you need to refer quickly to individual items in the list at a later time.

 To turn bullets on or off for selected lines, click the Bullets button.

If you want to specify what your bullets look like, follow these steps:

1. Select the bulleted text whose bullets you want to change.

2. Choose Format, Bullet.

   The Bullet dialog box appears, displaying all the symbol fonts.

3. From the Font drop-down list, choose the font to pick the bullet from.

   The Font list contains only fonts that have symbols in them, and any of these symbols can be used as your bullet

4. Click the symbol that you want to use as a bullet.

5. Using the Size box, specify how large you want the bullet to be in comparison with the text.

   If you want the bullet to be the same size as the text, choose 100 (percent). If you want the bullet to be larger than the text, pick a higher number— although you're more likely to want the bullet to be smaller than the text, in which case you should pick a smaller number.

6. Click the OK button.

   Your new bullet appears in place of the preceding bullet.

Part

I

Ch

4

TIP The fonts Wingdings and Wingdings 2 are good sources of interesting bullets.

CHAPTER 5

Working with Different Views

Working on a presentation involves adjusting slides, text, graphics, and interactions. No single view lets you make all adjustments, additions, and modifications easily. ◼

Change the view

As you work on your presentation, you can switch to use a view more appropriate to task-specific changes.

Use Slide Sorter view

Switch to a view that lets you rearrange slides easily.

View your outline

The Outline view lets you view, modify, and reorganize the text of your presentation easily.

Add speaker notes

Attach reminder notes to use during your presentation using Notes view. These notes can also be printed along with the slides to create a convenient handout.

Use Slide view

Switch to Slide view to add graphics to your slide and to design the visual aspects, such as colors and fonts, of your presentation.

Using Different Views to Prepare Your Presentation

Microsoft PowerPoint 97 has a number of views for different needs, each accessed with a single click of a button. The five view-changing buttons are along the lower-left edge of the window.

Button	View	Used For
	Slide View	Designing a slide
	Outline View	Organizing presentation text
	Slide Sorter View	Reordering slides
	Notes Page View	Adding speaker notes
	Slide Show	Watching the presentation

Viewing Slides in Slide Sorter View

Slide Sorter view shows miniature versions of as many slides as can fit on the screen, as seen in Figure 5.1. While in this view, you can't change the contents of the individual slides. Instead, this view is used for deleting and rearranging the slides and for configuring settings that apply to a whole slide (such as how long the slide gets displayed).

 To get into Slide Sorter view, click the Slide Sorter View button or choose View, Slide Sorter.

For information on how to use Slide Sorter view to sort slides, see Chapter 7, "Arranging Objects on Your Slide."

Organizing Your Presentation in Outline View

Outline view, seen in Figure 5.2, is the view that you've been working with up to this point. That's because Outline view is good for establishing the basics of your presentation. This is the only view that lets you see and change the text on all the slides at once, so that you can organize thoughts, rearrange topics, and see how the text on each slide relates to the slides around it. However, this view only allows you to work with the text on your slides. There's no way to work with graphics in this view, or with the layout of the slide.

This view includes a window with a miniature version of the slide that you are working on. You can turn this display on or off by choosing View, Slide Miniature.

 To get into Outline view from any other view, click the Outline View button or choose View, Outline.

For more information on using Outline view to build an outline, see Chapter 9, "Creating an Outline."

FIG. 5.1
Slide Sorter view shows as many slides on as will fit, according to your screen resolution.

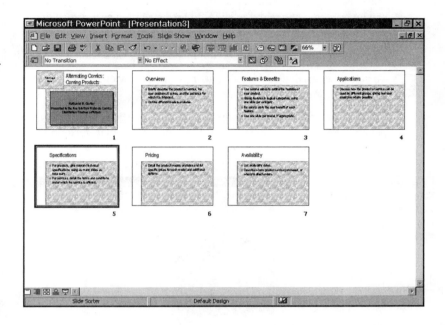

FIG. 5.2
Outline view is the best view for looking at the entire text of your presentation.

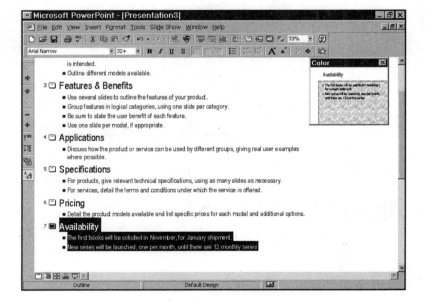

Part

I

Ch

5

Adding a Speaker Note in Notes Page View

PowerPoint gives you the capability to create notes to go along with each slide. These notes can be printed along with the slides to be distributed as a record of the presentation, or you can use them for reference when delivering your presentation.

A special view is used just for creating and editing these notes, as seen in Figure 5.3.

 To view the currently selected slide in Notes Page view, click the Notes Pages button or choose View, Notes Page.

To enter your notes, click the text area under the slide and begin typing. To edit existing notes, position your insertion point in the slide and use normal word processing procedures. All the standard text attributes can be used on the text here.

FIG. 5.3

Notes Page view helps you create a printout with notes about the slide.

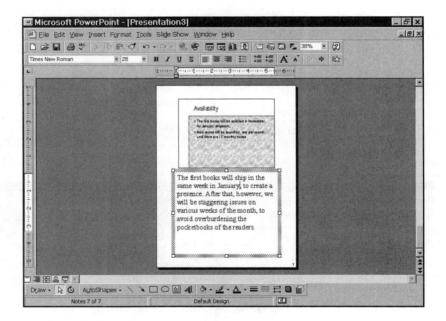

For information on printing out the notes pages, see Chapter 9, "Creating an Outline."

Designing Your Slide in Slide View

Slide view is designed to let you work on the layout of the slide, as seen in Figure 5.4. This view shows one slide at a time, as large as the PowerPoint window. You can zoom in even further by using the Zoom drop-down menu.

FIG. 5.4
Use Slide view for arranging and adding graphics to a slide.

Zoom menu

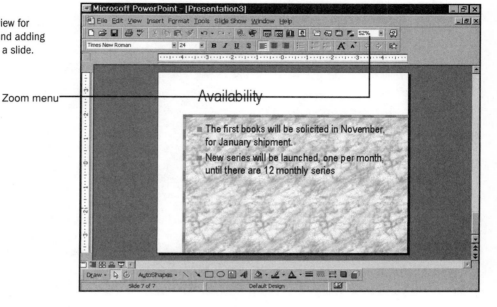

 To view the currently selected slide in Slide view, click the Slide view button or choose View, Slide.

For more information on using the Slide view to lay out your slide, see Chapter 6, "Arranging Your Slides."

T I P In Slide View and in Notes Page view, you can move from slide to slide either by using the scroll bar at the right of the screen, or by using Pg Up and Pg Dn.

Part
I

Ch
5

Arranging Your Slides

Slide Sorter view allows you to see all your slides at a glance and rearrange them easily. Build your presentation by bringing in slides from other presentations, expanding and duplicating slides, and adding summary slides. Eliminate unneeded slides and split up overcrowded slides so that your presentation contains information in easily digestible chunks. ■

Eliminate slides

Remove unwanted slides from your presentation.

Duplicate and rearrange slides

Switch the slides into the order you want and reproduce a slide to reemphasize a point.

Use slides from another presentation

Reuse slides from another slide show.

Expand a slide

Take a slide with a list on it and create a new slide for each statement in the list.

Create a summary slide

Add a slide that condenses the information from other slides, either for an introduction or for a recap.

Selecting Slides

The appropriate view in which to deal with entire slides and their place within the presentation is Slide Sorter view. To indicate which slides you're working with, you have to be able to select slides.

To select:

- One slide, click the slide
- A slide adjacent to the one currently selected, use the cursor keys
- Several slides, click the first slide you want; then, while holding the Shift key down, click the rest of the slides

Selecting Groups of Adjacent Slides

You can select a rectangular group set of slides by pointing to one corner of a rectangle containing the slides and dragging to the opposite corner, being careful that the corners you point to are outside the slide itself (see Figure 6.1).

FIG. 6.1
Rectangular selection allows you to select several slides in a single row or grouped sets of slides in several rows. In this case, every third slide is being selected.

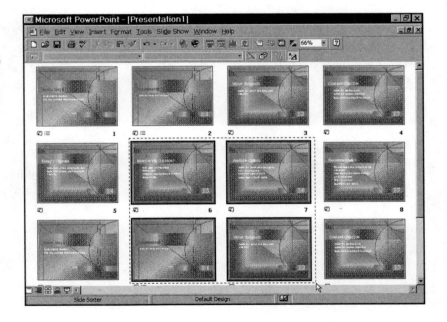

In most cases, this method is an awkward way to select a series of slides, unless the slides happen to be several complete rows on the screen, not skipping slides at the beginning of the first row or the end of the last. However, it does allow you one occasionally useful trick: selecting every other (or every third, or every fourth) slide.

To do this trick, resize the window so each row of slides contains as many slides as you want the interval to be. (If you want to select every third slide, for example, resize it so that it's three slides wide.) When you do so, the slides that you want to select are stacked in a single column, and you can easily select them in a rectangle.

 T I P If your interval is larger than the number of slides that fit in a fully open window, you can use the Zoom menu to shrink the size of the slides, allowing more to fit on-screen.

Deleting Slides

To delete slides, select them and then press Delete.

 If you accidentally delete slides that you did not mean to, click the Undo button, or press Ctrl+Z.

Reordering and Duplicating Slides

To move a slide or slides to another part of the presentation, follow these steps:

1. Select the slides that you want to move.
2. Drag the slides that you're moving.

   Instead of the slides themselves following the mouse pointer as you drag, a vertical insertion line will be dragged. The insertion line appears between slides.

3. Position the vertical insertion line at the point where you want to move the slides to; then release the mouse button.

   The slides move from where they were and appear where you placed the vertical insertion line. All the slides that were after that line will be placed after the slides you moved.

To copy slides, do the same thing, but hold down the Ctrl key as you drag. The new slide copies appear wherever you positioned the vertical insertion point.

Inserting Slides from Another Presentation

If you have slides already created for another presentation and want to copy them into the presentation that you're currently working on, follow these steps:

1. Select the slide that you want the copied slides to be inserted above.
2. Choose Insert, Slides From Files.

   The Slide Finder dialog box, shown in Figure 6.2, appears.

FIG 6.2

The Slide finder dialog box allows you to select slides from existing presentations to add to your current presentation.

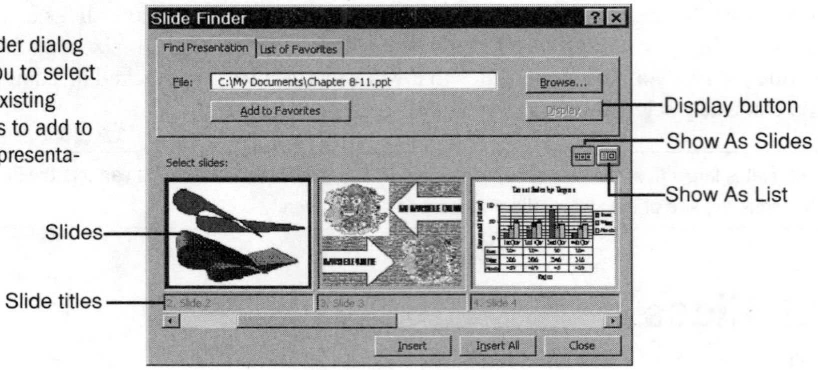

Slides

Slide titles

Display button

Show As Slides

Show As List

3. Click Browse.

   A file navigator appears. (Information on using file navigators appears in Chapter 1, "Getting Familiar with PowerPoint 97.") This file navigator has a preview pane, letting you see a sample slide from any presentation you select.

4. Use the file navigator to select the presentation file with the slides you want; then click the Open button.

   The navigator closes, but the Slide Finder dialog box is still open.

5. Click the Slide Finder dialog box's Display button.

   The slides appear in a scrollable row at the bottom of the dialog box. (If the presentation is long, click the Show As List button; the dialog box shows a list of the slide titles, and also displays a picture of one slide at a time.)

6. Select each slide that you want to copy into your presentation by clicking it.

   A blue frame appears around each selected slide. (If you've clicked the Show As List button, you can select multiple slides by holding down the Shift key and clicking each slide that you want.)

7. Click Insert.

   The selected slides are added to your presentation. (To insert an entire presentation quickly, click Insert All.)

The inserted slides may not look exactly as they did in the old presentation; they may take on aspects of the design and layout of the current presentation.

Expanding One Slide to Many Slides

If you have a slide with a series of *points* (individual lines from the outline) on it, you can quickly create new slides for each of those points. To do so, follow these steps:

1. Select the slide that you want to expand.

2. Choose Tools, Expand Slide.

   Each point on the slide that you selected is used as the header/title for a new slide. The new slides appear immediately following the original slide.

3. Switch to Slide view to add text to the expanded slides.

Creating a Summary Slide

A summary slide simply uses the titles (the first line of text) of several slides and makes the titles a list on a new slide. To create a summary slide, follow these steps:

1. In Slide Sorter view, select the slides that you want to summarize.

2. Click the Summary Slide button in the Slide Sorter toolbar.

   The summary slide is inserted before the first selected slide, with the title Summary Slide. You can now move the slide where you want it or change the title.

Part

I

Ch

6

Arranging Objects on Your Slide

All the items in slides—whether the items are text areas, tables, charts, or graphics—are considered *objects*. You can move objects, shape them, resize them, and restack them to create just the appearance you're looking for. ▪

Place objects

Put objects just where you want them in your slide. Put objects on top of other objects, and align them with the slide edges and with each other.

Copy and delete objects

Create multiple copies of an object in the same slide or different slides.

Group objects

Link several objects into a single object that's easy to move and copy.

Resize objects

Grow, shrink, and change the ratio of graphic objects. Change the amount of space for text.

Set tabs and margins

Control how your text flows within a text object.

Selecting Objects

In order to work with the objects that are on the slide, you have to be in Slide view. The only other view that lets you have any effect on the contents of the slide is Outline view, and that only lets you work with the contents of the text areas.

Before you can change an object in Slide view, whether it's a text object (which you've already been shown how to create), or a picture, chart, or table (covered in various upcoming chapters), you need to be able to indicate which object or objects you're working with.

To deal with objects properly, you need to understand that except for straight lines drawn with the Line or Arrow tool, PowerPoint considers every object to be a rectangle. For drawn shapes, the edges of the rectangle go along the highest, lowest, leftmost, and rightmost part of the object. A circle that's 1 inch across, for example, is part of an object that is 1 inch square.

To select objects, use any of the following techniques:

- To select a single object, click the visible portion of the object.
- To select a closely gathered group of objects, you need to indicate a rectangular area containing all those objects. Point to one corner of the object; then drag to the opposite corner. (Pick a corner that is not directly on top of any object; otherwise, you end up moving that object.) As you drag, a dotted outline of the rectangle appears. When you release the mouse button, any object that's completely contained within that rectangle is selected.
- To select additional objects without deselecting an already-selected object, hold down the Shift key and click the additional objects.
- To select all objects in the slide, choose Edit, Select All (or press Ctrl+A).
- To deselect all selected objects, simply click an area of the slide that contains no objects.

When objects are selected, *sizing handles* (little white squares) appears at all four corners and the middles of all four sides of rectangular objects (and at both ends of straight-line objects), as shown in Figure 7.1. Text objects also have a gray border.

Moving, Copying, and Deleting Objects

To move objects in Slide view, use any of the following techniques:

- To move a nontext object across a slide, point to the visible portion of the object and drag it to where you want it.
- To move a text object across a slide, select it and then drag the gray edge of its rectangle. (If you attempt to drag from within the rectangle, PowerPoint thinks that you're trying to select text.)
- To move an object to another slide, select the object; cut it to the Clipboard (choose Edit, Cut or press Ctrl+X); go to the slide where you want the object to appear; and paste it (choose Edit, Paste or press Ctrl+V).

FIG. 7.1
Notice that the edges of the object can extend off the edges of the slide.

A circle is a rectangular object

Line object

Rotated text object

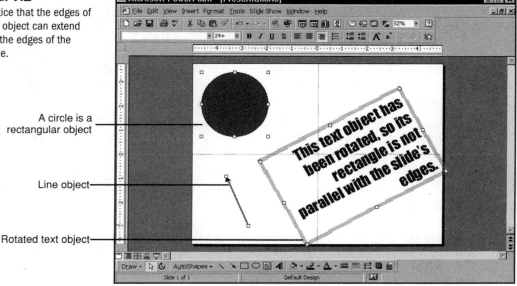

> **TIP**
> To drag an object in a straight horizontal or vertical path, hold down the Shift key while dragging.

To copy objects when in Slide view, use any of the following techniques:

- To copy an object to another spot on the same slide, hold down Ctrl and drag the object.
- To copy an object to another slide, select the object; copy it to the Clipboard (choose Edit, Copy or press Ctrl+C; go to the slide where you want the object to appear; and paste it (choose Edit, Paste or press Ctrl+V).

To delete any object, simply select it and then press Delete.

Aligning and Distributing Objects

Sometimes, you want to line up objects so that their edges are even or so that they're centered in the same line. To do so, follow these steps:

1. Select the objects that you want to align.
2. Click the Draw button on the Drawing toolbar to get the Draw menu.
3. In the Align Or Distribute submenu, make sure that the Relative to Slide command does not have a check next to it; if it does, choose it to remove the check.
4. Choose Draw, Align Or Distribute, and choose from the submenu one of the six Align options, indicating which edge (or center) you want to align the object with.

Part
I

Ch
7

If you use the same procedure with Relative To Slide checked instead of unchecked in step 3, your objects are aligned with the edge (or center) of the slide.

You can also make lining things up by hand easier. Choose Draw, Snap, To Grid to create an invisible grid that objects on the page are attracted to. Choose Draw, Snap, To Shape to have an object that you're moving snap to the edges of other objects that you move it by. Or drag the *guides* (dotted lines across the slides) to where you want things to snap to. (If you don't see guides, choose View, Guides to display them.)

If you select several objects and then choose Draw, Align Or Distribute, Distribute Horizontally, or Distribute Vertically, the objects move so that they space evenly. If Relative To Slide is selected, objects are spaced evenly between the edges of the slide; otherwise, they are spaced evenly between the two objects that are farthest apart.

Resizing Objects

You can make any object smaller or larger. In the case of most types of objects, this change of size makes every part of the object shrink or grow. In the case of text objects, you're resizing only the space provided for the text; the font remains the same size.

To resize any object, you first have to select it so that the sizing handles appear. Then use any of the following procedures:

- To make an object shorter or taller, drag the sizing handle in middle of the top or bottom edge until the object is the size that you want.

- To make an object thinner or wider, drag the sizing handle from the center of either side until the object is the desired size.

- To change both the height and the width at the same time, drag one of the corner sizing handles. If you want the object to maintain the same *aspect ratio* (the ratio of height to width), hold down the Shift key while you drag.

Normally, when you resize an object by dragging one edge, the opposite edge of the object stays stationary, which means that the center of the object is moving. If you want the center of the object to remain stationary, hold down the Ctrl key while dragging.

Rotating Objects

Most types of objects can be tilted at any angle, or even flipped horizontally or vertically. The exceptions are some types of graphics and all types of movies.

 To rotate or flip an object, select it. If the Free Rotate button is grayed out, you selected an object of a type that cannot be flipped or rotated. If, however, the button is not grayed out then you have the following options:

- To rotate the object 90 degrees, or to flip it horizontally or vertically, click the Draw button to get the Draw menu. From the Rotate Or Flip submenu, choose Rotate Left,

Rotate <u>R</u>ight, Flip <u>H</u>orizontal, or Flip <u>V</u>ertical. Be aware that if the object has been tilted, the horizontal and vertical are relative to the screen, not to the object. Also be aware that flipping a text box does not cause the text to become mirror-style backward.

■ To rotate the object at any angle, click the Free Rotate button. The sizing handles disappear, and *rotating handles* (little green circles) appear at the corners of the object. Drag one of those circles, and the object rotates around its center. (If you hold down the Ctrl key, the object rotates about the opposite corner rather than about the center.)

 After you click the Free Rotate button, anything rotatable that you select shows the rotating handles instead of the sizing handles. To return to seeing sizing handles, click the Select Objects button.

Ordering Objects

When the visible parts of two objects overlap, parts of one object are going to be hidden. As shown in Figure 7.2, which object is on top can make a big difference in the way that the slide appears.

FIG. 7.2
The order in which you stack your objects is important.

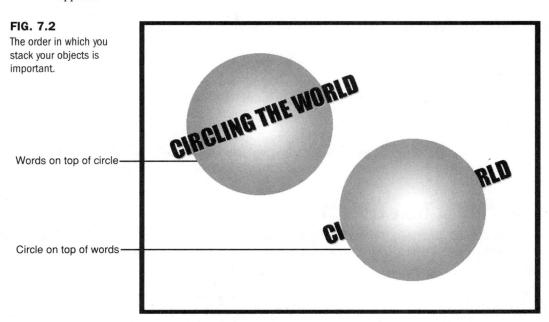

Words on top of circle

Circle on top of words

When you overlap things, PowerPoint automatically puts whatever was added to the slide first at the bottom and anything you add later on top of that. To switch this order, right-click any object. A shortcut menu appears. Choose O<u>r</u>der. Then, from the submenu, choose one of the following commands:

■ Bring To Fron<u>t</u> to put this object on the top of the pile.

- Send To Bac<u>k</u> to put this object on the bottom of the pile.
- Bring <u>For</u>ward to move the object up one position in the stack.
- Send <u>B</u>ackward to move the object down one position in the stack.

If you need to do some work on a hard-to-select object in the middle of the stack, try this:

1. Right-click the top item in the stack and choose O<u>r</u>der, Send To Bac<u>k</u> from the shortcut menu.
2. Repeat step 1 until the object that you want to work on is on top.
3. Do whatever you need to do to that object.
4. Send the top object to the back.
5. Repeat step 4 until the object that was originally on top is back on top again.

Grouping Objects

Sometimes, turning several objects into a single object is handy. That way, if you've built a design out of several objects, you can easily move or copy the complete design.

To group several objects into a single object, select the objects that you want to group. Right-click one of the objects and choose <u>G</u>rouping, <u>G</u>roup from the shortcut menu. All the separate sizing handles of the various objects disappear. Instead, one set of sizing handles appears for the entire grouped object.

If you want to undo the grouping, right-click the grouped object and choose <u>G</u>rouping, <u>U</u>ngroup from the shortcut menu. The grouped object is split into the individual objects.

If you need to change just one object in a group, ungroup the object and make the change; then right-click the object that you fixed (or any other object in the group) and choose <u>G</u>rouping, Regr<u>o</u>up.

Creating a Text Object

When you put text on a slide in Outline view, it automatically creates a text object to contain it. You can also create additional text objects while in Slide view. To do this, follow these steps:

1. Click the Text Box button. The mouse pointer turns into a downward-pointing arrow.
2. Drag from where you want one corner of the text object to where you want the opposite corner. A text box appears. The text box is the width of the dragged area, and one line deep, with a shaded rectangle around it.
3. Start typing. What you type appears in the object. You can use the buttons on the Formatting toolbar to format the text; these buttons work the same way that they do in Outline view.

You can also add text to most other types of objects by selecting the object then starting to type.

Positioning Text Within a Text Object

You can lay out text within the text object in Slide view in several ways. To work with text layout, you have to see the on-screen rulers, as shown in Figure 7.3. If you do not see the rulers, choose View, Ruler to display them. When you select a text object, you see a ruler that applies solely to that object.

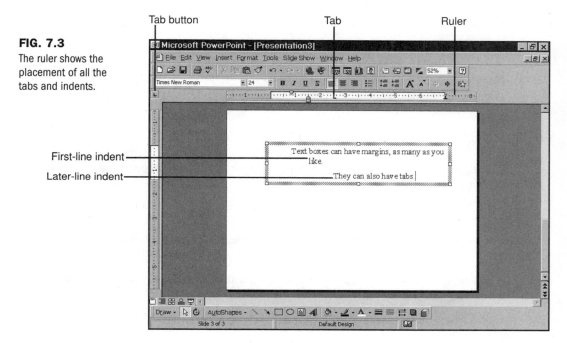

FIG. 7.3
The ruler shows the placement of all the tabs and indents.

To place the indents, just drag the first-line indent marker from the top-left edge of the ruler over to where you want the first line of each paragraph to start. Then drag the later-line indent marker along the bottom edge of the ruler to where you want the other lines to start.

To set tab stops on the ruler, follow these steps:

1. Click the tab button until it shows the type of tab you want.

Tab	Lines Up With
L	Left of text (standard)
⊥	Center of text
⌐	Right of text
⌐.	Decimal point

2. Click the ruler where you want the tab to appear.

You can move a tab by dragging it or eliminate a tab by dragging it off the ruler.

You can also align text within a text object. You can select the object's border to align the entire text or select text within the text box to align part of it. To set the alignment, click one of the following buttons:

Button	Puts Text
	Flush left
	Centered
	Flush right

To change the spacing between lines of text, select the text object without selecting any text within it. Then use any of the following techniques:

■ To increase the spacing, click the Increase Paragraph Spacing button.

■ To decrease the spacing, click the Decrease Paragraph Spacing button.

If you want these changes to affect only a few lines within a text object, select those lines before clicking the buttons.

You can also set further options about how text falls within a text box. To do this, follow these instructions:

1. Right-click the object.
2. From the shortcut menu, choose Format Text Box or Format Object or Format AutoShape (only one of these choices will appear, depending on the type of object you're working with). The Format dialog box appears.
3. Click the Text Box tab. You'll see all the options displayed in Figure 7.4. Use these options to configure your text box.

FIG. 7.4

The Text Box tab lets you control how text flows in your object.

Start new line when words hit right edge of text box

Expand text box when text exceeds box size

Tilt text on-edge

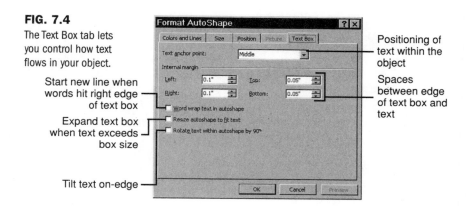

Positioning of text within the object

Spaces between edge of text box and text

CHAPTER 8

Creating a Presentation or New Slide from Scratch

Although the presentations created by the AutoContent Wizard are good, they do not cover all (or even most) presentation needs. By being able to start from a blank presentation, choose your own design template, and pick your own color scheme, you can build a presentation without relying on the wizard. ▪

Create a presentation from scratch

Start with a presentation without any text or even without any background design.

Add new slides

Put new slides in, with predesigned layouts, and just add the text.

Choose a different background and layout design

Switch templates to give your presentation a completely new look.

Change color scheme

Pick different colors for the design and the text of your presentation.

Change text color

Make individual words, phrases, or text objects a different color from the rest of the presentation text.

Starting with a Blank Presentation

You can start with a totally blank presentation; start with empty white slides; or choose to use a design template, which has a background or layout design but no text.

To start with a totally blank presentation, use one of the following methods:

- If you just started PowerPoint, choose the <u>B</u>lank Presentation option button in the initial dialog box; then click the OK button.

- If you've already been working in PowerPoint, click the New button.

When you do this, a dialog box appears, offering you a choice of slide layouts. See the next section of this chapter for details.

If you want to start a new presentation without any text, but with a background and style design already in place, do one of the following:

- If you just started PowerPoint, choose the <u>T</u>emplate option button in the initial dialog box; then click the OK button.

- If you've already been working in PowerPoint, choose <u>F</u>ile, <u>N</u>ew. When the New Presentation dialog box opens, click the Presentation Design tab.

When you complete one of these steps, you see a dialog box that looks like Figure 8.1. The dialog box shows a list of *templates* (presentation designs). Unfortunately, seeing the name of the design doesn't tell you much about it. PowerPoint provides an easy way to get a sense of what a given design looks like, however.

FIG. 8.1

The preview display shows a rough version of the typical slide from the selected template.

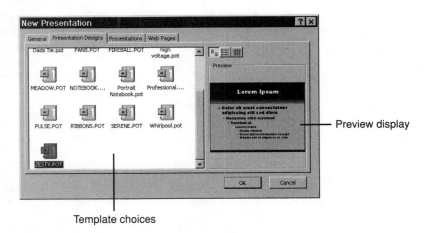

Template choices

Preview display

To find the template that you want, follow these steps:

1. Click one of the templates.

    A rough preview of what a typical slide in this presentation looks like appears in the preview window.

2. If you do not want to use this design, keep checking out other templates by clicking them, until you find one that you want to use.

3. When you find the template that you want, click the OK button.

You see a New Slide dialog box that allows you to select the layout for the first slide. See the next section for details on this dialog box.

Part
I
Ch
8

Adding a New Slide

To add a new slide to a presentation, follow these steps:

1. Select the slide after which you want to add the new slide.

You can do this in whatever view you choose. (In Slide view, the slide that currently appears in the PowerPoint window is considered to be the selected one.)

2. Click the New Slide button.

The dialog box shown in Figure 8.2 appears. You also see this dialog box when you start a new presentation from scratch.

FIG. 8.2

The slide designs in the New Slide dialog box use a little picture of a chart to indicate space for a chart, a picture of a man to indicate space for clip art, and a picture of a movie clapper to indicate space for a movie or sound clip.

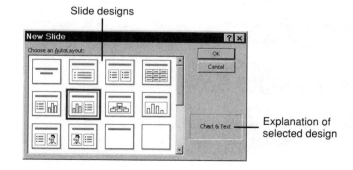

In the Choose an AutoLayout display area, you see several slide designs, with space already set aside for text (shown as gray bars), lists, graphs, charts, or other objects. (One blank slide is available, if you want to lay out the slide from scratch.)

3. Click a slide design that interests you.

A description of the areas in that design appears in the explanation area.

4. When you decide to use a design, double-click it.

The new slide is added to the presentation.

When viewed in Slide view, the new slide shows areas set aside for the various objects in the design. Clicking or double-clicking one of these areas starts the process of adding that object to the slide.

Adding Text to a Slide

You can also add additional text boxes, if you want multiple text areas on your slide.

▶ **See** "Creating a Text Object," **p. 56**

Choosing a Different Template

If you decide that you don't like the look of the template that you chose, you don't have to start over from scratch. Instead, you can choose a different template and have the presentation automatically reformatted to that template.

To do this, follow these steps:

1. Click the Apply Design button on the Standard toolbar.

   A file navigator appears, displaying a list of PowerPoint template files.

2. Click any of these templates to see it previewed in the file navigator's preview area.

3. When you find the template that you want, double-click it.

   Your presentation is automatically converted to the design of the new template.

If you're unhappy with the templates that come with PowerPoint, you can make your own.

▶ **See** "Creating and Editing PowerPoint Templates," **p. 115**

Changing the Color Scheme

Every template has its own built-in color scheme. This scheme sets the default color for various elements—titles, text, background, shadows, and so on. You can replace this color scheme with another color scheme and have it apply either to the currently selected slides or to all the slides in the presentation.

To change the color scheme to one of the alternative color schemes that come with the template, follow these steps:

1. Choose Format, Slide Color Scheme. The dialog box shown in Figure 8.3 appears.

   In the Color Schemes area of the dialog box is a series of little pictures, each depicting one color scheme. The picture shows the color for title text, normal text, and various drawing elements.

2. Click the color scheme that you want to use.

3. Click the Apply To All button to apply this color scheme to all the slides in your presentation, or click Apply to apply it to only the currently selected slides.

To create your own custom color scheme, follow these steps:

1. Choose Format, Slide Color Scheme.

2. When the Color Scheme dialog box appears, click the Custom tab to display what appears in Figure 8.4.

FIG. 8.3
The Standard tab of the Color Scheme dialog box gives you a choice of premade color schemes.

Color schemes

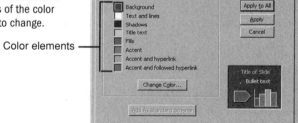

FIG. 8.4
The Custom tab allows you to select individual elements of the color scheme to change.

Color elements

3. Click the color box marked Background; then click the Change Color button.

   The color selector dialog box shown in Figure 8.5 appears.

FIG. 8.5
This color selector allows you to pick any of 144 colors.

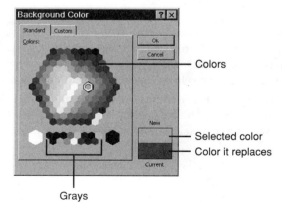

Colors

New

Selected color
Color it replaces

Current

Grays

4. Click the hexagon that has the color that you want.

   If you want to pick a shade that's a little different from any of the hexagons, click the Custom tab of the color selector and select the color, as shown in Figure 8.6.

FIG. 8.6

This color selector gives you three ways to select more than 16 million colors. All numeric values go from 0 to 255.

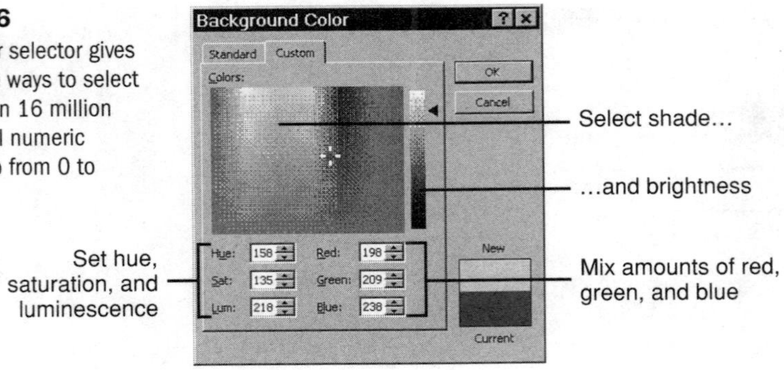

Set hue, saturation, and luminescence

Select shade...

...and brightness

Mix amounts of red, green, and blue

5. Click the OK button. The new color is set.

6. Repeat steps 3–5 for all the other color elements listed in the Color Scheme dialog box (Text and Lines, Shadows, and so on).

7. Click the Apply To All button to apply this color scheme to all the slides in your presentation, or click Apply to apply it to only the currently selected slides.

Changing the Text Color

If you want to change the color of all the text in a presentation, you're best off using the color-scheme settings to change it.

If you just want one word, phrase, or text object to have a different color, however, first select the text that you want to change in Slide view.

Then:

■ To change to the color displayed below the *A* on the Font Color button, click the Font Color button.

■ To change to another color from the slide's color scheme, click the down-arrow button to the right of the Font Color button, and from the drop-down list that appears, choose the square that has the color you want. (If you change the color scheme later, any text that you set to one of these color scheme colors will change color to match the new scheme.)

■ To change to any other color, click the down-arrow button to the right of the Font Color button, and from the drop-down list that appears, choose More Font Colors. Then select the color you want in a color selector dialog box, as shown in Figures 8.5 and 8.6.

Creating an Outline

The outline is the heart of most presentations. PowerPoint gives you a full outline editor, making it easy to set different levels of indentation for topics within topics within topics. The program also cooperates with other outline-making programs, allowing you to take an outline created elsewhere and use it as a basis for your presentation. By controlling your outline well, you can clarify for your audience what your major points are and what are minor details or clarifications. ■

Use an outline from another program

Import an existing outline created in Word or some other program for use in PowerPoint.

Send your outline to Word

Export your outline to Microsoft Word, where you can use it in other documents.

Create headings, topics, and subtopics

For each slide, choose what the header is to be, what points are going to be listed, and what points are listed as subtopics of other points.

Check your outline for clarity

Use the Style Checker to make sure that your slides aren't overcrowded and that the text is readable.

Check your capitalization and punctuation

Verify that you have capitals only where needed and that sentences have end punctuation.

Importing the Outline from Another Program

To import an outline created in (or readable by) Microsoft Word, open the outline file in Word and choose Word's File, Send To, Microsoft PowerPoint command. PowerPoint starts running (if it wasn't already running) and creates a new presentation with that outline as the text.

To open an outline created in another program, follow these steps:

1. Choose PowerPoint's File, Open command (or press Ctrl+O).

   A file navigator opens. (For information on using the file navigator, see Chapter 1, "Getting Familiar with PowerPoint 97.")

2. From the Files of Type drop-down list, choose All Outlines.

   The file navigator displays all files in formats that it can read outlines from, including Rich Text Format (.rtf), standard text (.txt), and HTML (.htm or .html).

3. Locate the file with your outline and double-click it.

   PowerPoint opens the outline as a new presentation.

N O T E If you are unable to find the file in the navigator, it is saved in a format that PowerPoint does not recognize. If you can, use the program that made the outline to save the outline in .rtf (Rich Text Format) or .txt format. Otherwise, you have to use the Copy (Ctrl+C) and Paste (Ctrl+V) commands to move the outline from the source program to PowerPoint. ▪

If your outline is formatted with the standard outlining styles, PowerPoint will organize the individual lines as follows:

- Any line marked as the style Header 1 is made the title for a new slide.
- Any line marked as the style Header 2 is made a list point on the slide in which the preceding Header 1 is the title.
- Any line marked with Header 3 is a continued subpoint of the preceding Header 2 line. Header 4 lines are considered to be subpoints of Header 3 lines, and so on.

If you're not using standard outlining, PowerPoint judges what are points and what are subpoints by the level of indenting, as shown in Figure 9.1. Anything that's flush left is treated as Header 1, anything indented one level is treated as Header 2, anything indented two levels is treated as Header 3, and so on.

Remember that when an outline is imported, it has no template attached to it yet. The outline is plain text on a white background until you apply a template design to it.

Creating an Outline from Scratch

To create an outline from scratch, click the New button. In Outline view, start typing. The first line that you type will be the header on the first slide.

FIG. 9.1
When reading text files as outlines, PowerPoint judges the level of a topic by how far it is indented.

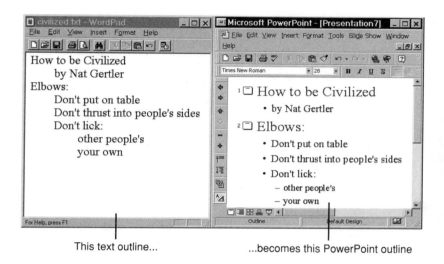

This text outline...　　　　...becomes this PowerPoint outline

Part

I

Ch

9

Whenever you press Enter, you start a new slide point. The point will be at the same indention level as the previous level. To indent the new line further, press Tab. To create less of an indent, press Shift+Tab.

Promoting, Demoting, and Rearranging Text in Outline View

You can easily change the level of any point, move any point, or change your view of the outline by using the buttons in the Outline toolbar, which appears at the side of the screen in Outline view. The functions of these buttons are seen in Table 9.1.

Table 9.1   Outline Toolbar Buttons

Button	Shortcut	Function
⬅	Alt+Shift+←	Promote: decrease this line's level of indentation, turning a subpoint into a point.
➡	Alt+Shift+→	Demote: increase the level of this line's indentation, turning a point into a subpoint.
⬆	Alt+Shift+↑	Move Up: place this line above the preceding line.
⬇	Alt+Shift+↓	Move Down: place this line after following line.

continues

Table 9.1   Continued

Button	Shortcut	Function
	Alt+Shift+-	Collapse: Show only the title for this slide. (The points still appear in the presentation—just not while you're editing the outline.)
	Alt+Shift+plus sign (+)	Expand: Show the entire contents of this slide.
	Alt+Shift+1	Collapse All: Show only the title for all slides.
	Alt+Shift+A	Expand All: Show the entire contents of all slides.
		Summary Slide: Create a slide summarizing the selected slides (as described in Chapter 7, "Arranging Objects on Your Slide").
	/ (numeric keypad)	Show Formatting: Toggles between showing all text formatting and showing unformatted text.

Because these functions affect an entire line at a time, you do not have to select the entire line before operating it. Placing the insertion bar anywhere in the line is enough to indicate the current line. If you want one of the line-oriented commands to affect multiple lines, however, you must select those lines.

Exporting an Outline or Presentation to Microsoft Word

If you want to turn a PowerPoint outline into a Microsoft Word outline, or if you want to create a Word document with pictures of your slides in it, follow these steps:

1. With the presentation loaded in PowerPoint, choose File, Send To, Microsoft Word. The Write-Up dialog box, shown in Figure 9.2, appears.

2. If you want to send just the outline with no graphics, select the Outline Only option button. To send pictures of your slides over, select the option button that best describes the format you want.

3. If you selected anything besides Outline Only, click either the Paste and Paste Link option buttons. If you choose Paste, the Word document always stays the same, no matter what you may later do to the PowerPoint presentation. If you choose Paste Link, every time you load the Word document, Word checks to see whether the presentation (as saved on the disk) has changed. If so, Word includes the changes in the document.

FIG. 9.2
The Send To command in Word offers several formats for the slides to be shown, as well as a way of sending over the outline.

Send slides ———

Send outline ———

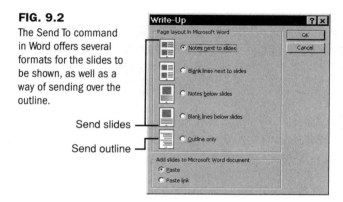

4. Click the OK button.

Word starts (if it's not already running), and a new document appears with your outline or slides in it.

Using Style Checker

PowerPoint has a built-in Style Checker program that looks over your presentation text. This tool offers three categories of checking:

- *Spelling* checks for the same spelling errors that would be caught by the spell checker that checks as you type.

- *Visual Clarity* makes sure that your slides are easy on the eyes by making sure that you're not using too many bulleted points, too small fonts, too many different fonts, and other such items.

- *Case And End Punctuation* makes sure that the sentences start with capital letters, that titles have every word capitalized, that titles don't end with periods, and so on.

To use Style Checker, follow these steps:

1. Choose Tools, Style Checker.

The Style Checker dialog box opens, offering you three possible types of style checking.

2. Check the check boxes for the type of style checking that you want to do.

Clicking the Options button allows you to configure the parameters for checking visual clarity, case, and end punctuation. You should do this at least once to see the full list of what Style Checker is checking.

3. Click the Start button.

Style Checker starts working. If the program finds any problems, it either fixes those problems itself or asks you whether you want to change or ignore the situation.

When Style Checker is done checking the presentation, a dialog box appears, telling you so.

4. Click OK.

CAUTION

Be sure to check the presentation yourself after the Style Checker finishes with it, because a good chance exists that Style Checker will have "fixed" something that wasn't wrong to begin with (such as a capitalized proper name in the middle of a sentence).

CHAPTER 10

Printing Your Presentation

The process of printing is used for more than just getting your presentation, outline, handouts, or notes onto paper; it's also something that you do if you put your presentation on overhead transparencies or slide-projector slides. PowerPoint is fairly flexible in the ways that it can print your presentation, and getting a good handle on those ways helps you get just the printout you want. ■

Check your presentation

Review how your hard copy will look if you're printing it on a black-and-white printer.

Set your print options

Choose which printer to send your presentation to, what layout to use, and other printing options.

Choose what to print

Choose whether you want to print an outline, handouts, notes, or the complete presentation, and specify which slides to print.

Start printing

Send the document to the printer for printing.

Fix print problems

Troubleshoot slow printing, nonprinting, and other printing errors.

Checking the Presentation

PowerPoint's tools give you access to a full range of colors to use in your presentation. If you are printing the presentation on a black-and-white printer, however, those colors are going to show up as grays, and a chance exists that they will be hard to read on printouts.

Even color presentations can be hard to view, if the colors don't contrast well. A slide that is hard to see in shades of gray will also be hard to see in color for many people.

To check how your presentation looks in shades of gray, follow these steps:

1. In Slide view, click the Black And White View button.

    The slides now appear in black and white. A small Color window shows how the slide looks in color.

2. Use the scroll bar to step through your presentation and check how each slide looks in gray.

3. After you check the entire presentation (or if you need to fix a slide), click the Black And White View button again to go back to working in color.

    If you're trying to fix the slide, choosing View, Slide Miniature opens a small window that shows how the slide you're working on looks in black and white.

Choosing the Right Printer

To start the print procedure, choose File, Print (or press Ctrl+P) to open the Print dialog box, shown in Figure 10.1. This dialog box is the center of all printing activities.

FIG. 10.1

The Print dialog box is the control center for printing to paper, transparencies, or slides.

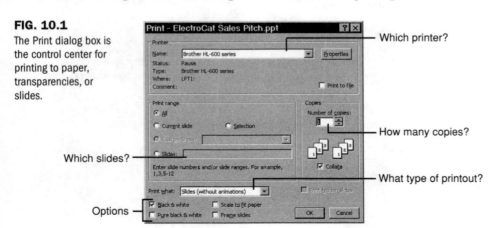

CAUTION

Make sure that you're happy with your most recent changes before opening the Print dialog box. After you open this dialog box (whether or not you end up printing), you cannot use the Undo command to undo earlier mistakes!

To select the printer that you are printing to, click the Printer Name drop-down list and choose a printer from the list of printers that are configured on the system. If you are making your own slides, choose your *film recorder* (a device that puts computer images on film), which should be configured as a printer.

If you're going to have the slides made by a *service bureau* (an outside company specializing in special computer input and output needs), you need to check the Print to File check box to save the output as a file. You also need to find out from your service bureau what printer driver to configure.

Part
I
Ch
10

CAUTION

If you are printing transparencies, make sure that you have the right type of transparency sheet for your printer. Using laser-printer transparency sheets in an inkjet printer can leave you with a multicolor puddle of ink. Worse yet, inkjet sheets may melt in a laser printer, causing extensive and expensive damage.

Selecting the Type of Printout

PowerPoint offers you a range of types of printouts for different needs. Choose the type that you want from the following types listed on the Print What drop-down list:

Table 10.1   PowerPoint Printout Types

Type	Printout Contents
Slides	Prints each slide, one per page. (This option is available only if the slides have are no animations.)
Slides (With Animations)	Prints multiple copies of each slide that has an animation—one copy of how the slide looks before any animations begin and then one copy apiece of how the slide looks after each animation. (This option is available only if at least one slide in the presentation has an animation.)
Slides (Without Animations)	Prints each slide as it appears after all animations on each slide are complete. (This option is available only if at least one slide in the presentation has an animation.)

continues

Table 10.1 Continued	
Type	**Printout Contents**
Handouts (2 Slides Per Page)	Prints two slides per page, stacked vertically, for use as a handout.
Handouts (3 Slides Per Page)	Prints three slides per page, plus a lined area for the viewer to take notes about each slide (as shown in Figure 10.2).
Handouts (6 Slides Per Page)	Prints three rows of two slides apiece.
Notes Page	Prints the slides with the notes that were attached in Notes Page view.
Outline	Prints the presentation's outline.

FIG. 10.2

The selection Handouts (3 slides per page) prints your presentation in a handy reference format with space for notes.

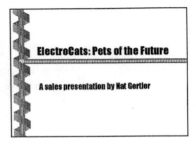

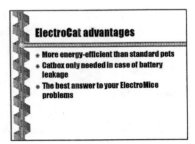

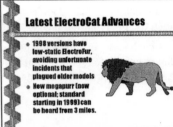

Choosing Which Slides to Print

In the Print Range area of the Print dialog box are several options for indicating which slides you want to include in the printout. These options include the following:

- To print all the slides, click All.
- To print just the slide that is currently displayed in Slide view or Notes Page view, click Current.
- To print all the slides that are currently selected in Outline view or Slide Sorter view, click Selection.
- If you are using PowerPoint's Custom Show feature and want to print all the slides used in one custom show, choose Custom Show; then choose the name of the show from the adjacent drop-down list.
- To specify now which slides to print, click Slides; then enter a list of slide numbers, separated by commas, in the adjacent text box. You can indicate a series of slides by listing the first slide in the series, followed by a dash and then the last slide. Entering **3,5-7,12**, for example, causes slides 3, 5, 6, 7, and 12 to be printed.

Setting Other Print Options

Other print options in the Print dialog box include:

- *Number of Copies*, a number box that allows you to set the number of copies of the presentation.
- *Collate*, a check box that has effect only if you choose to print more than one copy of more than one slide. If you check this check box, the entire first copy of the presentation prints, followed by the second copy, and so on. Otherwise, all the copies of the first page of the printout print, followed by the second page, and so on. (Printing without collation is faster than printing with collation, but you may lose a great deal of time putting the copies together.)
- *Print Hidden Slides*, a check box that is available only if you use the Hide Slide feature. Checking this check box causes those hidden slides to be included in your printout.
- *Black & White*, a check box that causes the slide to be printed in black, white, and shades of gray, even on color printers.
- *Pure Black & White*, a check box that causes the slide to be printed in black and white, without any shades of gray. This option can be handy if you're going to photocopy or fax the presentation, because grays do not turn out well on some copy and fax machines.
- *Scale To Fit Printer*, a check box that expands the printed version of the slide so that it fills the slide, no matter what the dimensions of your slide and paper are.
- *Frame Slides*, a check box that puts a black border around the printed version of your slides.

Printing Your Slides

After you make all your print settings in the Print dialog box, click the OK button. The presentation is sent to your printer.

 If you want to print again, using the same settings that you used the last time you printed, just click the Print button in the Standard toolbar.

Changing Slide Size

By default, PowerPoint assumes that you're designing your presentation as a computer slide show. This way, PowerPoint produces slides that fit the screen well and that also fit fairly nicely sideways on an 8.5" by 11" piece of paper. If your goal is to create a slide-projector slide show, or a presentation printed upright on paper or on some other size of paper, however, you want to change the dimensions of your presentation.

To change dimensions, follow these steps:

1. Choose File, Page Setup.

    The Page Setup dialog box, shown in Figure 10.3, appears.

FIG. 10.3

Using Page Setup to change the dimensions of your presentation causes your entire presentation to be reformatted. Doing this setting-up before doing much work on the presentation is wise.

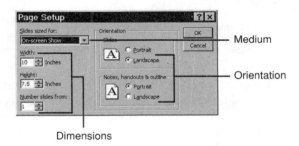

Medium

Orientation

Dimensions

2. From the Slides Sized For drop-down list, choose the size of paper or type of image output that you want.

    If you want something that is a different size from the items listed, choose Custom; then set the size of the item by using the Width and Height number boxes.

3. Specify the way that you want the slides to be oriented by using the Slide Orientation option buttons.

    If you want your slides to be taller than they are wide (as on a standard piece of paper), choose Portrait. If you want the slides to be wider than they are tall (as on a sideways piece of paper), choose Landscape. (You can also select the orientation for Notes, Handouts & Outline here.)

4. Click the OK button.

    PowerPoint changes the dimensions of your presentation.

5. Look through all your slides.

Although PowerPoint does resize everything to make it fit the new dimensions, the resizing sometimes comes out awkward, either stretching things strangely or pushing things right off the edge of the slide. You may need to fix some things.

Using Headers and Footers

You can set which information you want to appear in *headers* (information at the top of the page) and *footers* (information at the bottom of the page) of your notes pages and handouts. To do this, follow these steps:

1. Choose View, Header And Footer. The Header and Footer dialog box appears.
2. Click the Notes and Handouts tab. You see the tab shown in Figure 10.4.

FIG. 10.4

The page layout preview highlights the placement of the headers and footers that you select.

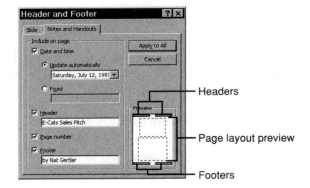

3. If you want the date to appear on each page, check the Date and Time check box; then specify whether you want PowerPoint to automatically update the date when the pages are printed (choose the Update Automatically option button) or whether you want the same date to appear no matter when the pages are printed (choose the Fixed Date option button).

   If you choose Update Automatically, you can select the format the date is shown in from the drop-down list. If you choose Fixed Date, just type the date as you want it shown into the text box.

4. If you want some other information to appear in the header (the presentation's title, for example), check the Header check box; then enter in the adjacent text box the information that you want to appear.

5. If you want every page to be numbered, check the Page Number check box.

6. If you want some additional information to appear in the footer (such as your name), check the Footer check box; then type the information in the adjacent text box.

7. After you make all your selections, click the Apply to All button. The dialog box closes.

Information about putting footer information directly on the slide is covered in Chapter 14, "Creating and Editing PowerPoint Templates."

Troubleshooting Common Printer Problems

If nothing prints, check the following items:

- Is your printer plugged in and turned on?
- Is it properly cabled to the computer?
- Is its warning light on? (If so, the problem probably is with the printer itself; check the printer documentation for information on the warning light.)
- Is the right printer selected in the Print dialog box?
- If a printer icon appears in the Windows taskbar, double-click it to open the printer status window. Is the print task paused? (If so, choose Printer, Pause Printing in the status window to get the task started again.)
- Do non-Office programs print? (If so, the problem is with PowerPoint or Office.)
- Do other presentations print? (If so, the problem is with this presentation.)

If the presentation prints slowly, check the following items:

- Are you running several programs? (If so, you're probably low on memory. Close some of the other programs.)
- Is your hard disk getting full? (If so, that's affecting your print spooling. Clear some space.)
- Are you printing on a networked computer? (If so, check how quickly files come up over the network. If that's slow, too, you could be experiencing network problems.)

If something is missing from the printed version, check the following items:

- Did you print Slides (With Animations)? (If so, you may be looking at the printout of what the slide looks like before an animation. Look at the next pages.)
- Check the slide: Is the item actually on the page, rather than over the edge? (You can accidentally move something off the edge of the slide, particularly if you change the dimensions or template of the page.)
- Is the proper printer selected in the Print dialog box?
- Is your printer driver current? (If you've changed the printer setup or operating system greatly since you installed the printer driver, you may need to reinstall the driver. Also, check with your printer manufacturer to see whether a newer driver is available.)

If the printed colors look wrong, check the following items:

- Is the proper printer selected in the Print dialog box?

- Is your printer driver current? (If you've changed the printer setup or operating system greatly since you installed the printer driver, you may need to reinstall the driver. Also, check with your printer manufacturer to see whether a newer driver is available. Color printers are particularly finicky about having their own driver, rather than a driver for a similar model.)

- Is the ink supply empty? (Being out of one primary color can affect the shades and tints of a range of colors.)

- Do the colors look right when you're printing from a non-Office program? (If not, the problem is either the driver or the printer.)

Part

I

Ch

10

Emphasizing Your Points with Organization Charts, Tables, and Graphs

CHAPTER 11

Adding Organization Charts

If you're giving a presentation that's about a company or other group, having a slide that shows how the organization is structured can be handy. PowerPoint includes a program called Microsoft Organization Chart that is designed to do just that. By allowing you to show the structure (and rearrange it, when need be), this tool can be a handy addition to your presentation arsenal. ■

Show the structure of your organization

Build a chart that shows whom each person or department reports to.

Change and rearrange your organization

Update your chart to reflect planned or existing changes.

Format your chart entries

Highlight entries in your chart through use of colors, fonts, and designs.

Mark up your chart

Add lines and boxes to indicate special areas and planned changes.

Save the chart

Keep the chart on disk for working with outside PowerPoint or for moving into other presentations.

What Is an Organization Chart?

An *organization chart* is a type of chart designed to show who reports to whom within a company, like the one shown in Figure 11.1. Generally, each person or workgroup in the company gets a single box. The head of the company gets the top box. Lines run from this box down to the boxes of all the people who report to him or her, from each of them to the people who report to them, and so on.

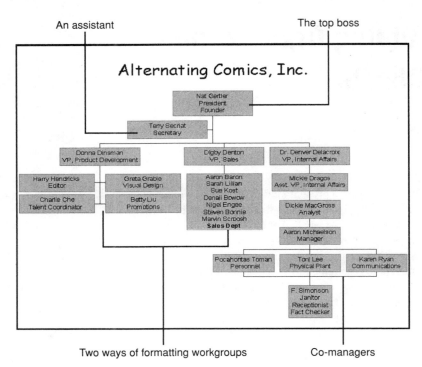

FIG. 11.1
The ways that the lines flow in an organization chart show how the members interact with one another.

The Parts of the Organization Chart Window

To start to put an organization chart on your slide, choose Insert, Picture, Organization Chart. This starts the Microsoft Organization Chart program, shown in Figure 11.2.

Double-clicking the menu bar expands the Organization Chart window so that it takes up the full screen, giving you room to work. You can also zoom in for a close-up look at your chart, or zoom back to look at it all at the same time, by using the four magnification settings in the View menu or their keyboard equivalents:

- F9 to show the entire chart in the window
- F10 to show the chart at half size
- F11 to show the chart at full size
- F12 to show the chart at double size

FIG. 11.2
The Microsoft
Organization Chart
window has its own set
of menus and its own
toolbar.

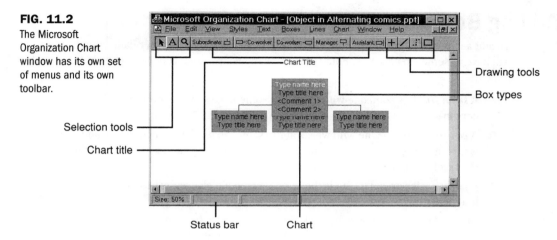

Drawing tools

Box types

Selection tools

Chart title

Status bar

Chart

Probably the first thing to do, before you forget, is select the text Chart Title and then type an actual title for your chart to replace that text. (You can then reselect it, right-click it, and choose Font from the shortcut menu if you want to change the font or size of the title.)

Part
II
Ch
11

Entering or Editing an Organization Member

To enter or change the name and job in a text box, follow these steps:

1. Click the text box to select it.

   The box turns to white text on black.

2. Press Enter.

   The text box opens to show four lines, and the first line is highlighted.

3. Type the name of the employee.

4. Press Enter.

   The next line is highlighted.

5. Type the person's job title.

   (You can repeat the press-Enter-and-then-type process twice more if you want to enter up to two lines of comments about the person.)

CAUTION

Before you put an organization chart for your company into a presentation that will be seen outside the company, check your company policy. Many companies consider their organizational structure to be confidential.

Adding Boxes

To add a new box to the chart, you first have to determine what sort of relationship this box will have to some existing box. Four types of relationships exist, represented by buttons on the toolbar:

- A *subordinate* is someone who works for someone else and whose box is below that person's.
- A *co-worker* is someone who works at the same job level as someone else and whose box is next to that person's. (The toolbar has two co-worker buttons: one to add the box to the right and one to add the box to the left.)
- A *manager* is someone who is the boss of someone else and whose box appears above that person's.
- An *assistant* is someone who works for someone else but can also be considered to be a route to that person. That person's box goes below and to the side of the boss's.

To add a box, follow these steps:

1. Click the button for the type of box that you want to add.

   The mouse pointer turns into a small box diagram.

2. Click the box that you want to attach the new box to.

   The new box appears in place (some other boxes may be automatically rearranged to make the box fit) and is selected.

3. Enter the information for the box, as described in the preceding section.

Selecting Boxes

As you've already seen, you can select a single box by clicking it. You can move from having that box selected to having an adjacent box selected by using the arrow keys.

To select multiple boxes at the same time, perform one of the following actions:

- For all boxes, press Ctrl+A.
- For an entire group or all boxes of one type (all assistants, all managers, and so on), choose Edit, Select and then choose the type of box from the submenu.
- For a set of boxes that are close together, drag from one corner of a rectangle that contains those boxes to the opposite corner.
- For any mix of boxes that you want to select, hold down the Shift key while clicking each box.

Removing and Rearranging Boxes

To get rid of a box (if someone gets fired, for example), select that box and then press Delete.

To move an employee from one spot to another, drag his box on top of a box that you want to attach it to.

- If you drag onto another box from below, the mouse pointer turns into a subordinate box diagram. Release the box to make the dragged box a subordinate of the box that you are placing it on.

- If you drag onto another box from the side, the mouse pointer turns into a sideways-pointing arrow. Release the box to make the dragged box a co-worker of the box that you are placing it on.

To change how employees are grouped, follow these steps:

1. Select the boxes that you want to change.

2. Choose the Styles menu.

   The graphic menu shown in Figure 11.3 appears.

FIG. 11.3

The program has six formats for displaying workgroups.

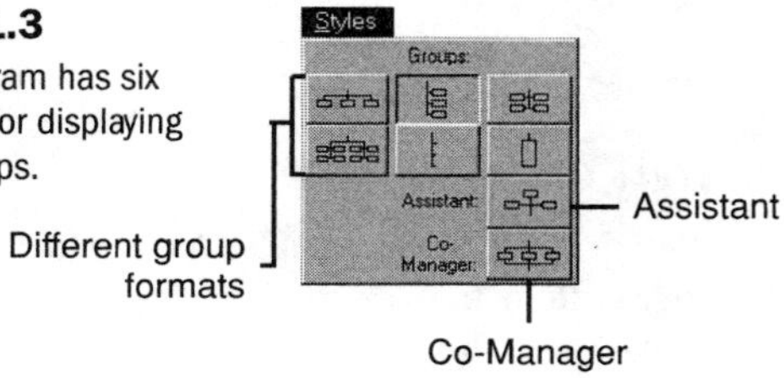

Different group formats

Assistant

Co-Manager

3. Choose the format that you want to use.

   Six buttons change the way that a workgroup is displayed; the picture of the button indicates the format. Also, one button turns the selected boxes into assistant boxes attached to the boss's box. The final choice turns the selected employees into co-managers, arranged so that a single group of employees reports to all of them.

Formatting Lines and Boxes

You can change the color of the boxes, the font of the text, and the style of both the box borders and the connecting lines on your organization chart.

To make any changes, first select the items that you want to change. Then to change, select the appropriate command from the following table:

Item to Change	Menu Command
Font	Text, Font; then choose the font and size in the Font dialog box.
Text color	Text, Color; then choose a color from the grid that appears.
Text alignment	Text, Left or Text, Right or Text Center, depending on the desired alignment.

continues

continued

Item to Change	Menu Command
Box color	Boxes, Color; then choose a color from the grid that appears.
Box shadow	Boxes, Shadow; then choose a style from the menu that appears.
Box border	Boxes, Border Style; then choose a style from the menu that appears.
Border color	Boxes, Border Color; then choose a color from the grid that appears.
Border	Boxes, Border Line Style; then choose a style from the menu that appears.
Line width	Lines, Thickness; then choose a width from the menu that appears.
Dashed line	Lines, Style; then choose a style from the menu that appears.
Line color	Lines, Color; then choose a color from the grid that appears.

Adding Other Items to the Chart

The Organization Chart program has some built-in drawing tools that allow you to further highlight items on your chart. These tools are four buttons that appear at the right end of the toolbar. If these buttons are not present, press Ctrl+D, and they appear. The function of these buttons are listed in Table 11.1.

Table 11.1 Organization Chart Drawing Tools

Button	Function
⊞	Draws horizontal and vertical lines; drag mouse pointer from one end of line to the other.
╱	Draws diagonal lines; drag mouse pointer from one end of line to the other.
⠢	Draws a line connecting two boxes; drag mouse pointer from the edge of one box to the edge of the other, and the line is automatically routed around other boxes.
▭	Draws a rectangle; mouse pointer from one corner to the opposite corner.

You can also set the background color of the chart by using the Chart, Background Color command.

To add text to the chart outside the boxes, follow these steps:

1. Click the Enter Text button.

2. Click the chart where you want the text to appear.

3. Type the text.

Saving the Organization Chart

You can save a copy of the chart to a disk file, separate from your presentation. This makes it easy to move the chart to other presentations and to work with it with chart software outside PowerPoint. To save the chart, follow these steps:

1. Choose File, Save Copy As.

   The Save Chart file navigator opens.

2. Type a name for your file into the File Name text box.

3. Click the OK button.

   The file is saved with the extension .OPX, and is readable by the program Org Plus for Windows.

Leaving and Re-Entering Organization Chart

To leave the Organization Chart program, click the Close button. A dialog box asks you whether you want to save the changes in the chart. Click the Yes button.

To resume editing this chart at a later date, bring up the slide with the chart on it in Slide view; then double-click the chart.

Part

II

Ch

11

Importing an Organization Chart from Another Program

Organization Chart basically is a less powerful version of a program called Org Plus for Windows, manufactured by Banner Blue Software. Organization Chart can load an Org Plus chart (use the File, Open command). You can also run Org Plus from PowerPoint, if you have it installed on your system; just choose Insert, Object and then choose Org Plus in the Insert Object dialog box that appears.

To insert charts from other chart programs, if the program is designed to be directly compatible with PowerPoint, go through the same procedure that you do for Org Chart, but choose the name of your chart program in the Insert Object dialog box. If your chart program is not listed, follow these steps:

1. Load your chart into your chart program.

2. Select the entire chart (press Ctrl+A).

3. Copy the chart to the Clipboard (press Ctrl+C).

4. Switch to PowerPoint.

5. Paste the chart into the slide (press Ctrl+V).

CHAPTER 12

Creating and Customizing Charts and Graphs

Microsoft Graph is a numerical charting program built into PowerPoint. It is extremely flexible, allowing for a broad range of chart types and many formatting options. Fully exploring its capabilities can take a while because almost every aspect of your chart is configurable.

Despite the program being called *Graph*, Microsoft sometimes refers to the images it creates as *charts* instead of calling them *graphs*. To be consistent with Microsoft terminology, both terms are used here. However, the charts that this program creates should not be confused with organization charts that are created by the Organization Chart program. ■

Enter data

Give Microsoft Graph the data that you want charted.

Choose a chart type

Pick a bar graph, pie chart, line graph, or one of many other general and specialty chart types.

Add titles and labels

Make it clear what each item on your chart is meant to represent and what the chart as a whole is about.

Format your chart

Set colors, labels, shadows, grid lines, and many other factors that affect the visual appearance of the chart.

Use Excel data

Take existing spreadsheet data and use it as the basis for a new chart.

Starting Microsoft Graph

 To start the Graph program, click the Insert Chart button:

A *datasheet* will open up, as seen in Figure 12.1. A datasheet looks like a spreadsheet (such as you might make with Excel), but it has no capability to calculate. It's just a gridwork in which you enter the values to be graphed and the labels to mark the data.

FIG. 12.1

The datasheet holds all the raw data that will be used to make the chart.

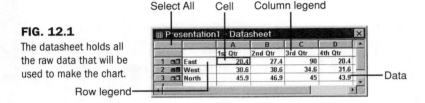

As with most spreadsheets, the rows are numbered, and the columns are lettered. Unlike spreadsheets, however, there is a row above row 1 and a column to the left of column A. These unlabeled lines are used for *legends*, which are names for the data in the rows and columns. For example, if you're graphing what your sales were in different states during each month of the year, you might have a row with the legend Michigan and a column with the legend March. The rows and columns combine to break the datasheet into little rectangles called *cells*. In the cell where the Michigan row intersects with the March column, you would enter the number for the sales in Michigan during March.

To enter data into a cell, click the cell and then type in the data. To move to the next cell, press Enter to move down, or use the cursor keys to move in whatever direction you want.

 The steps involved in making the datasheet disappear and reappear are as follows:

- You can hide the datasheet by clicking its Close button or by clicking the View Datasheet button.

- When you stop viewing the datasheet, you are still in Microsoft Graph. The screen looks a lot like Slide view, but the toolbars and menus are different.

- To resume working with the datasheet while you're still within Microsoft Graph, click the View Datasheet button. To re-enter Microsoft Graph after leaving it and get back to the datasheet, double-click the chart.

Formatting Data

The datasheet is a good place to set the look of the text for your chart. The legends you've entered will probably be appearing on the chart, and depending on how you format the chart, the data values may appear as text as well. You can format the data in terms of both font appearance and numeric format: how many digits after the decimal point, whether there's a dollar sign before the figures, and so on.

You don't necessarily want the same format for all your data. For example, one chart might show both the rising sales rate and the rising inflation rate over time. You'll want to display the sales figures as dollars, but the interest rates would be best shown as percent figures. As such, before you can format data, you need to be able to select the data you need to format. Use any of the following methods:

- To select any one cell, click it, or use the arrow keys to move to it.
- To select any row, click the button at the left end of that row.
- To select any column, click the button at the top of that column.
- To select any rectangular grouped set of cells, point to one corner of the rectangle and drag to the opposite corner.
- To select the entire datasheet, click the button in the upper left-hand corner of the sheet (where the row buttons meet the column buttons).

To set the numeric formatting for the selected cells, follow these steps:

1. Right-click the selected area.
2. Choose Number from the pop-up menu. A dialog box appears showing a list of categories of formats on the left.
3. Choose the category of number format that you want (currency, scientific, fraction, and so on). On the right half of the dialog box, fields appear where you can configure the details of the format; the exact fields depend on the category that you choose. (Note: The General and Text formats have no fields.)
4. Use the fields to set the exact design of the number format you want.
5. Click OK. The numeric data is formatted as you indicated.

To set the text formatting for the selected cells, do the following:

1. Right-click the selected area.
2. Choose Font from the pop-up menu. A dialog box appears with fields for the font, size, color, and other attributes.
3. Set the font, size, and attributes that you want.
4. Click OK. The text is formatted as you requested.

 If a number appears as a string of #s, the number is too wide to fit in the cell. To make that column of cells wider, point to the right edge of the button at the top of the column. When the pointer turns into a line with two arrows, drag the edge of the column to the right.

Rearranging Data

To rearrange the rows or columns on the datasheet, perform the following steps:

1. Select the row or column that you want to move by clicking the button at the beginning of the row or column.

2. Right-click the selected area and choose Cut from the pop-up menu. The selected area becomes blank.

3. Right-click the area again and choose Delete. This removes the blank row or column, sliding the following rows or columns over to take up the space.

4. Select the row that you want to put the removed row on top of, or the column that you want to put the removed column to the left of.

5. Right-click the selected area and click Insert from the pop-up menu. A new blank row or column appears, and it is selected.

6. Right-click the selected area and click Paste. The information that you cut earlier now appears in this column.

 TIP If you have a column or row that you want to keep on the datasheet but do not want to appear on the chart, double-click the button at the start of the row or column. To reverse this, double-click again.

Selecting a Chart Type

When you start Microsoft Graph, it automatically displays your data using the default chart type (which is a column chart, unless you have changed it). To get the type of chart you want, follow these steps:

1. Choose Chart, Chart Type. The dialog box shown in Figure 12.2 appears.

2. From the Chart Type area, select the general kind of chart you want. Small pictures of that type of chart appear in the Chart Sub-type area.

3. Click the picture that looks most like the chart you want.

4. Click the Press And Hold To View Sample button. A sample area appears to show you roughly what your data would look like in that type of chart. You can choose another type or sub-type if this doesn't look right.

5. After you've found the right type of chart, click OK. Your chart now takes that format.

FIG. 12.2
The Chart Type dialog box lets you choose from more than 70 chart designs in more than a dozen categories.

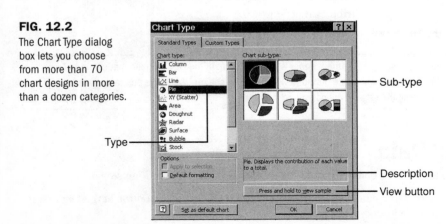

The type of chart that you choose should depend on what sort of data you're graphing:

- *Bar charts*. This type, which includes column, bar, cylinder, cone, and pyramid, shows shapes of varying heights. These are good to compare different values that do not have a natural order (for example, total sales in each of the various stores). Some versions stack the items so that you can see, for example, how sales of men's clothing and sales of women's clothing add up to total clothing sales for each store.

- *Continuity charts*. These charts, which include types line, area, and surface, as well as some XY (scatter), connect the points of your graph to make lines or shapes. Only use these graphs if the connecting line actually means something. For example, if your data points are your total sales for each month, then the line connecting the February sales to the March sales suggests how the sales rose between the months. However, a line connecting your total moped sales to your chain saw sales really wouldn't mean anything.

- *Dot charts*. This type includes the XY (scatter) chart and shows a single dot for each point of data. These are good when charting two measurements against each other. (If you want to show a general pattern to a dot chart with many points, choose the Chart menu and select Add Trendline to display a line that shows the average relationship of one measurement to the other.

- *Slice charts*. This type, including pie and doughnut charts, shows how a total amount is made up of individual portions. Use the doughnut chart to show more than one total at a time.

- *Specialty charts*. These charts include radar, bubble, and stock charts and are used in certain fields for special purposes. If you're not used to seeing one of these chart types, don't use them because your audience won't know how to interpret them.

The Chart Type dialog box also has a Custom Types tab with a number of charts for special uses. These are not all types that can be designed using Microsoft Graphs design tools, but they are good examples of what can be designed. (Later in the chapter, you'll see how to add your own designs to the Custom Types list.)

Basic Chart Formatting

A handful of buttons on Graph's Standard toolbar let you quickly and easily add components to your chart. These are listed in the following table.

Button	Name	Function
	By Row	Treats the rows of your datasheet as the primary data grouping. For example, on a line graph, each row of data would be a different color line, with the cells on that row being different points on the line.

Part
II

Ch
12

continues

Button	Name	Function
	By Column	Treats the columns of your datasheet as the primary data grouping. For example, on a line graph, each column of data would be a different color line, with the cells in that column being different points on that line.
	Data Table	Puts a table on the graph, displaying the data from the datasheet.
	Category Axis Gridlines	Adds vertical lines to the graph, making it easier to see which points on the graph line up with which items along the base of the graph.
	Value Axis Gridlines	Adds lines across the graph, making it easier to see what the value of each point is.
	Legend	Adds a legend to the chart, a box indicating what each of the different colored lines or areas in the chart means.

For further formatting, choose Chart, Chart Options. A dialog box appears with six tabs, each with a different group of options for your chart.

- The Titles tab lets you set a title that appears at the top of the chart, as well as titles for each axis of the chart.
- The Axes tab is where you choose whether there are numbers along each axis and the format for those numbers.
- The Gridlines tab lets you set whether there are straight lines across the graph that make it easier to tell where each point is. *Major* gridlines are at major steps (10, 20, 30, and so on), whereas *minor* gridlines are thinner lines that appear between major gridlines (5, 15, 25, and so on). There is also an option to choose between 2-D and 3-D gridlines and *walls* (the surfaces that hold the gridlines).
- The Legend tab lets you choose to include and position the legend.
- The Data Labels tab lets you place a label with the value of each chart point right next to the point.
- The Data Table tab lets you set up the data table.

Selecting Chart Elements

As shown in Figure 12.3, many individual elements go into making up a chart. Each of these elements has its own dialog box for formatting, where you can change line widths, colors, shadows, fonts, and more. This is a far greater array of options than can be set with the Chart Options dialog box.

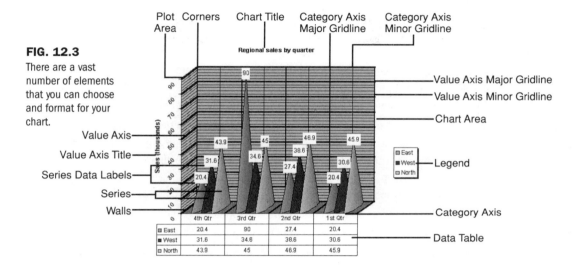

FIG. 12.3
There are a vast number of elements that you can choose and format for your chart.

To be able to format an element, you have to be able to select the element you're formatting. There are two ways of doing this:

- *Click the element.* This can be tricky because many elements overlap one another. Magnifying the chart by choosing View, Zoom can help. Also, if you point to the element and pause, a note will pop up, telling you which element you're pointing to.

- *Select the element from the Chart Objects drop-down menu.* This menu on the Standard toolbar lists all the elements that exist on this chart. (Not all charts have all elements.)

When you select an element, black sizing handles appear on it. However, most elements cannot be separately resized, and only a few can be moved.

Formatting Elements

To format a selected element, choose Format, Selected (the exact name of the Selected item on the menu will change based on what type of element is selected, such as Selected Data Series), or use the shortcut Ctrl+1. A dialog box appears with a set of tabs appropriate to that element. The different tabs that may be included are as follows:

- The Patterns tab sets the color that fills the element (including the option of using fancy fills and fades; see Chapter 15, "Drawing Graphic Objects," for more on these). It also has controls for the color, thickness, and style of lines or outline, and a shadow for the object. Other, element-specific settings are here as well.

- The Font tab has controls for the font, font size, attributes, and color of text.

- The Alignment tab lets you tilt text at an angle, or stack the letters vertically. It also controls the justification of text within the space allotted it.

Part
II

Ch
12

- The Scale tab lets you set the top and bottom values for an axis and the spacing of the gridlines. (People doing scientific presentations should note that this tab includes the capability to use logarithmic scaling.)

- The Number tab controls the format of a number, in the same way as the number formatting done on the datasheet.

- The Placement tab has options for where in the chart area an element appears.

- The Shape tab lets you select the shape of the bars used in a bar-style chart.

- The Axis tab lets you select whether a data series is being marked against the standard range of values for the axis (marked on the right edge of the chart, if used).

- The X and Y Error Bar tabs let you set up marks around the data point showing the degree of the precision of the measurement.

- The Data Label tab has options controlling the appearance of data labels.

- The Type option lets you pick the sort of trendline used on an XY Scatter chart.

- The Options tab has additional options for this element that aren't appropriate for the other tabs.

You can quickly set simple text options using the Formatting toolbar, as shown in Figure 12.4.

FIG. 12.4
The Formatting toolbar gives you quick control over the appearance of text, although not as detailed control as using that element's Settings dialog box.

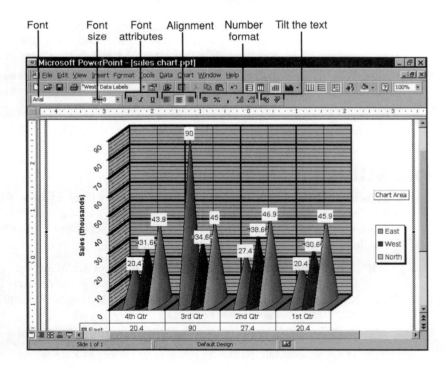

Rotating a 3-D Chart

If you're using a 3-D chart type, you can change the angle from which the chart is being viewed. This can improve more than just the aesthetics; for some charts, the default angle can hide important data points.

To change the angle, follow these steps:

1. Choose Chart, 3-D View. The dialog box shown in Figure 12.5 appears.
2. Use the Elevation buttons to tilt the demonstration chart up and down. Remember that these buttons (and the Perspective buttons) are changing where the viewpoint is relative to the chart, so pushing the Up button tilts the chart down.
3. Use the Rotation buttons to turn the chart from side to side.
4. If you want the chart to have no *foreshortening* (nearer parts looking bigger than farther parts), check the Right Angle Axes check box, and the perspective controls disappear. Otherwise, use the Perspective buttons to control the degree of foreshortening.
5. Click OK, and these settings will be used for your chart.

Elevation controls   Perspective controls

FIG. 12.5
The 3-D View dialog box lets you change the view by using buttons or set view values directly.

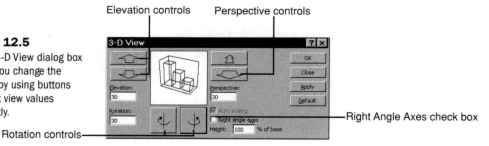

Rotation controls

Right Angle Axes check box

TIP To quickly change the tilt and rotation, click the Chart Objects drop-down list and select Corners. Sizing handles appear on the eight corners of the 3-D chart. Drag one of these corners, and the chart is replaced by a box shape that you can rotate. Drag until the box is at the angle you want the chart to be; then release the mouse button.

Storing a Custom Design

Getting a chart to look just as you want it to can take a lot of formatting. If you come up with a chart design that you want to use again and again for additional charts, you don't have to repeat all that formatting. Instead, you can save the settings to use again with other charts. Follow these steps:

1. After you've designed your chart, choose Chart, Chart Type. The Chart Type dialog box appears.

Part
II

Ch
12

2. Click the Custom Types tab.

3. Click the Uuser-defined option button, and a list of the chart types you've defined appears above it, as shown in Figure 12.6.

4. Click the Add button, and an Add Custom Chart Type dialog box appears.

5. Enter a name for the chart design into the Name field, and a description of the design into the Description field.

6. Click OK, and your chart is added to the list of user-defined custom charts.

7. Click OK in the Chart Type dialog to return to working with your chart.

FIG. 12.6

The Custom Types tab of the Chart Type dialog box lets you store your own designs for later reuse.

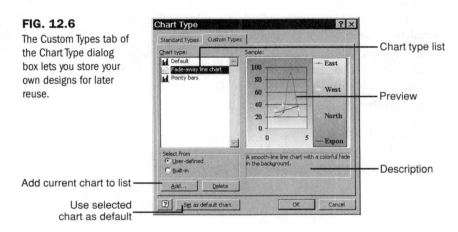

To apply this design to a new chart, perform the following steps:

1. Choose Chart, Chart Type.

2. Click the Custom Types tab.

3. Click the Uuser-defined option button.

4. Select the chart from the Chart Type list.

5. Click OK.

If you find that you are using the same chart type regularly, you can set it to be your default chart design. That way, every time you start a new chart, it will have that design without you having to set it. Just select the chart type in the Chart Type dialog box, as described earlier, but click the Set As Default Chart button before clicking OK.

Importing Spreadsheet Data

If you have data on a spreadsheet that you want to turn into a PowerPoint chart, you don't have to retype it. There are two quicker ways to set it up, each with its own advantages.

The first way copies the data exactly as it is now, so that your chart always reflects the status at the time you designed the chart:

1. Load the spreadsheet in the spreadsheet program. (Note: If you don't have the proper program, try using whatever spreadsheet you do have. Most can read files created by other programs.)
2. Select the range of cells that you want to base your chart on.
3. Press Ctrl+C to copy these cells to the Clipboard.
4. In PowerPoint, select the datasheet cell where you want the upper-left corner of the copied cells to go.
5. Press Ctrl+V to copy the cells into place.

If, on the other hand, you're going to keep changing the spreadsheet and you want the presentation to always reflect the latest information on the spreadsheet, follow these steps:

1. Copy the cells as described in the preceding steps 1 through 3.
2. In PowerPoint, start the chart and open the datasheet.
3. Choose Edit, Paste Link. A dialog box appears, warning you that this action will erase all the existing information on the datasheet.
4. Click OK. The data from the spreadsheet appears in the datasheet. Remember that if you want to change the data later, change it in the spreadsheet and save the changes. Don't change it in the datasheet.

 If you don't have a Windows spreadsheet program that can read the file, you may still be able to use it. Choose Edit, Import File, and then select the type of file from the File Type drop menu on the file browser.

Part
II

Ch
12

13

Working with Tables

A table format is a good way of presenting organized information. A large table allows you to put complex information in an easy-to-read format. A simple, small table is a good way to highlight key points, as in product-comparison tables. ■

Create a table

Put a grid of information in your presentation.

Enter data

Put figures and text in the table.

Rearrange the table

Add, delete, and move rows and columns.

Design the table's appearance

Change the size of the table cells, and add border lines and shading.

Import a Word table

Transfer a table from Word to PowerPoint.

Creating a Table

Realizing that PowerPoint cannot really create tables on its own is important. Although table features seem to be built into PowerPoint, PowerPoint is really using Microsoft Word to create the table. If you don't have Word installed on your system, you cannot use PowerPoint's table tools. (You could draw up your own table grid by using PowerPoint's line, box, and text tools, however.)

To create a table, follow these steps:

1. In Slide view, click the Insert Microsoft Word Table button.

   A grid like the one shown in Figure 13.1 appears below the button.

FIG. 13.1

The selected area in the table-sizing grid indicates the dimensions of your table.

2. Drag to select the number of rows and columns that you want in your table.

   If you just click a cell, you can select a table with up to 4 rows and 5 columns, but when you drag, the grid expands with your drag, allowing you to select up to 6 rows and a larger number of columns. (If you need more columns, start your table by using the command Insert, Picture, Microsoft Word Table instead.)

   The table grid appears on the slide, as shown in Figure 13.2. Although the title bar still says Microsoft PowerPoint and the view is still Slide view, the menus and the toolbars are Word toolbars.

If you have an existing table that you want to resume work on, double-click it. To stop working on a table and return to the PowerPoint menu and toolbars, click outside the table area.

Entering and Editing Text

Entering text in cells is simply a matter of putting the insertion point in the cell and typing. Use the following methods to set the insertion point:

- Click any cell to place the insertion point there.
- To move to the next cell in the row, press Tab. (If you're at the end of the row, this action moves the insertion point to the first cell of the next row.) If the cell contains text, the text is selected.
- To move to the preceding cell, press Shift+Tab.
- Press the up-arrow and down-arrow keys to move between rows.
- Press the Pg Up or Pg Dn key to move several rows at a time.

FIG. 13.2

When you're working on a table, Microsoft Word takes control.

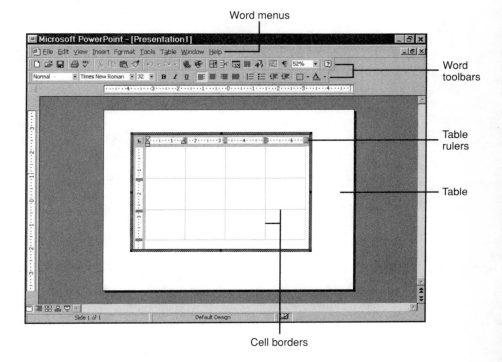

Word menus

Word toolbars

Table rulers

Table

Cell borders

Within a cell, editing is the same as in ordinary text. Press Delete or Backspace to remove characters; type to add characters; and press the cursor keys to move between characters without destroying them.

Selecting Rows, Columns, and Cells

To perform various operations on parts of the table, you need to know how to select the parts.

To select:

- *a cell*, click the space between the line bordering the left of the cell and the place where the text begins. If the cell contains no text, you can tell that you're clicking in the right place when the mouse pointer is an arrow, not an insertion bar.

- *a rectangular range of cells*, click the cell in one corner of the range, hold down the Shift key, and click the cell in the opposite corner.

- *complete rows*, point to the space between the first row's left edge and the vertical ruler. (To see this space, you may have to put the insertion point in a cell and press Tab until you're in the first cell of the next row). Drag down to the last row that you want to select.

- *complete columns*, point to the top line of the first column that you want to select. The mouse pointer should turn into a down arrow; if it doesn't, the top row of cells is not visible, and you should press Pg Up until it is. Drag to the last column that you want to select.

Part

II

Ch

13

■ *the entire table*, press Ctrl+A.

When cells are selected, you can use the standard text-formatting commands to format the text in them.

Adding and Deleting Rows and Columns

To delete a row or column, first select what you want to delete; then choose Table, Delete Column (or Delete Row). You can also issue the Delete command by right-clicking the selected area and choosing Delete from the shortcut menu.

To add a column or row, select the row that you want to add the new row above or the column that you want to add a new column to the left of. Then use the Table, Insert Row or the Insert Column command. The Insert command is also available on the shortcut menu you get when you right-click the selected area.

Copying and Moving Cells

To move cells, first select the cells that you want to move; then drag them until the mouse pointer is where you want to put the top-left corner of the range. When the range is moved, any nonblank cells where the range is being moved to are overwritten, so make sure that you have nothing important there. The range where you moved the cells from now is blank.

You copy cells the same way, but you have to hold down the Ctrl key while dragging the cells into place.

To rearrange the entire table so that rows are in alphabetical or numerical order, follow these steps:

1. Select the rows that you want to sort. (You may want to not select the top row, using it instead to label the columns.)

2. Choose Table, Sort.

   A Sort dialog box appears.

3. From the Sort By drop-down list, choose which column you want to sort by.

4. From the Type drop-down list, choose Text or Number.

5. Choose the Ascending option button if you want to go from A to Z or from the lowest number to the highest; otherwise, choose Descending.

6. If you have several rows with the same value in the column you're sorting by, you should select a column to use as a tie-breaker to decide which of the matching entries comes first. To do this, repeat steps 3–5 using the boxes in the upper Then By area of the Sort dialog box. (If you're sorting by a column of last names, for example, and you have multiple Smiths on the table, then choosing the first name column as your Then By column will keep all the Smiths together, in the alphabetical order of their first names.)

If there's a chance that there will be rows with the same values in both the Sort By and Then By columns, you can select another tie-breaker column using the lower Then By area of the Sort dialog box.

7. Click the OK button.

Your table is sorted.

Merging and Splitting Cells

You can remove the dividing wall between selected cells, making a single cell that spans several rows or columns, as shown in Figure 13.3. To do so, select the cells (you must select a rectangular range of cells) and then choose Table, Merge Cells.

FIG. 13.3
Merging cells turns several cells into one; splitting cells does just the opposite.

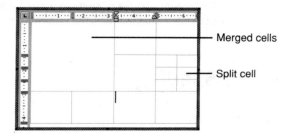

Merged cells

Split cell

To divide one cell into several cells, creating a mini-table within a cell, follow these steps:

1. Select the cell that you want to divide.

2. Choose Table, Split Cells.

The Split Cells dialog box appears.

3. In the Number Of Rows box, enter the number of rows that you want to create.

4. In the Number Of Columns box, enter the number of columns that you want to create.

5. If you have multiple cells selected, you can use the Merge Cells Before Split check box to create one big grid among the cells. Otherwise, each of the cells is split to the same degree. Setting this check box resets the rows and columns boxes, so set it first.

6. Click the OK button.

The splitting takes place.

Part

II

Ch

13

Resizing Columns and Rows

To resize a column or row, point to the gray line on the ruler that represents the edge that you want to move. The mouse pointer turns into an arrow with two heads pointing in opposite directions. You can now drag the line away from the cell to expand it or toward the cell to reduce it.

When you do that, however, you are actually changing the position of all the later rows or columns. If you just want to move a column divider, changing the size of two adjacent columns without effecting any of the other columns, hold Shift while you drag the divider. (The Shift technique does not work on row dividers.)

If you hold down the Alt key while dragging, the rulers display the exact measurements of the column or row.

To resize several rows so that they're all the same size, select those rows and then choose Table, Distribute Rows Evenly. The space for these rows is split equally among them. To do the same for columns, select them and then choose Table, Distribute Columns Evenly. This technique does not work, however, if you have a merged cell that is partly but not fully included in the selected range.

You can resize the entire table after leaving Word's editing mode (by clicking outside the table area). When you resize by dragging the sizing handles, the fonts automatically change size proportionately.

Adding Borders and Shading

PowerPoint (actually, Word) has some nice built-in designs that you can apply to your table. To use these designs, follow these steps:

1. If you have one or more rows with labels for the column, select those rows and then choose Table, Headings.

   This action marks those rows for special formatting.

2. Choose Table, Table AutoFormat.

   The dialog box shown in Figure 13.4 appears.

FIG. 13.4
In the Table AutoFormat dialog box, you can specify which attributes of the design you want to apply to your table.

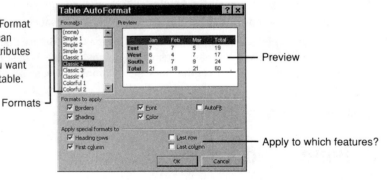

3. Select a format in the Formats list.

   A picture of what that format looks like appears in the Preview area.

4. Repeat step 3 until you find the format that you want.

5. Click OK.

The format is applied to your table.

If you want to make your own design choices for the table, follow these steps:

1. Choose Format, Borders and Shading.

The Borders and Shading dialog box appears, as shown in Figure 13.5.

FIG. 13.5
The Borders tab of the Borders And Shading dialog box allows you to select which borders to change.

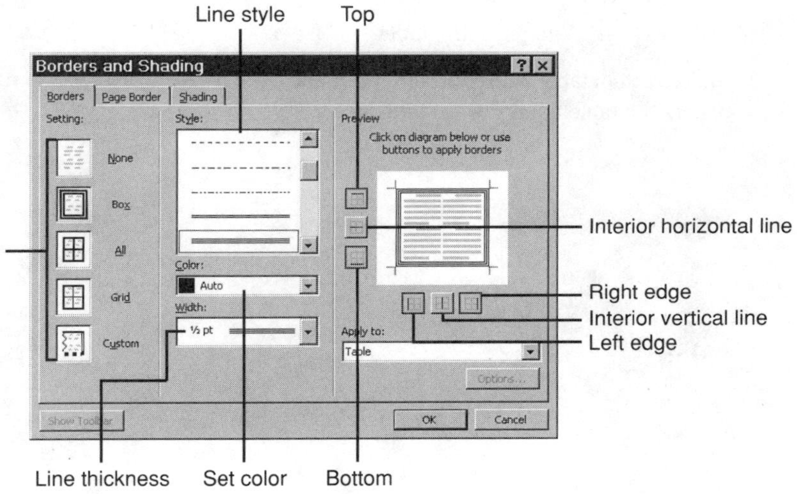

2. In the center of the Borders tab, select the style, color, and width for the border lines.

3. Use one of the Settings buttons on the left side of the tab to have border lines only on the edges pictured on the button.

To apply the selected style to only specific types of borders (top, bottom, individual side, or horizontals or verticals), use the buttons in the Preview section to select those edges. (If you want it just to apply to the borders around currently selected cells, select Cell from the Apply To menu.)

4. In the Shading tab, select the color that you want to set as the background.

(Again, to apply the color just to currently selected cells, choose Cell from the Apply To menu.)

5. Click the OK button to apply these changes.

Part
II

Ch
13

CAUTION

Don't touch anything on the Page Border tab. Although this tab is useful while you're working in Word, it isn't useful in PowerPoint. Beyond not being useful, selecting things on this tab can really mess up the handling of the table in the slide.

Importing a Table from Microsoft Word

If you've created a table in Word, you can easily send it over to PowerPoint to include it in a slide. Just follow these steps:

1. Select the table in Word.
2. Press Ctrl+C to copy the table to the Clipboard.
3. Switch to PowerPoint.
4. Press Ctrl+V to paste the table.

If you're comfortable with Word, you can use most of the Word tools in making tables, even if you start the table from PowerPoint. ●

Adding Visual Elements to the Presentation

CHAPTER 14

Creating and Editing PowerPoint Templates

A good presentation has a consistent look. That way, people viewing the presentation spend their time focusing on the information, rather than how you're presenting it. By creating slide masters that set the design for each slide, you can create a consistent interesting look for all the slides in your presentation. By saving these designs in a template file, you can reuse these designs in future presentations, or reformat existing presentations. ■

Design a look for your slides

Create a slide layout, with background and colors, that can be used repeatedly.

Set automatic text formatting

Plan the look for all the text on your slides.

Plan the text flow

Set indenting and bullet design for your entire presentation at once.

Design handouts and notes pages

Create custom looks for your printed copies.

Save your design

Create a template file so that you can apply this design to other presentations.

Understanding PowerPoint Templates

A *template* is PowerPoint's way of storing the design of a presentation. The template file doesn't include any of the text of your presentation, nor any of the graphic elements that you might add to individual slides. Instead, it contains:

- The *Title Master*, which is the design for the title slide. This includes the background design for the slide, the placement, font, size, and attributes for the title and the other text that goes on the title slide.

- The *Slide Master*, which is like the Title Master, only it contains the design for every slide except the first one. In addition to the type of things set for the title slide, you also set the degree of indentation and the bullets for points and sub-points from your outline. You can also set *footers*, information to appear at the bottom of each slide, such as the date, slide number, or presentation name.

- The *color schemes* that can be applied to this presentation. These schemes set the colors for the text, bullets, and other elements of the presentation. You can store several color schemes with a template, allowing you to change quickly between several color designs.

- The *Handout Master* sets the background design and the placement of the headers and footers on handouts.

- The *Notes Master* sets the background and the placement of the slide picture and text areas for notes pages.

Remember that the template only sets the default for all these things. You can always override the default for any given item on any given slide. If, for example, you set the default font for your text to be Times New Roman, that doesn't stop you from selecting some text later and changing it to Courier.

N O T E Reformatting your presentation by changing a Master is a safe procedure. It will not delete or destroy anything you've added to the slides. It may cause some of the things on the slides to be moved or resized. After you change your master, check all your slides again, because you may have changed something so that it no longer fits on the slide. If, for example, if you increase your text font size, text that fit on the slide may now be too large to fit. ■

Using the Slide Master

To start working with the slide master, choose View, Master, Slide Master. As seen in Figure 14.1, the view you get will be Slide view-style, with all the toolbars that you expect in Slide view.

- To set up a basic color, fade, or texture fill for the background of your slides, choose Format, Background to get the Background dialog box. Click the drop-down list to select a color to fill the background with, or one of the more complex fills.

  ▶ **See** "Changing the Fill," **p. 129**

FIG. 14.1

The Slide Master view has sample text for titles and points that you can use to set the formatting for all the presentation text. Click the Close button on the Master Toolbar when you're finished.

Master toolbar   Slide title area

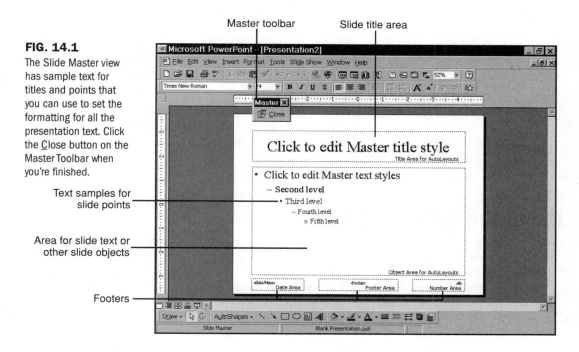

Text samples for slide points

Area for slide text or other slide objects

Footers

- You can use all the standard graphic tools (also discussed more in Chapter 15, "Drawing Graphic Objects") to add items to the background. Anything you put on the Slide Master automatically appears on all slides except for the Title Slide. Anything you put on the slides appear in front of anything you put on the Slide Master, so don't worry about whether what you put will hide text.

- You can also move and resize the areas on the master. When new slides are created using AutoFormat, the layout will be based on where you position the title area and the *object area*, which is for everything on the slide except the title (text points, pictures, charts, and so on).

 While working with the Slide Master, you see dotted outlines surrounding areas. These outlines will not actually appear on the slide. To see a window with a better example of what the slide will look like, choose View, Slide Miniature.

When you're done working with the Slide Master, return to your presentation by clicking the Close button on the little Master toolbar.

Formatting Text on Masters

The text formatting that you set on the Slide Master will affect all the slides. This applies not only to the font, size, and attributes, but also to the indentation, the spacing between lines, and the bullets.

Part
III

Ch
14

You can create separate settings for the slide title and for each of the levels of points, sub-points, and so on. To change the setting for a given line, just click it to place the insertion point there; you don't need to select the whole line. (If you want to change several lines at a time, select them. To select all the various point levels at once, click one of them, and then press Ctrl+A.)

Once you've selected what you want to alter, you can use any of the methods shown in Chapter 4, "Changing the Look of Text," to change the look of the text and the bullet. Use the information on tab setting in Chapter 7, "Arranging Objects on Your Slide," to set the tabs which control how far the different points indent.

▶ **See** "Positioning Text Within a Text Object," **p. 57**

Using the Title Master

By default, the slides in your presentation have only one master, the Slide Master. You have to tell PowerPoint to create a second master that's just for title slides. This Title Master will be the design for any slide AutoFormatted as a title slide (which is the first slide design on the first row of the AutoFormat dialog box.) Usually, this is only used for the first slide in the presentation.

To create a Title Master:

1. View the Slide Master by choosing View, Master, Slide Master. You must have the Slide Master showing to create the Title Master.

2. Create the Title Master by choosing Insert, New Title Master (or press Ctrl+M).

   The Title Master appears as shown in Figure 14.2.

When the Title Master is created, PowerPoint automatically copies onto it anything that you've put on the Slide Master. As such, if you're going to use a lot of the same graphic elements on both Masters, it's a good idea to fully design your Slide Master and then create your Title Master. On the other hand, if your Title Master is going to be very different from your Slide Master, you can save yourself a lot of deleting by creating your Title Master before putting things on your Slide Master.

When you're done working on your Title Master, click the Close button on the Master toolbar to return to what you were editing before. To restart editing the Title Master, just choose View, Master, Title Master at any time.

Working with the Footers

The Slide and Title Masters have several areas at the bottom devoted to footer information. You can move and change the formatting of these areas in just the same way as you do other areas on the Masters. However, that still does not dictate whether those footers actually appear on the slide.

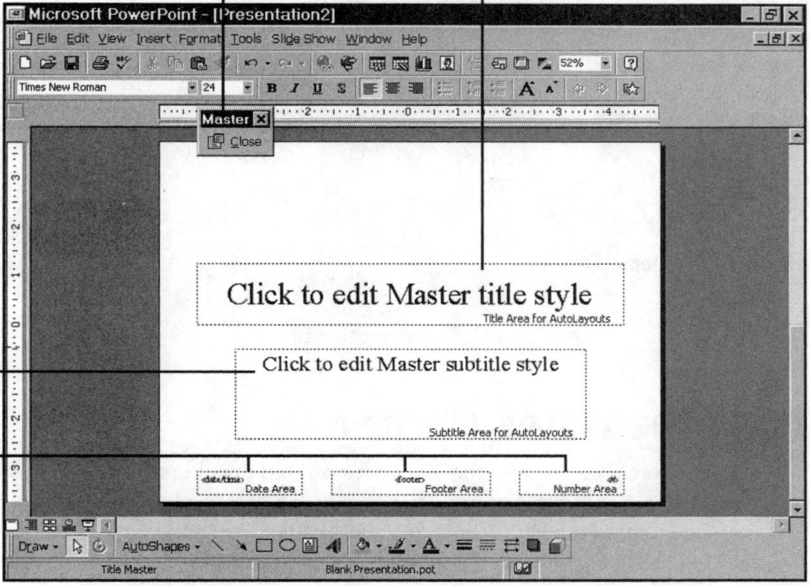

FIG. 14.2

The Title Master is like the Slide Master, but applies only to slides formatted as title slides.

Master toolbar   Presentation title area

Presentation subtitle area

Footers

To choose which footers appear:

1. Choose View, Header And Footer. The dialog box shown in Figure 14.3 appears.
2. Select which footers you want using the check boxes.
3. If you chose to include the Date And Time footer, select whether you want it to stay Fixed or to Update Automatically by choosing the corresponding option button. If you choose Fixed, the footer will always show whatever date you type into the field next to the option button. If you choose Update Automatically, PowerPoint will always show the current date, and you can select the style of date from the drop-down list.
4. If you include the general purpose Footer, type whatever information you want into the adjacent field.
5. Check the Don't Show On Title Slide check box if you want to keep your title slide clear of such things.
6. Click the Apply To All button.

If you later want to create individual slides with different footer settings, select those slides, then use the View, Header And Footer command. Finish with the Apply button instead of the Apply To All button.

Part
III

Ch
14

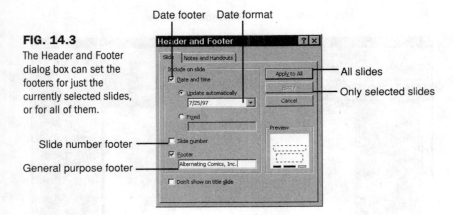

Date footer   Date format

FIG. 14.3

The Header and Footer dialog box can set the footers for just the currently selected slides, or for all of them.

All slides

Only selected slides

Slide number footer

General purpose footer

Using the Notes Master

The Notes Master sets the format for printed Speakers Notes. To work on it, choose <u>V</u>iew, <u>M</u>aster, <u>N</u>otes Master. In this view, you can create a background and rearrange and resize the placement of the slide, the notes, and the headers and footers.

You can also change the text formatting on this page, in the same way as you change text formatting on the Slide Master. However, you will probably have to use the Zoom drop-down list to enlarge your view of the text so that you can see what you're doing.

▶ **See** "Using Headers and Footers," **p. 79**

Using the Handout Master

The Handout Master lets you change the placement of the headers and footers on the handouts, and you can set the background color and add design items to the background. You cannot change the size or placement of the slides on these handouts.

To work with the Handout Master, choose <u>V</u>iew, <u>M</u>aster, Han<u>d</u>out Master. The Handout Master appears. Handout Master has a special toolbar with buttons to pick whether you're looking at the layout for 2, 3, or 6 slides per page, or for an outline handout.

Adding a Color Scheme to Your Design

In Chapter 8, "Creating a Presentation or New Slide from Scratch," you saw how to create your own color scheme. To take the current color scheme and make it a standard color scheme for this slide design:

1. Choose F<u>o</u>rmat, Slide <u>C</u>olor Scheme. (If you're working on one of the Masters, the menu option will read a little differently, but will end in <u>C</u>olor Scheme.) The Color Scheme dialog box appears.

2. Click the Custom tab. If you have not already designed the color scheme, do so now.

3. Click the Add As Standard Scheme button. If this button is grayed out, the color scheme you are working with will be added as a standard color scheme for this slide design.

If you want to remove a color scheme from the list of standard schemes from that slide design, select the scheme on the Color dialog box's Standard tab, then click the Delete Scheme button.

Saving Master Changes as a Template

To store the Masters so that you can apply them to another presentation:

1. Choose File, Save As and a file explorer appears.

2. From the Save As Type drop-down list, select Presentation Template (*.POT). The file explorer will automatically switch to the directory where PowerPoint stores all its templates.

3. Type a name for this template into the File Name text box.

4. Click the Save button to store the template file.

   ▶ **See** "Creating a Presentation or New Slide from Scratch," **p. 61**

Drawing Graphic Objects

Drawing objects can be used for a wide range of purposes, whether to create a simple eye-catching highlight or to design a fancy graphic representation of an object. PowerPoint allows easy creation of a broad range of simple drawing objects, which can be combined to create complex items. Every fancy PowerPoint design is made up of combinations of these simple items. ■

Draw shapes

Add circles, squares, lines, and more complex drawn objects to your slide.

Set the shape's outline

Choose outline color, thickness, and dashed or multiple line styles.

Fill the shape

Give the shape a color, or fill it with a pattern or drawing.

Create depth

Cast a shadow, or expand your shape into 3-D.

Design a logo

Shape, warp, and color text to create an eye-catching logo.

Viewing the Drawing Area

Drawing is done in Slide view. As shown in Figure 15.1, many elements in Slide view are designed specifically around drawing, or are particularly useful when drawing.

FIG. 15.1

If the drawing toolbar is not visible, right-click any other toolbar and choose Drawing from the pop-up menu.

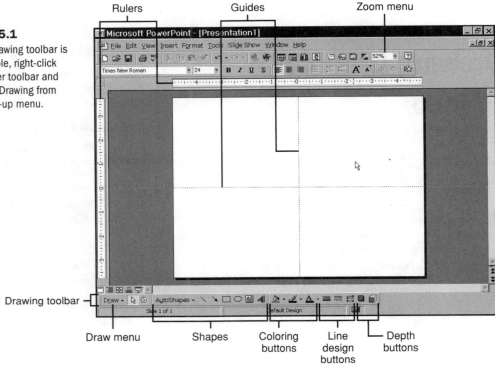

Rulers   Guides   Zoom menu

Drawing toolbar

Draw menu   Shapes   Coloring buttons   Line design buttons   Depth buttons

T I P   The Zoom drop-down list can come in handy while drawing. Select a higher magnification percentage to get a close-up view of your slide so that you can make small changes.

▶ **See** "Arranging Objects on Your Slide," **p. 51**

Placing Objects Precisely with Rulers and Guides

If you don't see the rulers on the screen in Slide view, choose <u>V</u>iew, <u>R</u>uler to make them appear, as shown in Figure 15.2.

Use the following features to take advantage of the rulers:

■ The rulers each have a thin dotted line that shows the position of the pointer, helping you see precisely where you are putting things. When using drawing objects, the center of each ruler is zero. This makes it easy to make your slide symmetrical; just put items at the same distance from both edges.

FIG 15.2
If you want to move a guide, just drag it. As you drag, the pointer will show the exact ruler measurement for where you've moved it.

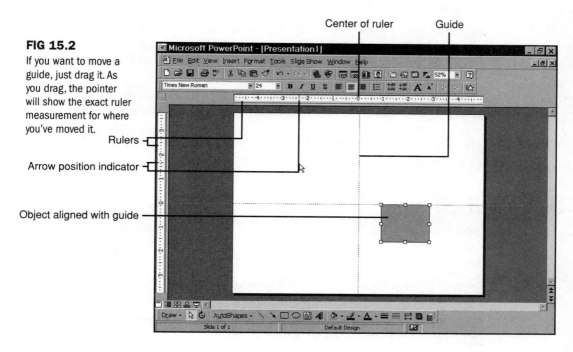

- *Guides* are dotted lines that run across the slides, which are handy for lining things up. When you start to draw an object near a guide, it automatically sticks to the guide. (If the guides are not visible, you can make them visible by choosing View, Guides.)

- To create an additional guide, hold down the Ctrl key while dragging.

Drawing Basic Shapes

There are four basic shapes, each with its own button. Clicking the button lets you draw one of the objects, and then you return to normal slide editing mode. The shapes are as follows:

To draw a line, click the Line button and then drag from one end of the line to the other.

To draw an arrow line, click the Arrow button and then drag from the non-pointy end of the line to the end with an arrow on it.

To draw a rectangle, click the Rectangle button and then drag from one corner of the rectangle to the opposite corner.

To draw an oval, click the Oval button and then indicate the rectangular area that the oval would fit tightly in by dragging from one corner to the opposite corner.

Some additional tips on drawing basic shapes are as follows:

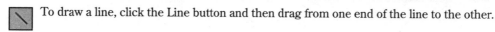

- If you want to draw several of the same objects in a row, double-click the object's button rather than single-clicking. Then you can draw as many of the object as you want. When you're finished, click the Select Objects button to return to normal editing mode.

■ If you hold down Ctrl while dragging to place your object, where you start dragging is considered the center of the object. As you drag, the object expands away from the center in all directions. This is particularly useful if you're trying to draw a circle with a center at a given point.

■ If you hold down Shift while drawing an oval or a rectangle, PowerPoint keeps the object the same width and height. That way, you can make perfect circles or squares.

■ Holding Shift while dragging a line or arrow keeps your line at an angle that's an exact multiple of 15 degrees, which is particularly useful for making exactly horizontal or vertical lines.

Using AutoShapes

PowerPoint has a large array of additional built-in shapes, as shown in Figure 15.3. Click the AutoShapes button to see a menu of types of other shapes that PowerPoint will let you draw. The sub-menus include the following:

■ Lines include not only straight lines, but also curved lines.

■ Connectors have series of lines designed to connect things in flow diagrams.

■ Basic Shapes includes rectangles, triangles, arcs, and more decorative items.

■ Block Arrows include various large arrow shapes that include an outline and an interior area (as opposed to the arrows drawn with the Arrow button, which are just lines.)

■ Flowcharts includes special symbols used in programming and designing flowcharts.

■ Stars and Banners includes star shapes, medallion shapes, and ribbon shapes that are good for creating certificates. (The numbers inside the images of some of the star shapes on the menu indicate how many points those stars have.)

■ Callouts have text areas with pointers, good for highlighting items in an image on the slide. These include comics-style speech and thought balloons.

■ Action Buttons include special button shapes designed for uses on interactive presentation. These buttons have special attributes that are discussed in Chapter 17, "Adding Multimedia Effects."

FIG. 15.3
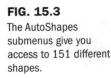
The AutoShapes submenus give you access to 151 different shapes.

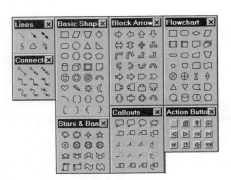

To draw any of these shapes, first select the shape from the menu. Then do one of the following:

- To draw a line, drag from one end of the line to the other.
- To draw a callout, drag from where the callout is supposed to be pointing to where the callout text area should appear.
- To draw a curved line, click the start of the curved line and then on points along the line where the curve changes direction, ending with the line's end point. Then click somewhere off the slide to indicate that the line is complete.
- For all other objects, drag from one corner of a rectangle tightly surrounding the object to the opposite corner.

Changing a Shape

To work with the shape of an AutoShape, first select the object by clicking it. Most AutoShapes, when selected, display not only sizing handles but also a yellow diamond. Dragging this diamond changes the shape. The exact change depends on the type of shape. For example, on a star shape, moving the diamond changes how far from the star's center the rays start. On the happy face shape, dragging the diamond changes the angle of its smile, even turning it into a frown. The best way to learn what the diamond does on a specific shape is to experiment.

▶ **See** "Arranging Objects on Your Slide," **p. 51**

A curved line is a special case, with its own special ways to change. First, right-click it and select Edit Points from the pop-up menu. The points that you had selected on the curve will show up as little black boxes. Using these boxes, you can do the following:

- Move a point by dragging a little black box to a new place.
- Add new points to the curve by simply dragging part of the curve edge where you want it to be.
- Delete a point by right-clicking it and choosing Delete Point from the pop-up menu.
- To change the amount that the curve flexes at a point, right-click the black box and select either Smooth Point or Straight Point. A blue line shows up going through the black box, and by dragging the sizing handles at the end of the blue line, you can change the angle of the curve.
- To create a precise, tight angle, right-click a black box and select Corner Point. Two blue lines appear emanating from the black box. Drag the sizing handles at the end of these lines to move them into the exact angle you want at the point.
- Turn a curved part of the line into a straight part by clicking it (not on a black box) and choosing Straight Segment.

With practice, you can used the curve line tools to make any shape you want, no matter how irregular.

Changing the Line or Outline

Every object has lines associated with it. For lines and arrows, the line is basically everything, whereas for solid shapes, there's an outline. For any of these lines on a selected object, you can set the following:

■ Visible or invisible line

■ Solid or one of several styles of dashed line

■ Line thickness

■ Multiple lines

■ Color or two-color pattern

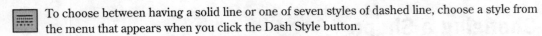 To choose between having a solid line or one of seven styles of dashed line, choose a style from the menu that appears when you click the Dash Style button.

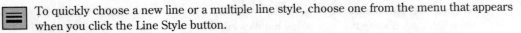 To quickly choose a new line or a multiple line style, choose one from the menu that appears when you click the Line Style button.

To set the line color to the color on the bottom of the Line Color button, click that button.

To choose another color or an invisible line, click the down arrow at the right side of the Line Color button. A menu like the one shown in Figure 15.4 appears.

FIG. 15.4
The Line Color menu lets you select from any color already used in the presentation or a new color entirely.

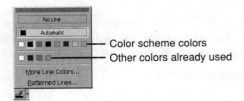

Color scheme colors
Other colors already used

After you have access to the Line Color menu, you can do any of the following:

■ To make the line invisible, choose No Line.

■ To set the line color to the color scheme's default line color, select Automatic.

■ To set the color to any of the eight colors in the color scheme, choose that color from first line of colored boxes. If you choose one of these colors and then change the color scheme, the color of the line changes to match.

■ To set the color to any non-color scheme color already used in this presentation, select that color from the colored boxes below the first line.

■ To set the color to any other color, choose More Line Colors. Then use the colors selector dialog box described in the "Changing the Color Scheme" section of Chapter 8, "Creating a Presentation or New Slide from Scratch."

■ To choose a two-color pattern for the line, click Patterned Lines. The Patterned Lines dialog box appears, as shown in Figure 15.5. Choose the pattern you want from the 48 presented. Then use the drop-down list to choose the two colors to make up the pattern.

FIG. 15.5
The menus on the
Patterned Lines dialog
box have many of the
same options as the
Line Color menu.

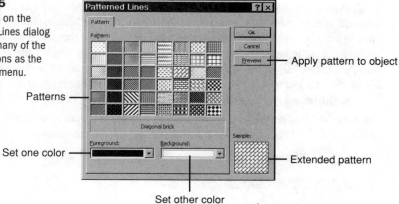

Patterns

Set one color

Set other color

Apply pattern to object

Extended pattern

 If the line is an arrow, you can choose the style of arrow pointers (including creating an bi-directional arrow) by clicking Arrow Style.

You can also set all the line attributes using the Format AutoShape dialog box described later in this chapter.

Changing the Fill

 To change the color that fills the shape, use the Fill Color button. This button works much like the Line Color button described in the previous pages. Clicking the button itself sets the color of the object to the color at the bottom of the button. Clicking the down arrow gets you a menu with most of the same choices as the Line Color menu. The choices that are different are as follows:

- *No Fill is like No Line.* Choosing this makes the fill area of the object invisible; only the line of the object is visible. (Choosing this option makes selecting the object more difficult; when the fill is invisible, you have to click the object's outline to select the object.)

- *Fill Effects brings up a Fill Effects dialog box.* The Fill Effects dialog box is a powerful tool that lets you choose from four different methods of filling the object with more than just a simple single color. Each method has its own tab:

  - The Picture tab lets you choose a graphic file (such as a scanned photograph or drawing) by clicking the Select Picture button and choosing the picture using a file browser. The picture will be stretched or squashed to fit the dimensions of the rectangular area that holds the object. Only the parts of the picture that fit in the actual area of the object will be shown.

  - The Pattern tab works just like the Patterned Line dialog box shown earlier in this chapter.

- The Texture tab lets you fill the object with a repeating image that can give it a look of a something real. The tab comes with a number of built-in patterns to choose from, such as marble, crumpled paper, wood, and fabric. You can choose any of the built-in textures by clicking it. You can also use a graphic file of your own by clicking the Other Texture button. The difference between choosing the file on this tab and on the Picture tab is that here the picture is not stretched to fit. Instead, the image is repeated until it fills the whole area.

- The Gradient tab, shown in Figure 15.6, lets you select a pattern that fades between colors. This is good for creating sunset effects, shiny metal effects, and other subtle looks.

FIG. 15.6

With all the colors available and the different styles, the Gradient tab gives you access to a substantial array of fades.

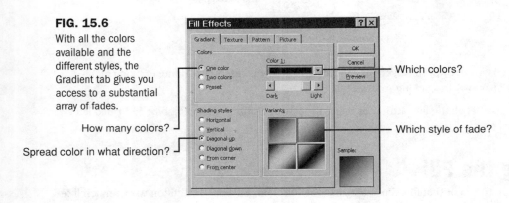

The Gradient tab is the most complex of the Fill tabs to use. To design your gradient, follow these steps:

1. From the Colors option buttons, choose One Color to use one color and just fade its brightness; choose Two Colors to create a range of colors going from one to another; or choose Preset to use one of PowerPoint's predesigned advanced gradients, including metallic and sunset patterns.

2. If you chose One or Two Colors, color drop-down lists appear. Use them to choose the colors you want. If you chose One Color, a slider also appears for you to select how light a tone you want to fade it to. If you chose Preset, a drop-down list appears listing two dozen possible gradient designs. The choices you make here are reflected in the Sample area, giving you a sense of how the color choice looks.

3. From the Shading Styles option buttons, choose the direction in which you want the lines of color to run.

4. The Variants area shows several different styles for the fade, with different placement for the highlights of the fade. Click the one that you want.

5. Click OK, and the gradient design is applied to the object.

Advanced Formatting Techniques

You can set most attributes of a drawing object (including attributes that are not set in any other way) by using the Format AutoShape dialog box. This dialog box appears when you select the object, then choose F_ormat, Aut_oShape. For a shortcut, right-click the object and choose Format Aut_oShape from the pop-up menu.

The Format AutoShape dialog box has five tabs. The Picture tab is always grayed out for drawing objects. (This tab is only for use with pictures inserted from graphics files, as seen in Chapter 16, "Inserting Predesigned Artwork.") The other tabs are as follows:

■ *Colors and Lines.* This tab includes all the settings for the fill, color, style, and thickness of the line and the ends of the arrows. Features available on this tab that you cannot use otherwise include selecting any thickness you want for the line and making a single-color fill *semitransparent*, so that whatever is under the object can be seen through the object.

■ *Size.* This tab lets you set the exact dimensions of the object (down to a hundredth of an inch), as well as the rotation (in degrees).

■ *Position.* The Position tab lets you set the exact placement of the object on the slide, down to a hundredth of an inch. The positioning sets the placement of the upper-left corner of the rectangle containing the object, and it can be set relative to the upper-left corner of the slide, or relative to the center of the slide.

■ *Text Box.* The Text Box tab is grayed out unless the object is being used as a text container. Here you can set the margins and how the text is justified within the text area. Settings available only here include the capability to tilt text 90 degrees, for words to automatically wrap to the next line within the text box, and to automatically stretch the object to fit the text provided.

Using this dialog box is handy if you want to change many settings at once. For most purposes, however, simply using the individual commands and menus is quicker.

Putting Text in a Shape

You can turn any solid drawing object into a text box. Callouts are designed to have text in them and have a built-in text box, which is visible immediately when you draw the object.

To add a text area to another drawing object, select the object and start typing. A gray rectangle appears around the object, and the text you type appears. Now, you can format the text just as with any other text object.

Be aware that after you add text to a drawing object, the object becomes more difficult to drag to another place. You can't just drag anywhere on the object because PowerPoint will think you're trying to select some of the text in it. Instead, you have to select the object and drag it by the gray rectangle around the text area.

Casting Shadows

You can make your object appear to be casting a shadow. Usually, this is used to make the object look like it is hovering slightly above the slide, but there are a variety of other styles of shadows available.

To quickly set a shadow, perform the following steps:

1. Select the object you want to add the shadow to.
2. Click the Shadow button to get the menu of shadow styles shown in Figure 15.7.
3. Click the style of shadow that you want. Not all shadow styles are available with all shapes.

FIG. 15.7
Note that the shadow styles that make the object looked pressed into or out from the slide cause your object's outline to disappear.

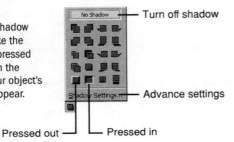

Turn off shadow

Advance settings

Pressed out — Pressed in

TIP You can remove a shadow from a selected object by choosing No Shadow from the Shadow menu.

To fine-tune your shadow, choose <u>S</u>hadow Settings from the shadow menu. A Shadow toolbar appears with the following buttons:

	Turns the shadow on or off.
	Moves the shadow up a little.
	Moves the shadow down a little.
	Moves the shadow left a little.
	Moves the shadow right a little.
	Sets the color of the shadow. This works the same as the other color menus. It also has the additional command <u>S</u>emitransparent Shadow, which makes what is on the slide under the shadow still somewhat visible.

Making Objects 3-D

Until now, everything you've been shown has been about moving, sizing, and reshaping objects in two dimensions. Using PowerPoint's 3-D capabilities, you can rotate your object in three dimension and give it thickness, making it look like a solid item.

 To do this, select the object; then select a 3-D style from the menu shown in Figure 15.8, which appears when you click the 3-D button:

FIG. 15.8

The 3-D menu gives you quick access to 20 different combinations of 3-D rotation and extrusion.

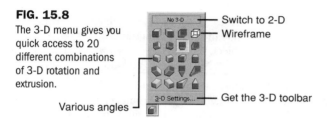

When you go to 3-D, any text associated with the object will not turn 3-D. Instead, the text will just appear in 2-D, in front of the 3-D object.

N O T E When you go to 3-D, the outline disappears and any shadow you have set disappears. (If you have the object fill set to No Fill, the object disappears altogether.) If you want to create a shadow under the 3-D object, copy the object, use the Fill Color menu to make the copy's color black, and use the Order commands to set the copy under the original. The copy will look like a black shadow on the slide. (You will have to adjust its position to make the lighting angle look right.)

Most objects look fine in 3-D. However, if you draw a freeform curved line and the line crosses itself, PowerPoint does not know how to properly draw the depth area, and it will look odd.

If you want to have more control over the rotation and the look of your 3-D, choose the 3-D Settings command from the 3-D menu. This brings up a toolbar with the following buttons:

Turns on or off the 3-D effect.
Tilts the object toward the viewer.
Tilts the object away from the viewer.
Spins the object toward the left.
Spins the object toward the right.

	Brings up a menu to set the thickness of the object. The menu has six preset thicknesses from zero thickness to infinitely thick, plus a field you can use to set the thickness to exactly what you want.
	Choose the direction that the object is angled in. Nine different basic angles are displayed. In addition, you can choose between a Perspective view (where the far end of the object looks smaller than the close one, as in real life) or a Parallel view (the distant parts are the same size as the close parts).
	This button has a menu (see Figure 15.9), with two areas to choose from. The top area lets you select the angle of the lighting; this angle is relative to the object, so if you rotate the object, the lighting moves with it. The lower area lets you select from Bright, Normal, or Dim light.
	This button lets you select the material that makes up the object, which affects how it reflects light. The first choice, Wire Frame, causes a line structure to be drawn. This makes working with the angle of the object much quicker. The other three (Matte, Plastic, and Metal) vary in the degree that they reflect light.
	The last button sets the color of the sides of the 3-D object. This works like PowerPoint's other color buttons, letting you select from the scheme colors, other colors used in the presentation, or any other color from the palette. It does not change the color of the front face of the object, which is set by the Fill Color button.

FIG. 15.9
The Lighting menu lets
you choose the angle
and brightness of light.

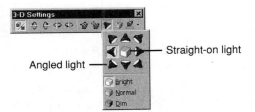

Drawing Connectors

Connectors are special types of lines used to connect one item to another. They are frequently used for flow charts.

To use connectors, follow these steps:

1. To place a connector, first choose a type of connector by clicking the AutoShapes menu and selecting Connector.

2. Point to the edge of the first object you're connecting, and then drag it to the edge of the second. PowerPoint automatically attaches the connector to the middle of the selected edges.

Some connector types are straight lines, whereas others can change direction along their paths. The non-straight ones automatically are routed for you; you don't need to draw their path.

N O T E If you move either of the objects that the connector is connected to, the connector's end moves with it, ensuring that the connection is maintained. ▓

If you wish to change a connector, keep in mind the following:

- When you select a connector, white sizing handles do not appear. Instead, you see red or green squares at the ends of the connection. Red means that the connector is properly attached to the edge, whereas green means that it isn't (a connector can become unattached if you accidentally drag the connector line itself). To change the connection being made, drag the box from the edge that it was connecting to the edge that you want to connect instead.

- When you select a connector that has not attached as a straight line, one or more diamonds appear in the middle of the line. Drag these to change the path of the connection. It does not change which edges are being connected, merely the path of the line.

Replacing an AutoShape

To replace one AutoShape with a different AutoShape, perform these steps:

1. Select the AutoShape to be changed.
2. From the drawing toolbar, choose Draw, Change Autoshape. A submenu of AutoShapes types appears. This is the same as the AutoShape menu, except that it doesn't have lines or connectors. (You cannot change lines or connectors in this method.)
3. Choose the category of AutoShape you want, and from its submenu, the exact type of AutoShape.

Using WordArt

WordArt gives you the capability to shape text and treat it as a drawing object. Using the WordArt feature, you can color text, fill it, outline it, cast shadows with it, and draw it into 3-D. Figure 15.10 shows you an example of WordArt at work.

To create WordArt, perform the following steps:

1. Click the Insert WordArt button:
2. The WordArt Gallery dialog box appears (see Figure 15.11). Double-click the design that looks the most like the way you want your words to appear.
3. An Edit WordArt Text dialog box appears. Choose the font design for your text using the font menu, the font size menu, and the Bold and Italic buttons. You can only choose one set of attributes that apply to your entire text. The font size attribute won't really change the size of your WordArt; it's only there because some fonts have different designs depending on the size.

4. When the dialog box opens, the words Your Text Here appear selected in the <u>T</u>ext field. Type the text you want, and that line is replaced. If you want multiple lines of text in your object, press Enter to start a new line. (If you type past the edge of the field and the text wraps to a new line, this does not cause a new line in the finished piece.)

5. Click OK, and your WordArt object appears. A WordArt toolbar also appears, allowing you greater control over the look of your text.

CAUTION

PowerPoint considers WordArt to be art, not text, and will not spell check it for you.

After you've created your WordArt piece, you can use the usual drawing buttons to set the outline color, fill, or shadow, or to make the object 3-D. (WordArt text will turn properly in 3-D, unlike text box text.) There will also be one of those yellow diamonds that you can drag to change the shape. While you drag the diamond, the text disappears, and you'll find yourself working with an outline of the basic shape of the WordArt. The exact change it makes depends on the basic shape of the WordArt.

The WordArt toolbar should appear when you create your WordArt object; if not, bring it up by right-clicking the object and choosing Show WordArt Toolba<u>r</u>. You can use the buttons on this toolbar to control other aspects of the object's appearance. These buttons are as follows:

 This does not affect the current piece of WordArt. Instead, it starts creating a new WordArt object.

Edit Text...	Reopens the Edit WordArt Text dialog box, so that you can change the text or the font.
	Reopens the WordArt Gallery, letting you select another design for this object. This wipes out all your current shape and color settings.
	Opens the Format WordArt dialog box, which is the same as the Format AutoShape dialog box described earlier in this chapter.
Abc	Displays a menu of WordArt shapes (see Figure 15.12). Choose one to reshape your art.

FIG. 15.11

The WordArt Gallery offers 30 WordArt designs to start your work with. You can then alter your WordArt in many ways.

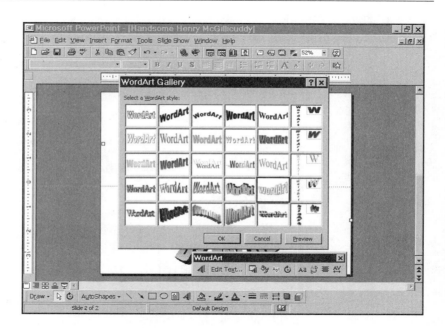

FIG. 15.12

The shapes on the WordArt shape menu with multiple segments are designed to hold multiple lines of text.

⟳	Displays the rotation handles on the WordArt object, allowing you to rotate it.
Aa	Makes all the letters the same height. In text with capitals and lowercase mixed, this usually looks goofy (reminiscent of some psychedelic 1960s rock posters), and it ruins most punctuation. However, it has the added benefit of reducing the space between lines of text, making it handy if you have multiple lines of all-capital text.
Ab	Stacks the text vertically, instead of horizontally.
≡	Pops up a menu letting you choose how to place or stretch shorter lines of text for multiline WordArt objects. See Figure 15.13 to see the effect of the different options.
AV	Displays a menu to choose spacing between letters. Choices include five preset settings (from Very Tight to Very Loose) and a Custom field, which lets you select the spacing as a percentage of the normal spacing.

FIG. 15.13
The different options on the WordArt Alignment menu apply only to multiline WordArt.

Left Align

Word Justify expands word spacing

HANDSOME HENRY MCGILLICUDDY
USED CAR LOT

HANDSOME HENRY MCGILLICUDDY
USED   CAR   LOT

Center

HANDSOME HENRY MCGILLICUDDY
USED CAR LOT

HANDSOME HENRY MCGILLICUDDY
U S E D   C A R   L O T

Letter Justify expands letter and word spacing

Right Align

HANDSOME HENRY MCGILLICUDDY
USED CAR LOT

HANDSOME HENRY MCGILLICUDDY
USED CAR LOT

Stretch Justify expands letters and spacing

TIP WordArt is useful for more than just text. Many fonts have interesting little drawings and shapes as bullets and dingbats, and you can work with those just as you work with any other text.

CHAPTER 16

Inserting Predesigned Artwork

PowerPoint allows you to use two kinds of images made outside of PowerPoint. One is standard computer-format pictures, whether created by scanning in a photograph or by using a computer art program. The other is clip art, a type of colored line-based drawing that is designed to be resizable. Either type of image can be used to enhance your presentation, and various editions of Office 97 come with a large number of both, with more available on the Web. The capability to scan or design your own pictures and add them to your presentation lets you show your audience just what you're talking about. ■

Add pictures
Put scanned photographs and computer-designed pictures on your slides.

Use clip art
Use hundreds of drawn graphic images from the Office CD-ROM or from the Web.

Change the image
Trim, resize, and change the colors of pictures or clip art.

Ungroup clip art
Turn clip art into a set of drawing objects that you can rework and alter.

Organizing your art
Add your own art and images to PowerPoint's collection, in a way that you can find what you need.

Getting a Picture from a File

PowerPoint has the capability to read a broad range of graphic files. File formats supported include:

File Extension	Name
.GIF	Graphic Interchange Format
.JPG or .JPEG	Joint Photographic Experts Group
.PCX	PC Paintbrush
.TIF	Tagged Image File Format
.BMP, .DIB, or .RLE	Windows Bitmap
.EMF	Windows Enhanced Metafile
.WMF	Windows Metafile
.PNG	Portable Network Graphics
.CGM	Computer Graphics Metafile
.EPS	Encapsulated PostScript
.WPG	WordPerfect Graphics
.PCD	Kodak Photo CD
.PCT	Macintosh PICT
.TGA	Targa Graphics Adapter
.DXF	AutoCAD 2-D
.CDR	Corel Draw
.DRW	Micrografx Draw

Almost every graphics program currently available can save their images in one or more of these formats.

To take a picture from a file and put it on your slide:

1. In Slide view, choose Insert, Picture, From File. A file browser appears.
2. Find the file you want, and click it. A small version of the picture appears in the browser's preview window.
3. Click OK, and the image appears on your slide.

Scanning in a Picture

A *scanner* is a device that takes a picture of an image from outside the computer (such as a photograph or the printed page) and translates that into an image that the computer can store and display. Most scanners these days are compatible with the *TWAIN* (Toolbox Without An

Interesting Name) standard for communicating with programs. If you have a TWAIN-compatible scanner, you can start the scanner software from PowerPoint and have the image automatically placed on your slide.

To do this:

1. In Slide view, choose Insert, Picture, From Scanner. PowerPoint starts Microsoft Photo Editor, a graphics-editing program, and Photo Editor starts your scanner's software.

2. Scan in the image and close the scanner software. The picture now appears in Photo Editor. (Photo Editor does have an array of tools that you can use to modify your picture in various ways; it's worth spending some time exploring its menus to see what it can do.)

3. In Photo Editor, choose File, Exit And Return To (name of presentation). The scanned image appears on your slide.

Choosing a Picture from the Clip Gallery

Depending on which version of Office or PowerPoint you purchased, you may have Microsoft-provided photos that you can use, on your hard disk and/or on the installation CD-ROM. These are organized by type (clip art or digitized picture) and by picture contents.

To access these pictures:

1. If you have access to it, insert the Office CD-ROM into your CD-ROM drive while holding down the Shift key. Keep the key held down for several seconds after insertion; this tells Windows that you don't want to run any programs from the CD-ROM.

2. In Slide view, choose Insert, Picture, Clip Art. A large Microsoft Clip Gallery dialog box appears. (Clip Gallery is actually a separate program that works with PowerPoint and other Office components.)

3. Choose the Pictures tab. Figure 16.1 shows you how this tab appears.

4. If no pictures are displayed, then you don't have any picture files on your CD-ROM (if installed), nor any others on your hard disk that the Clip Gallery program knows about. (In "Adding to the Clip Gallery" later in this chapter, you will learn how to add files to the gallery, both files already on your hard disk and files taken from the Web.) If this is the case, click the Close button to leave the Clip Gallery, and skip the rest of this procedure.

5. Click the category name for the type of picture you want to see. The categories are listed to the left of the panel. Pictures that fall into that category are displayed in the center area of the dialog box.

6. Find the picture you want. You can use the scrollbar to view more pictures in that category, if there are any. Be patient when you scroll down; Clip Gallery doesn't try to read the image's file until you scroll down, and with the relatively slow speed of the CD-ROM, some waiting may be involved.

7. Double-click the picture you want. The Clip Gallery closes, and the picture appears on your slide.

FIG. 16.1
The Clip Gallery manages categorized clip art, pictures, movies, and sound.

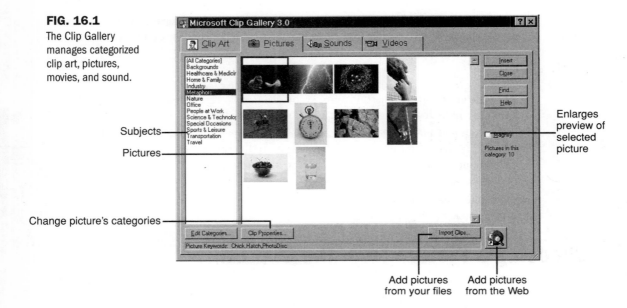

Subjects

Pictures

Enlarges preview of selected picture

Change picture's categories

Add pictures from your files

Add pictures from the Web

▶ For information on using the Clip Gallery to add sounds and movies to your presentation, **see** Chapter 17, "Adding Multimedia Effects to Your Presentation."

Cropping a Picture

Sometimes, you just want to use part of the picture in your image. You can trim a picture, cutting away from all four sides, until just the part of the picture you want remains. This is called *cropping*.

To crop a picture:

1. Select the picture, and a Picture toolbar should appear. If you don't see a Picture toolbar, right-click the picture and choose Show Picture Toolbar from the pop-up menu.

2. Click the Crop button.

3. The pointer will now look like the image on the cropping tool button. With this pointer, point to the sizing handle on the side of the picture that you want to cut away from, and drag that toward the center of the picture. A dotted outline shows what portion of the picture remains. When you release the mouse button, the image will be reduced to what was inside the outline.

4. Click the Crop button again, and the pointer returns to normal. Dragging the sizing handle now would squash or stretch the picture.

When you crop a picture, PowerPoint does not forget what the cut-away portions looked like. If you use the cropping tool to drag the sizing handle away from the image, you add back parts of the picture that had been cut. To instantly restore the entire picture (and remove any color changes), click the Reset Picture button.

Changing Picture Colors

The Picture toolbar has several buttons to adjust the colors of the picture:

Button	Name	Function
	Less Brightness	Makes the entire picture darker.
	More Brightness	Makes the entire picture brighter.
	Less Contrast	Makes the bright parts darker and the dark parts brighter.
	More Contrast	Makes the bright parts brighter and the dark parts darker.
	Image Control	Drops a menu, where you can choose from Automatic (normal), Grayscale (turns all colors into shades of gray), Black & White (no grays; dark colors become black, light colors become white), or Watermark (everything becomes extremely light; good for pictures that will be background decorations behind text).

 You can undo all color changes (as well as all cropping) by clicking the Reset Picture button.

Making Part of a Picture Transparent

You can choose one color from the picture and make it transparent, so that everywhere it appears in the picture you can see what's behind it on the slide. This doesn't do much good on scanned photos, where there are often thousands of colors and there are not usually large areas of the same color. It's meant more for computer-created art, which often is made up of just a few colors.

 To select the color, click the Set Transparent Color button. The pointer changes. Then click on part of the picture that is the color you want to change. Every part of the picture that is that color will turn clear.

Usually, this is used to remove the edge of the picture, allowing you to show a non-rectangular image. Be careful when you use this, however, as other portions of the picture may have that color as well, so you may end up with unintended holes in the picture.

If you have the picture cast a shadow (using the Shadow button), the transparent parts will cast no shadow. However, if you give the picture an outline, it will be rectangular, going around both the visible and transparent parts of the picture.

Adding Clip Art

Clip art is a Microsoft term for images made of lines and colors that they package with Office. Additional clip art images are also available. The images range from very designy to very cartoony. Because they're stored as a collection of lines and shapes, rather than as a gridwork of colored dots (the way pictures are), they don't turn grainy if you stretch or shrink them.

You can select clip art from the Clip Gallery using the same technique described earlier for pictures. Just select the Clip Art tab from the Gallery, rather than the Pictures tab. You can also use all the same tools on the clip art that you use on the pictures, except for setting a transparent color. (The areas between the edges of the clip art image and the rectangle that contains it are already transparent).

Letting AutoClipArt Suggest Images

PowerPoint has a built-in feature that will look through your presentation and suggest pictures and clip art. It looks for words that it recognizes, and suggests images that it associates with those words.

To use this feature:

1. Choose Tools, AutoClipArt. PowerPoint displays a message telling you that it's scanning through your presentation. When it's done, the dialog box seen in Figure 16.2 appears.

2. The first drop menu has a list of words that PowerPoint recognized. Choose a word from that list that you would like to illustrate with a picture or clip art.

3. The second drop menu now lists all the slides that contain that word. Choose the slide that you'd like the image to appear on.

4. Click the View Clip Art button. The Clip Gallery opens, displaying only items associated with the chosen concept.

5. Using the techniques described earlier, choose an item that you would like to insert from the Clip Art or Pictures tabs. (It is possible that there will be no items on those tabs; AutoClipArt also associates words with items on the Sounds and Videos tabs. See Chapter 17, "Adding Multimedia Effects to Your Presentation," for information on using sounds and videos in PowerPoint.)

6. Click the Insert button to add the image to your slide. (If you didn't find an image worth adding, click the Close button to leave the Clip Gallery without adding an image to your slide.)

7. You now return to the AutoClipArt dialog box. Repeat steps 2–6 until you've selected all the clip art and pictures that you want to add.

8. When done, click the Close button of the AutoClipArt dialog box.

FIG. 16.2
AutoClipArt looks for words that it recognizes on your slides.

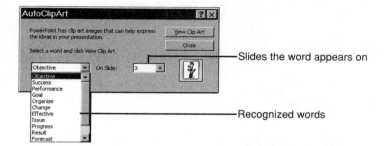

Changing Clip Art Colors

In addition to the buttons used to lighten and darken pictures, you can also change any individual color in a clip art image.

To do this:

1. Click the Recolor Picture button on the Picture toolbar.

2. The dialog box pictured in Figure 16.3 appears. In the Change area, choose between Colors (which means working with all the line and fill colors in the image) and Fills (no line colors, just fill colors).

3. On the Original color list, find a color you want to change. Then use the adjacent standard color menu to choose between the color scheme colors, additional colors already used in this presentation, or choosing a color from the color selector. When you choose your color, a check will appear in the check box at the left of the color entry.

4. Colors that are used in multiple areas of the image may have multiple entries. If you find that you've changed the wrong entry for the color, clear the check from the check box, and the change will be undone.

5. Repeat step 3 for all the colors that you want to change. As you make each change, the color changes in the preview of the picture.

6. Click OK, and the color changes are applied to the clip art on the slide.

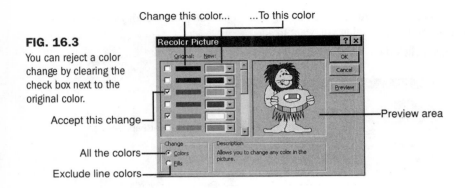

FIG. 16.3
You can reject a color change by clearing the check box next to the original color.

Change this color...   ...To this color

Accept this change

All the colors

Exclude line colors

Preview area

Converting Clip Art to PowerPoint Objects

Clip art is like computer pictures in many ways. There are things that you can do with it that you cannot do with drawing objects, such as cropping. On the other hand, there are also things that you can do with drawing objects that you cannot do with clip art or pictures, such as rotating them.

Luckily, you can change any piece of clip art into a grouped set of PowerPoint drawing objects. This allows you not only the capability to rotate it, but the capability to take the clip art apart into pieces, enlarge pieces, shrink pieces, and so on. In many pieces of clip art, the pieces are grouped into logical sub-groups, so that you can, for example, simply remove the stone tire seen in Figure 16.4, or enlarge it, shrink it, or change its color as a single item.

To make this change:

1. Select the clip art in Slide view.
2. Choose Draw, Ungroup. PowerPoint will display a dialog box, warning that If You Convert It To A Microsoft Office Object, Important Data Or Linking Information Will Be Lost.
3. Click Yes. The object turns into a collection of drawing objects, all of which are selected, as seen in Figure 16.4.
4. Before doing anything else, choose Draw, Group. It's important that you do this even if you're going to immediately turn around and ungroup it again so that you can work with the pieces. The reason is that when making the conversion, PowerPoint forgets that these items were a group. If you don't group them immediately while they're still selected, it may be hard to properly select them later to regroup them.

This is a one-directional change; after you've turned the clip art into a grouped set of drawing objects, there's no way to turn it back.

FIG. 16.4
Clip art turns into a
group of PowerPoint
drawing objects, many
of which are groups of
smaller objects.

 The grouped object will not cast a shadow properly, since when you click the Shadow button, each
element of the group will cast its own shadow. Instead, make a copy of the grouped object, set all
colors to the color scheme's shadow color, and put it under the original as the shadow.

▶ **See** "Arranging Your Slides," **p. 45**

Adding to the Clip Gallery

If you have your own pictures, videos, or sounds that you would like to add to the Clip Gallery:

1. Choose Import, Picture, Clip Art to open up the Clip Gallery.
2. Click the tab for the sort of clips you want to add (Clip Art, Pictures, Sounds, or Videos.)
3. Click the Import Clips button. A file browser appears.
4. Use file browser to select the clip you want. Once you've selected the clip, click OK.
5. The Clip Properties dialog box seen in Figure 16.5 appears. Type some words that you relate to this clip in the Keywords field. These words are used by the AutoClipArt feature; when it finds any of these words on a slide, it recommends this clip.
6. The Categories section has a list of clip categories. Check the check boxes of all the categories you think this clip fits into. Whenever you ask for a checked-off category of clips, this clip will be one of the ones that appears. (You can add more categories by clicking the New Category button.)
7. Click OK. Your clip will be added to the category.
8. Once you've added all the clips you want, click the Clip Gallery's Close button to exit.

Part
III

Ch
16

FIG. 16.5
The Clip Properties dialog box lets you set what categories and concepts the Clip Gallery associates with a clip.

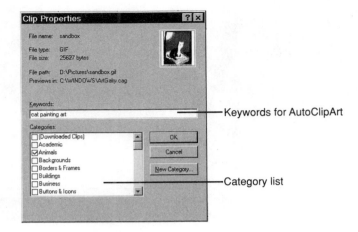

Keywords for AutoClipArt

Category list

Organizing Pictures, Sounds, and Videos in the Clip Gallery

In addition to adding various sorts of clips to the Clip Gallery, you can delete clips, change the category for each clip, change the list of available categories, and even change the keywords that AutoClipArt searches for to suggest that clip. However, you cannot do this with clips that are stored on CD-ROM, since you cannot write to the CD-ROM to change their properties.

To do any changes, you will have to open the Clip Gallery by using the Insert, Picture, Clip Art command. Then you can use any of the following changes:

- To change the keywords and categories of a clip (or add a new category), select the clip, then click Clip Properties. (See the previous instruction list for information on using this dialog box.)

- To delete a clip, right click the clip entry in the gallery, and choose Delete Clip from the pop-up menu.

- To remove a category from the displayed list of categories, click the Edit Categories button. From the dialog box that pops up, select the category to eliminate, then click the Delete Category button. Click the Close button when you're finished deleting categories.

Getting Clip Art from the Web

Microsoft has a Web site called Clip Gallery Live where they offer free addition clips of all types. If you need the right clip to make your presentation perfect, check it out and you may find what you're looking for.

If you have Web access and want to get to the Web site:

1. Start the Clip Gallery by choosing Insert, Picture, Clip Art.

2. Click the Clip Gallery Live button.

3. If a dialog box opens explaining If You Have Access To The World Wide Web, Click OK To Browse Additional Clips From A Special Web Page, put a check in the Don't Show This Message Again check box, then click OK.

4. Your Web browser starts up, and displays a page from Microsoft's web site. Click the First-Time Help link to get instructions on using the site to add clips to your Clip Gallery.

Part

III

Ch

CAUTION

Some of the clips (particularly movie clips) can be rather large. Using a 28.8 modem on typical busy Web conditions, you can expect to transfer around 1K of data per second. As such, you may have to wait 15 to 20 minutes for a 1 megabyte file.

Using the Internet

CHAPTER 17

Adding Multimedia Effects to Your Presentation

Add movies to a slide

Use your own computerized film clips, or take advantage of Microsoft-offered animations.

Add sound effects

Use sound to highlight the appearance of a new slide or a new item on a slide.

Narrate your presentation

Add your own recorded voice to the presentation, so that you can be heard without being present.

Play a CD

Use PowerPoint to play music from your CD-ROM drive, giving your presentation background music.

Get multimedia from the Web

Search the World Wide Web for the multimedia you need.

Previous chapters of this book have treated each slide as being still—a single image that does not change with time, until it is replaced by another slide. Starting with this chapter, we'll see that each individual slide can have a life of its own; by adding digital movies and sound to a slide, you can communicate things that are not possible with a silent, still image. However, these features only apply to presentations delivered immediately on a computer. After all, there is no way to print a moving picture on a piece of paper, or have sound come off of a slide projector slide. Additionally, PowerPoint's conference presentation feature does not support using movies and sounds, so those items cannot be used on a presentation delivered to a group over a network. ■

Adding a Movie

You can add a digitized movie clip to your presentation either from the Clip Gallery or from a file on your disk. This operation must be done in Slide view.

■ To add a movie from the Clip Gallery, choose Insert, Movies And Sounds, Movie From Gallery. The Clip Gallery opens. Double-click the image for the clip you want. (The features of using Clip Gallery described in Chapter 16, "Inserting PreDesigned Artwork," also apply here. Plus, you can click a movie image then click the Play button to see what the whole movie looks like.)

■ To insert a movie from a file, choose Insert, Movies And Sounds, Movie From File. Using the file browser that opens, find and select the movie file. PowerPoint supports a broad range of movie formats, although you may need to have the proper Windows drivers configured for those formats. (This is important to remember if you'll be playing the movie on someone else's machine later, as they may not have the same drivers installed that you do.)

After you've properly inserted the movie, it appears on your slide. You can view the movie by double-clicking it. You can reposition it by dragging it, like any object.

N O T E You can resize a movie by dragging the sizing handles—but you probably shouldn't. A digital movie has built-in measurements, measured in *pixels* (computer screen dots) that it expects to be played at. PowerPoint automatically sizes the movie clip to the right size for being displayed as part of an on-screen presentation on your computer. If you make it larger or smaller, the movie may play back erratically, as the computer has to work to resize each frame of the film as it plays. Plus, if you make it larger, it may look grainy or blocky. ■

If you click the Slide Show button to test your movie now, the slide show will come up, but the movie won't play automatically. You have to click the movie to start it playing. To make the movie play automatically when the slide is displayed:

1. Select the movie.
2. Choose Slide Show, Custom Animation. A dialog box opens with a Play Settings tab displayed. (This Custom Animation dialog box is discussed more in Chapter 18, "Using Special Effects in your Presentation".)
3. On the Play Settings tab, put a check in the Play Using Animation Order check box.
4. Click the Timing tab.
5. Click the Animate option button, then click the Automatically option button.
6. Click OK, and your movie will now be set to start playing when the slide is displayed.

If you position some object over the movie, the movie will automatically come to the front when it starts to play.

> **CAUTION**
>
> Some of AutoFormat's slide designs have an area designated for multimedia clips. If you double-click these areas, you will be taken through a different procedure to install the clip, one that does not allow you as much control. Avoid this.

Adding Sound

Adding sound from a sound file is done in almost the exact manner as described for movies. The differences are as follows:

- To start getting a sound from the Clip Gallery, choose Insert, Movies And Sounds, Sound From Gallery.
- To start getting a sound from a file, choose Insert, Movies And Sounds, Sound From File.
- When the sound is added to the slide, it will be represented by the picture of a speaker. There is no reason not to resize this, if you want.
- If you've set the sound to play automatically, there's probably no reason to have the speaker picture on the slide. If you slide it off the side of the slide, the picture will not appear during the presentation, but the sound will still be heard.

N O T E Two types of sound files are supported by PowerPoint. *Digitized sound files* (any file with the extension .wav) are actual recordings of sounds stored on the computer. *Score files* (.mid or .rmi extensions) are more like sheet music—the files have a list of instrument types and the notes that they are playing. These score files are only good for music, but are handy because you can store several minutes of music in the same file space as a few seconds of digitized sound. File size can be very important if you want to distribute your presentation via disk or e-mail. ▨

Playing Multimedia Continuously

Normally, a sound or a movie will stop either when the end of the file is reached or you switch to the next slide. In most cases, this is fine. However, you may want a movie to carry over from one slide to the next, or to have a song keep repeating until the end of the presentation is reached.

To make a movie or sound repeat once the end of the file is reached:

1. Right-click the object and choose Edit Sound Object or Edit Movie Object from the pop-up menu. A Play Options dialog box appears.
2. Put a check in the Loop Until Stopped check box.
3. Click OK.

Part

IV

Ch

17

This Play Option dialog box has another option for movies; if you're not looping the movie, you can choose whether it should show the first frame or last frame when it stops.

To have a movie or sound continue even after the slide is replaced with the next one:

1. Right-click the movie or sound, and choose Custom Animation. A Custom Animation dialog box appears.
2. On the Play Settings tab, select the following options: Play Using Animation Order, Continue Slide Show, and After.
3. In the numerical field next to After, select the number of slides that you want it to continue for.
4. Click OK.

This dialog box has a different option for what to do with a movie after it's finished; by checking the Hide While Not Playing option, you can make the movie disappear altogether.

Triggering Multimedia with the Mouse

If you want the sound or movie to start when the item of the slide is clicked or when the pointer passes over the slide in an interactive presentation:

1. Right-click the movie area or the speaker icon, and choose Action Settings from the pop-up menu.
2. A dialog box might pop up, recommending that you save the presentation before creating a hyperlink, and asking Do You Want To Save This Document Now? Click No; you won't be creating a hyperlink, so there's no need answer yes.
3. The dialog box shown in Figure 17.1 will show up, with two identical tabs, one marked Mouse Click, the other marked Mouse Over. Select the Mouse Click tab.
4. If you want the sound or movie to play when the viewer clicks them, click the Object Action option button. Otherwise, click the None option button.
5. Select the Mouse Over tab. This sets what happens when the mouse just passes over the object. This is particularly useful for kiosk presentations, where the user may have a trackball with no button and may not be able to click anything.
6. If you want the sound or movie to play when the pointer passes over it, click the Object Action option button. Otherwise, click the None option button.
7. Click OK.

FIG. 17.1
The Action Settings dialog box has a lot of options that will be grayed out for movies and sounds. They will be used for other interactive features.

Don't play the sound or movie

Play the sound or movie

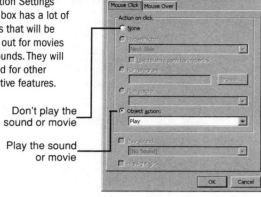

Recording a Sound

If you have a properly configured sound card you can record a sound file from within PowerPoint, and make it a built-in part of your presentation.

1. Connect your microphone or other sound input device to the proper port on your sound card.

2. Choose Insert, Movies And Sounds, Record Sound. The Record Sound dialog box shown in Figure 17.2 appears.

FIG. 17.2
The buttons on the Record Sound dialog box have standard VCR-style diagrams.

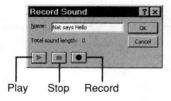

Play   Stop   Record

3. Type a name for the sound into the Name field. This name lets you select this sound for various uses in other places of the presentation.

4. Click Record, and start talking into the microphone or playing the sound into the sound card.

5. At the end of the sound, click Stop.

6. Check the sound by clicking Play. If it didn't come out properly for some reason, go back to step 4.

7. Click OK. A speaker icon for this sound appears on the slide.

▶ **See** "Using Special Effects in Your Presentation," **p. 161**

Recording Voice Narration for Self-Running Shows

There's a large difference between presentations that are designed to be delivered in person and presentations that are designed to be viewed completely from the slides. If the presentation is to be given completely from the slides, you will have all the relevant information built into the slide show. If you're giving it in person, the items on the slide are generally just a jumping-off point for your discussion of their contents.

You can record a narration to go along with your slide show. That way, you can design a show to deliver yourself, and then have the same slide show with recorded narration for people to view when you're not around.

To record narration:

1. Choose Slide Show, Record Narration. You will see the dialog box shown in Figure 17.3, telling you how much space you have left on your hard disk, and how much narration time that allows you, given the current settings.

2. Put a check in the Link Narrations In check box. This option means that you're storing the narrations in separate files, rather than in the main presentation file. Linked narrations play back more smoothly than narrations stored in the main presentation file. (If you don't like the directory that it says it will store the files in, click Browse to select another directory.)

3. Click Settings. A Sound Selection dialog box will appear.

FIG. 17.3

The time limit in the Record Narration dialog box presumes the current recording settings. You can change these settings as well, depending on the sound quality desired.

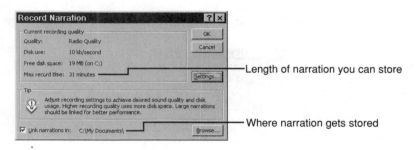

Length of narration you can store

Where narration gets stored

4. From the Name drop-down menu, select a recording quality. CD Quality is the best, but takes up a lot of disk space. For most purposes, Radio Quality doesn't sound that much worse (after all, you're not recording this in a CD-quality recording studio), and takes up only 1/12th as much disk space. Telephone Quality takes up even less disk space, although the drop in quality is noticeable.

5. Click OK to save this setting and return to the Record Narration dialog box.

6. Click OK. The Slide Show starts.

7. Narrate the current slide, then click the mouse button when it's time to advance to the next slide.

8. Repeat step 7 for every slide in the presentation. (If you need to take a break from recording, right-click and select Pa<u>u</u>se Narration, then right-click and select <u>R</u>esume Narration when you want to continue.)

9. After you've completed the entire presentation, a dialog box appears, asking if you want to save the timings also. *Timings* (discussed further in Chapter 18, "Using Special Effects in your Presentation") are time measurements that PowerPoint sometimes uses to automatically advance through the presentation, or to let you know when your presentation is running too fast or too slow. Choose <u>Y</u>es or <u>N</u>o.

10. If you chose Yes, you are asked if you want to be taken to Slide Sorter View. Click <u>Y</u>es or <u>N</u>o.

Playing a CD During a Presentation

If your computer has the CD-ROM drive properly configured to play audio CDs through the speakers, you can have PowerPoint take control of the CD and play whatever tracks you want. This is a handy way of adding musical background to your presentation without filling your disk with large wave files.

To play a CD with your presentation:

1. In Slide View, go to the slide where you want the CD to start playing.

2. Insert the CD you want to play with the presentation into the CD-ROM drive. Hold down the Shift key while you insert the CD, and for ten seconds afterward. (This will keep Windows from automatically playing your CD, which would interfere with the steps you're about to take.)

3. Choose <u>I</u>nsert, Mo<u>v</u>ies And Sounds, Play <u>C</u>D Audio Track. The dialog box in Figure 17.4 appears.

FIG. 17.4

In the Play Options dialog box, the Start and End times are automatically set to the beginning and end of the track.

Start with which track?——

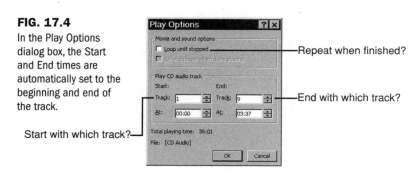

——Repeat when finished?

——End with which track?

4. In the Start area, put the track number for the first track you want to play into the Tra<u>c</u>k field. (If you want to start somewhere besides the beginning of the track, put the starting point in the <u>A</u>t field, in the format minutes:seconds.)

5. In the End area, put the track number for the last track you want to play into the Track field. (If you want to stop somewhere before the end of the track, put the stopping point in the At field.)

6. Click OK.

A picture of a CD appears on the slide. You can set whether the CD starts playing by being clicked, or if it starts automatically when the slide appears, using the same commands described earlier for sounds and movies.

TIP When you play this presentation, remember to put the CD in while holding down the Shift key before starting the presentation, or Windows may start the CD immediately.

CHAPTER 18

Using Special Effects in Your Presentation

This chapter focuses on features only available on a computer-presented slide show. You can set the way that one slide changes to the next, using fancy graphic transitions or setting the slides to change automatically after a fixed period of time. You can animate the slide, having objects move, text fly onto the screen, and parts of your charts appear in order. By setting up interactive links on your slides, you can give the person viewing the slide on his PC quick point-and-click access to other slides, or even to World Wide Web sites. ■

Add a stylish transition

Choose from a number of fancy ways to replace one slide with the next.

Set the timing of slide transitions

Have one slide disappear and the next appear after a fixed amount of time.

Animate your slide

Have objects move on and off your slide.

Add interactivity

Let the viewer navigate your presentation by clicking parts of your slide to move to other slides.

Link to the Web

Create interactive access to Web sites.

Setting Slide Transitions

Instead of simply having one slide instantly replaced by the next, you can have the old slide dissolve away, be replaced piece by piece, or simply move away.

The styles of transitions available include the following:

- *No Transition.* The new slide just appears in place.
- *Blinds.* The slide is replaced as if the new slide is on venetian blinds closing in front of the old slide.
- *Box.* The old slide is replaced from the edges to the center (*in*) or from the center to the edges (*out*).
- *Checkerboard.* The slide breaks into little squares, wiping first half the squares and then the other half.
- *Cover.* The new slide is dragged into place over the old one.
- *Cut.* This is the same as No Transition.
- *Cut through Black.* This briefly shows black between slides. (It looks better than Cut on projection screens.)
- *Dissolve.* This treats the new slide as a lot of little squares revealed one at a time.
- *Fade through Black.* The old slide fades away to black; then the black brightens into a new slide.
- *Random Bars.* This transition puts up short lines of the new slide until it's whole.
- *Split.* The new slide is treated as halves, wiping in opposite directions.
- *Strip.* This is a diagonal wipe.
- *Uncover.* The old slide is pulled away to reveal the new one.
- *Wipe.* The slide is replaced a bit at a time, moving from one side to the other.
- *Random Transition.* This transition randomly picks a style and direction each time the transition takes place.

To set up a transition for your slide, follow these steps:

1. In Slide Sorter view, right-click the slide that you want to transition to and click Slide Transition from the pop-up menu.
2. The dialog box shown in Figure 18.1 appears. Choose one of the transition styles from the drop-down list. When you choose, the transition style is simulated in the preview area. (If this is the only setting you want, you don't need this dialog box at all. Instead, just select the style using the Slide Transition Effects drop-down list, which is the first drop-down list on the Slide Sorter toolbar.)

CAUTION

Be careful of the Cover and Uncover transitions. They can look clumsy on slower computers.

3. Use the option buttons below the menu to set the speed for the transition (Slow, Medium, or Fast). Again, the transition is simulated.

4. If you want a sound effect to accompany the transition, choose one of the built-in sounds from the Sounds drop-down list. If you choose Other Sound, you can select any sound from a file. (This does not include audio CD tracks.)

5. Click the Apply button. (If you want to set the same transition for all the slides, click the Apply To All button.) The transition is demonstrated on the miniature of your slide in Slide Sorter view.

FIG. 18.1

The Slide Transition can also be used to set slide timings, but those are better set via Rehearse Timings.

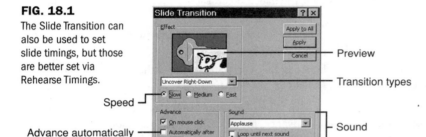

Preview — Transition types — Sound — Speed — Advance automatically — Repeat sound until next sound

Setting the Timings

You can set an amount of time for each slide to appear on the screen. This can be used for two purposes:

- To automatically advance the slides, without anyone having to click. This can be good for kiosk displays; the presentation can proceed without anyone doing anything.

- To create a set of expected times. You can use the Slide Meter feature while delivering a presentation to make sure that you aren't going too fast or too slow.

You can set the timings using the Slide Transition dialog box discussed in the preceding section. However, a better way to do it is to actually run through your presentation, stepping through each slide as if you were giving the presentation, and have PowerPoint record how long you paused at each slide. To do this, follow these steps:

1. Choose Slide Show, Rehearse Timings. Your slide show begins, but a Rehearsal dialog box appears over the slide, as shown in Figure 18.2.

2. Stay on the slide for as long as you want it to appear (if you're going to narrate your presentation in front of the audience, try giving your spoken presentation for the slide in a slow, even voice); then click the Advance button to go to the next slide. If you mess up the timing, click the Repeat button to restart the timing for the slide.

3. Repeat step 2 for all the slides in your presentation.

Time for show to this point

FIG. 18.2

Rehearse Timings lets you measure the time for stepping through your presentation.

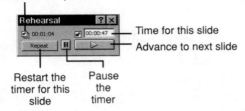

Time for this slide

Advance to next slide

Restart the timer for this slide

Pause the timer

4. When you've finished all the slides, the dialog box disappears. If your last slide is still showing, click it.

5. Another dialog box appears, asking Do you want to record the new slide timings and use them when you view the slide show?. Click Yes.

6. Another dialog box appears asking whether you want to review the timings in Slide Sorter view. Click Yes, and you will be in Slide Sorter view.

Once you've completed this, all the slides in your slide show will be set for automatic advance. If you want to set some slides to manual advance, bring up the Slide Transition dialog box for the slide and select On Mouse Click.

Easy Animation

PowerPoint lets you animate your objects, having them move onto the slide or suddenly appear in place. Many styles of motion are available. You can use a *preset animation*, using predesigned animation styles with sound effects, or you can make your own *custom animation*, making your own choices of the animation style and sound effects.

Only one object can move at a time. With preset animation, PowerPoint animates the objects in the order that you set the animation. When you give the presentation, it waits until you click the mouse button before moving on to the next animation. However, after setting up a preset animation, you can use the custom animation tools to make the animation happen automatically, without waiting for the mouse click.

To set a preset animation, perform the following steps:

1. In Slide view, position the object on the slide where you want it to end up. Make sure that object is selected.

2. Choose Slide Show, Preset Animation. A submenu of animation styles appears.

3. Choose the animation style you want from the submenu. The exact list that you have to choose from depends on the type of object you are working with. The list includes some of the following choices:

- *Off.* Removes any existing animation from the object, setting the object to be on-screen when the slide first appears.

- *Drive-In.* The object moves into place from the right side of the screen.

- *Flying.* The object moves in from the left side of the screen.
- *Camera.* The center of the object appears first; then it grows in a circular shape until the entire object appears.
- *Flash Once.* The object appears, disappears for a moment, and then reappears.
- *Laser Text.* Letters in a text box appear one at a time, flying in from the upper-left corner of the screen.
- *Typewriter.* Letters in a text box appear one at a time, in place.
- *Reverse Order.* The bottom item of a list appears; then after a mouse click, shows the line above it, and so on until the whole list is shown. (This is good in presentations where you want to discuss a list of points starting with the least significant and moving up to the most important or exciting.)
- *Drop In.* The text appears one word at a time, falling into place from the top of the slide.
- *Wipe Right.* The left edge of the object appears in place first, expanding until the whole object is in place.
- *Dissolve.* Treats the object as a bunch of little squares that appear in random order.
- *Split Vertical Out.* Shows the vertical center line of the object in place first; then expands that until the whole object appears.
- *Appear.* The object suddenly appears in place.
- *Fly from Top.* The object comes down from the top of the screen.

> **CAUTION**
>
> If your presentation might be shown on anything slower than a 100MHz Pentium, you should avoid moving anything but small objects because their movements can be erratic and jerky. It's safe to use any of the animations that have the object appear right in place, however.

To quickly see how the animation looks, choose Slide Show, Animation Preview. A small window appears showing the animation for the slide, without waiting for any mouse clicks to advance it.

 T I P You can quickly set a simple text animation for the AutoFormatted text area on a slide. In Slide Sorter view, select the slide; then choose an animation style from the Text Preset Animation drop-down list, the second drop-down list on the Slide Sorter toolbar.

Custom Animation

You can mix your own animation effects, choosing where the object moves in from, how it moves, and what happens when it gets there. To do this, follow these steps:

1. In Slide view, position the object on the slide where you want it to end up. Make sure that object is selected.

Part
IV

Ch
18

2. Choose Slide Show, Custom Animation. The dialog box shown in Figure 18.3 appears.

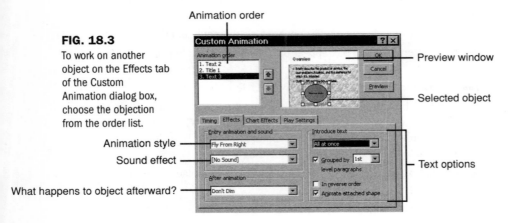

Animation order

FIG. 18.3
To work on another object on the Effects tab of the Custom Animation dialog box, choose the objection from the order list.

Preview window

Selected object

Animation style

Sound effect

What happens to object afterward?

Text options

3. Select a motion or appearance type from the Entry Animation drop-down list. Motion entry types include your choice of directions. The basic types include the following:

- *Appear.* The object appears in place.
- *Fly.* The object moves into place quickly.
- *Blinds.* Reveals the object as if venetian blinds are opening in front of it.
- *Box.* Shows the object from the edges to the center (*in*) or from the center to the edges (*out*).
- *Checkerboard.* Treats the object as a grid of squares, first wiping alternating squares into place, and then wiping the remainder.
- *Crawl.* The same as Fly, only slower.
- *Dissolve.* Treats the object as small squares that appear in random order.
- *Peek.* Slips the object in from the edge of the object's box.
- *Random Bars.* Puts up lines from the object until it's whole.
- *Spiral.* The object moves onto the screen along a spiral path. The object starts small and expands to full size as it moves.
- *Split.* A wipe that starts at the center.
- *Stretch.* Expands a shrunken version of the object until it's full size.
- *Strips.* A diagonal wipe.
- *Swivel.* The object repeatedly grows and shrinks horizontally, making it look as though the object is dangling from a string.
- *Wipe.* Starts by revealing one edge of the object, expanding it until the whole object is seen.
- *Zoom.* The object grows (*in*) or shrinks (*out*) in place, until it becomes normal size.

- *No Effect.* Removes any motion effect.
- *Random Effect.* The computer chooses a different effect each time the presentation is shown.

4. From the Sounds drop-down list, select a sound to accompany the animation. In addition to the list of sound effects, the options include No Sound, Stop Previous Sound, and Other Sound (which lets you select a sound file using a file browser).

5. From the After Animation drop-down list, select what is to happen to the object after the animation is completed. The menu is mostly a standard color menu, letting you pick which color the object turns after the animation is complete. (PowerPoint calls this change of color *dimming*, but you can choose a brighter rather than dimmer color.) The other choices include Don't Dim (that is, keep the object the same color), Hide After Animation (get rid of the object altogether), and Hide On Next Mouse Click.

6. Click the Preview button to see the whole slide's animation take place in the Preview window.

7. Click OK when you're happy with the animation.

 TIP You can make an object move fully across the slide and disappear off the other side by placing the object off the slide to begin with. For example, if you drag the object off the left side of the slide into the gray area in Slide view and then use Fly From Right animation style, the object will fly across the slide.

If you want to start with an object on your slide and then make it disappear, there are no animation styles designed just for that. However, if you're using a solid-color background and your object is not ovetnapping any others, here's a trick you can use:

1. In Slide view, make a copy of the object.

2. Place the copy directly over the original; then use the color tools to make both the fill and the outline (if any) the same color as the background.

3. Use the animation tools to make this copy dissolve into place. In effect, you'll be painting over the original object using the background color!

Custom Animating Text

Animating a text box is done basically like animating other objects, except that you have an additional set of options to consider. These options let you choose whether the whole block of text moves as a single unit or appears piece-by-piece. The options are grayed out until you choose your Entry Animation.

The additional settings on the Effects tab of the Custom Animation dialog box are as follows:

- The Introduce Text drop-down list lets you select whether the text appears all at once, a word at a time, or a letter at a time.

- The Grouped By check box lets you select whether the text is grouped by the level of outline indentation (if checked) or treated as a single unit.

■ The Grouped By drop-down list lets you select how big the groups are. Choose 1st Level to make each main point and its subpoints a single group. Choose 2nd Level to make each point its own group and each subpoint (with all sub-subpoints) its own group. Choose 3rd Level to make each point, subpoint, and sub-subpoint its own group.

■ The In Reverse Order check box causes text to appear with the bottom group first, rather than the other way around. (Words within the group always appear in forwards order.)

■ The Animate Attached Shape causes any shape attached to the text box to be animated. Unless the Introduce Text option is set to All At Once and the Grouped By check box is not checked, the shape will animate on first, followed by the text.

Animation Order and Timing

PowerPoint cannot animate more than one object at a time. By default, objects are animated in the order that you set the animation to them. Also by default, PowerPoint waits for you to click the mouse before starting each animation. However, you can change both of these using the Timing tab in the Custom Animation dialog box, as shown in Figure 18.4.

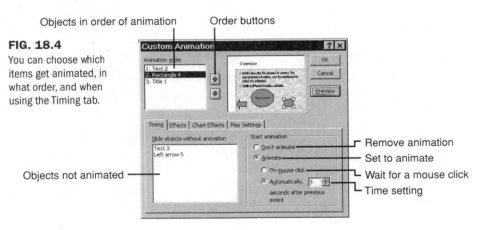

FIG. 18.4
You can choose which items get animated, in what order, and when using the Timing tab.

The controls that you have with the Timing tab include the following:

■ The Animation Order list displays all the animated objects on the slide, as well as all the sounds and movies set to play automatically, in the order that they are animated or played. Click an item on the list, and it becomes selected as the current working object. Items are named with the type of object they are and a number.

■ The order buttons move the currently selected item up or down through the animation list, making the object animated earlier or later.

■ The Slide Objects Without Animation list shows all the slide objects not on the Animation Order list. Click an item, and it becomes selected as the current working object.

- The <u>D</u>on't Animate option button moves the selected object from the Animation <u>O</u>rder list to the <u>S</u>lide Objects Without Animation list.

- The <u>A</u>nimate option button moves the selected object from the <u>S</u>lide Objects Without Animation list to the Animation <u>O</u>rder list.

- The On <u>M</u>ouse Click option button causes the presentation to wait for the mouse to click before animating this item or playing this sound or movie. For individual objects with multiple animated parts (such as a text object that is animated by the word), a mouse click is required before each part of the animation.

- The A<u>u</u>tomatically option buttons cause this animation to start after the number of seconds in the following field. The time can be set to the tenth of a second. For individual objects with multiple animated parts, this length pause takes place between animations.

Animating Charts

Charts created using Microsoft Graph have their own animation capabilities. You can bring the data up one graphed item at a time, letting you discuss that item before bringing up the next.

To animate a chart, select it, and choose Sli<u>d</u>e Show, Custo<u>m</u> Animation. The Chart Effects tab of the dialog box appears. In addition to the <u>E</u>ntry Animation, Sound, and <u>A</u>fter Animation drop-down lists seen on the Effects tab, two more items are on this tab.

The first is the <u>I</u>ntroduce Chart Elements drop-down list. This selects the order in which the charted data is introduced onto the chart. For an example case of a sales chart with a red column and a green column for each of four quarters, choosing the following options from the list will have these effects:

- *All At Once* treats the entire chart like a single image, animating it as you would any other object.

- *By Series* brings all the red columns on at once and then all the green columns on.

- *By Category* brings both of the first quarter columns on at once, then both of the second quarter, and so on.

- *By Element In Series* brings each of the red columns on, one at a time, and then each of the green columns.

- *By Element In Category* brings up the red column for the first quarter, then the green column for the first quarter, then moves on to the second quarter, and so on.

Unless you select All At Once, you are limited to animation styles that cause the object to appear in place (such as wipes and dissolves). You cannot use anything that moves the object or changes its size.

The other item on the tab is the Ani<u>m</u>ate Grid And Legend check box. If you check this, the chart's grid and legend animate onto the slide before the data.

Adding Interactive Links

If your presentation is going to be viewed by a person directly on her own computer or on a kiosk, you can make the presentation interactive. You can give an object properties so that when the user clicks it or when she just passes the pointer over it (your choice), something happens.

1. To select what happens, right-click the object and select _A_ction Settings. When you do this, a dialog box appears recommending that you save this document before creating a hyperlink.

2. Click _Y_es, and your file is saved. (If you have not yet saved this file, you are taken through the usual file naming procedure.)

3. The Action Settings dialog box shown in Figure 18.5 appears. This dialog box has two near-identical tabs, one marked Mouse Over to set what happens when the mouse passes over the visible portion of this object, and one marked Mouse Click to set what happens when the visible portion of the object is clicked.

FIG. 18.5

The Mouse Click and Mouse Over tabs of the Action Settings dialog box are functionally identical. You can set separate actions on each tab.

The option buttons for choices of action are as follows:

- _None_. Nothing happens.
- _Hyperlink To_. Select from the drop-down list to move to another slide in the presentation (Next, Previous, First, Last, Last Viewed, or just Slide, which lets you pick a specific slide); to a custom show within this presentation (Custom Show); to another PowerPoint presentation (Other PowerPoint Presentation); to end this presentation altogether (End Show); to any other Windows file (Other File); or to a file on the World Wide Web (URL).
- _Run Program_. Start up another Windows program listed in the attached field. (Use the Browse button to get a file browser so that you can select the program you want.)
- _Run _M_acro_. Starts a macro. (See Chapter 24, "Automating Your Work with Macros," for information on creating and using macros.)

■ *Object Action.* Choose a command related to the object. (Information on using this option is covered in Chapter 17, "Adding Multimedia Effects to Your Presentation"; it also applies to certain Add-In objects, discussed in Chapter 22, "Customizing PowerPoint.")

Two check box options are on the tab:

■ *Play Sound.* Plays a sound, in addition to any other action. Use the drop-down list to select from various sound effects, sounds you've recorded for this presentation, or Other Sound, which lets you select any sound file.

■ *Highlight Click or Highlight When Mouse Over.* Temporarily changes the colors of the object to draw attention to it.

Better Linking for Web Presentations

If you plan to publish this presentation on the Web, you should take advantage of the capability to set a base Web address and have all the links set as relative links. For example, if you have the base Web address of **http://www.gertler.com/** and you link to another presentation that's stored at **http://www.gertler.com/sales.ppt**, a relative link to that slide simply lists the link as `sales.ppt`.

When you use relative links, it's easier to move a Web-based presentation from site to site because you won't have to change where all the links point. Otherwise, when you move your files from your hard disk to the Web or if you move your presentation from one Web site to another, all the links on the page still link to the old location.

Part

IV

Ch

18

 TIP The use of links to an URL will open up your Web browser and bring up what's at that Web address. This can be a distracting change of environment for someone who is not viewing the presentation on the Web and does not know what to expect. It makes much more sense if your presentation is being delivered on the Web, so that the viewer is already using his Web browser.

To set the base Web address, follow these steps:

1. Click the File menu and select Properties. A dialog box opens.

2. Type the base URL into the Hyperlink Base field on the Summary tab. (You don't have to do this immediately; by default, PowerPoint assumes that all relative links are made relative to the location where the presentation file is stored.)

3. When you're adding a link to a slide, put a check in the Use Relative Path For Hyperlink check box on the Action Settings dialog box.

Interactive Action Buttons

One of the shape types on the AutoShapes menu is Action Buttons. These shapes are specifically designed for interactivity. When you place one of these button shapes on your slide, the Action Settings dialog box automatically pops up. An action for Mouse Click the shape will already be set (although you can choose another action, if you desire.) As shown in Table 18.1, most of these buttons are designed for a specific action.

Table 18.1 Action Buttons

Button	Action
	No pre-set action
	Link to first slide
	None (used for Help link)
	None (used for Information link)
	Link to previous slide
	Link to next slide
	Link to first slide
	Link to last slide
	Link to last slide viewed
	Run a program
	Play a sound
	None (used for Video link)

These buttons all have a nice two-tone raised look. The yellow diamond can be used to adjust the depth of the button.

N O T E The buttons for the Help, Information, and Video links don't have actions pre-set for them. It's up to you to decide how you are implementing your presentation's Help, Information, or Video systems (if you use them at all), and to set the appropriate action for the button. ■

Delivering the Slide Show

CHAPTER 19

Playing to a Live Audience

This chapter focuses on delivering your presentation to a gathered audience. Although much of the information here pertains specifically to showing your presentation from a computer, there also is much on addressing an audience effectively, which works whether you are using computer projection, slide project, overheads, or not using PowerPoint at all. ■

Show your presentation

Move from slide to slide, or jump out of order.

Use two screens

Have one screen set up for everyone to see and a separate screen with the controls that is just for you.

Set up a kiosk

Create a stand-alone presentation that anyone can view using just a mouse or trackball.

Take notes

Store notes about the points on the slides, or draw right on the slides to illustrate a point.

Communicate effectively

Prepare yourself and your environment to help your audience understand your message.

Displaying Your Presentation

To show your presentation, follow these steps:

1. Load your presentation into PowerPoint.
2. Choose Slide Show, Set Up Show. The Set Up Show dialog box appears.
3. Click the Presented By a Speaker option button.
4. If you recorded a narration for this presentation, indicate whether you want to use it by using the Show Without Narrations check box.
5. If you recorded timings to go with the slides, select either to use those timings to automatically advance the show (Using Timings, If Present check box) or to always have PowerPoint wait for you to click before going to the next slide (Manually check box).
6. Click OK.
7. Choose Slide Show, View Show. (Do *not* just click the Slide Show button because that starts at the currently selected slide, which may not be the first slide.)

While viewing the slide show, you can move ahead to the next slide or animation by clicking the mouse button (making sure that you're not clicking an interactive part of the slide), or by pressing any of these keys: N, right arrow, down arrow, spacebar, or Enter.

You can move to the previous slide by pressing any of these keys: P, left arrow, up arrow, or backspace.

There is a pop-up menu in viewing mode. To see this menu, either right-click or press Shift+F10 or move the cursor to the lower left of the slide and click the raised arrow that appears.

To end the presentation, either click past the end of the presentation, choose End Show from the pop-up menu, or simply press Esc.

If you're running an automatic timed slide show and want to pause it, choose Screen, Pause, or simply press S.

If you want to hide the pointer and the button just until you next move the mouse, choose Pointer Options, Hide Now (shortcut: Ctrl+H). If you want it to remain hidden, choose Pointer Options, Hide Always (shortcut: Ctrl+L). Although the pointer is hidden, you will still see it when you bring up the pop-up menu. To unhide the pointer, choose Pointer Options, Hide Now; then move the mouse.

Viewing Slides Out of Order

You can jump to any slide at any point. To do so, choose Go, By Title from the pop-up menu. The submenu that appears lists all the slides in your presentation, if there's room. Each slide is listed by the title of the slide (if the slide has a title field) and by slide number.

If you have more slides in your presentation than the menu can show, choose Go, Slide Navigator from the pop-up menu to get a scrollable list of slides.

Hiding a Slide

You can create a *hidden slide*, a slide that won't normally be played as part of your presentation but that you can reach from the slide before it when you need it. This is a good place to keep a slide with answers to questions that might (but won't definitely) arise.

 To hide the slide, go into Slide Sorter view, select the slide, and then click the Hide Slide button on the Slide Sorter toolbar.

When viewing the slide show, you can get to the hidden slide from the slide before it by choosing Go, Hidden Slide from the pop-up menu (keyboard shortcut: H).

Whenever you bring up a numbered list of slides (such as when you click the Go menu and select By Title), you can identify the hidden slides because they will have parentheses around the number.

Viewing on Two Screens

If you have two computers, you can run the presentation on two screens at once. This is generally done when you have one computer with a large screen or some form of projection screen (such as a video projector or an LCD panel on an overhead projector).

The advantages of running a presentation on two screens are as follows:

- The audience doesn't see all the presentation control information. While your screen displays the pop-up menu, the speaker's notes, or the slide timer when you request them (as described later), the viewers just see the slide. You can even switch to another running program (by using Alt+Tab) without your audience seeing.

- You can see the slide without facing away from your audience.

To run a slide show on two screens, follow these steps:

1. Connect the communications ports (COM ports) on both computers using a *null modem cable* (a cable designed to hook up two computers directly as if they were connected by modems). Do not try hooking up the machines via modem; it won't be fast enough.

2. Start PowerPoint on both machines. You must have PowerPoint 97 on both; running a PowerPoint Viewer program is not enough.

3. On the computer you'll be using to control the show, load the presentation.

4. On the computer the audience will see, choose the Slide Show, View On Two Screens command. The dialog box shown in Figure 19.1 appears.

5. In the dialog box, click the Audience option button, choose the communications port you connected the cable to from the Select drop menu, and then click OK.

6. On the computer you'll use to control the show, choose Slide Show, View On Two Screens command. The same dialog box appears again.

7. In the dialog box, click the Presenter option button, choose the communications port you connected the cable to from the Select drop menu; then click OK.

FIG. 19.1
Configuring a two-screen show requires you knowing which COM port on your computer is which.

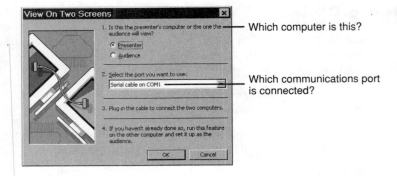

Which computer is this?

Which communications port is connected?

Using the Slide Meter

As shown in Figure 19.2, the Slide Meter shows you how much time you've used to present the current slide and to present the show so far. If you've used the Rehearse Show command (discussed in Chapter 18, "Using Multimedia Effects in Your Presentation") to set the timings for the slide, the Slide Meter shows you whether you're running faster or slower than that time, which can help you adjust your speed accordingly.

Time spent on slide...

FIG. 19.2
The Slide Meter shows you how long you're taking, compared to how long you expected to take.

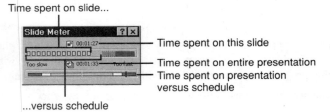

Time spent on this slide

Time spent on entire presentation

Time spent on presentation versus schedule

...versus schedule

To view the slide meter while running the slide show, choose Slide Meter from the pop-up menu. You can get rid of it at any time by clicking its Close button.

Creating a Custom Show

Sometimes you want to have a special, shorter version of your presentation for a specific audience. For example, you might have a full-length slide show aimed at engineers, full of technical details, but just want to show a shorter highlights version to executives.

To create a custom show for your current presentation, follow these steps:

1. Choose Slide Show, Custom Shows. The Custom Shows dialog box shown in Figure 19.3 appears.

2. Click the New button to create a new show. The Define Custom Show dialog box shown in Figure 19.4 appears. (Alternatively, if you have an existing custom show that's close to what you want, use the Copy button to copy it and then double-click the Copy Of *show name* entry to rename and edit it.)

FIG. 19.3

The Custom Shows
dialog box lets you
organize and display
your custom shows.

Existing custom shows ⎯⎯⎯⎯

Create a new show
Edit selected show
Get rid of selected show
Copy selected show to a new name

Show selected show in slide show mode

3. In the Slide Show Name field, type a name for this custom show.

4. The Slides In Presentation list has the names of all the slides in the presentation. Double-click the slide that you want first in the presentation.

5. Continue by double-clicking each slide you want to add. If you accidentally add the wrong slide, select it on the Slides In Custom Show list and then click the Remove button. You can also change the selected entry's place in the show using the Order buttons.

FIG. 19.4

Choose the slides for
the custom show in the
Define Custom Show
dialog box.

Slides to choose from ⎯⎯⎯⎯

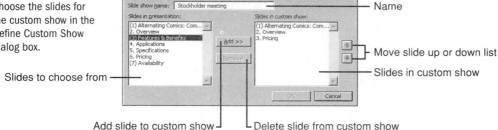

Name

Move slide up or down list

Slides in custom show

Add slide to custom show ⎯⏌ ⎿⎯ Delete slide from custom show

6. When you're finished setting up the custom show, click OK to go back to the Custom Shows dialog box.

7. Click the Close button to leave the Custom Shows dialog box.

To view a Custom Show, follow these steps:

1. Choose Slide Show, Custom Shows.

2. Click the name of the show you want in the Custom Shows dialog box.

3. Click the Show button.

To set a custom show as the default show for viewing, perform the following steps:

1. Choose Slide Show, Set Up Show.

2. Select the show you want from the Custom Shows drop menu.

3. Click OK.

Part
V

Ch
19

Reading and Taking Notes During a Show

You can view your speaker's notes (as discussed in Chapter 5, "Working with Different Views") and add or change notes. Simply right-click to get the pop-up menu then choose Speaker Notes. A dialog box displaying your speaker's notes in an editable field appears.

You can leave the dialog box open while moving through your presentation. As you advance to each slide, the notes for that slide appear.

If you want to take one set of notes for your complete show rather than slide-by-slide notes, choose Meeting Minder from the pop-up menu. In the Meeting Minder dialog box (see Figure 19.5) is a Meeting Minutes tab with a large editable text field, good for taking notes.

FIG. 19.5

The notes in the Meeting Minder can be sent to Microsoft Word by clicking the Export button.

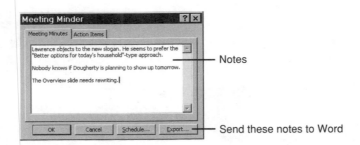

Any changes you make in the Meeting Minder notes or speaker's notes during the presentation will be saved with the presentation, *if* you remember to save the presentation after you're finished viewing it.

Planning Your Project with the Meeting Minder

Many presentations are part of a planning meeting, and often during the presentation decisions are made about who in the company is to take which next step. PowerPoint provides a tool to let you track these plans.

To use this tool, follow these steps:

1. Choose Meeting Minder from the pop-up menu. The Meeting Minder dialog box appears.
2. Click the Action Items tab. The dialog box shown in Figure 19.6 appears.
3. Enter a Description of the planned item, the name of who it's Assigned To, and the item's Due Date into the listed fields.
4. Click the Add button, and the item is added to the list. (You can edit or remove items from that list; just click an item, and then click the Delete button to remove it, or the Edit button to bring the item back up to the fields where you can edit it.)
5. Click OK when you're finished with the Meeting Minder.

FIG. 19.6

The Action Items tab helps you coordinate the project.

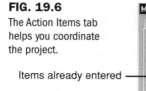

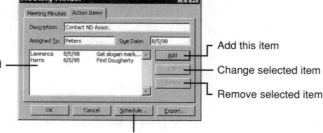

Items already entered

Add this item
Change selected item
Remove selected item

Transfer items to Outlook

If your office is using Microsoft Outlook (part of Microsoft Office) to keep track of projects, you can link this information right into Outlook. Just click the Schedule button to have the schedule e-mailed to Outlook. Outlook adds the listed items to the schedule of the named individuals.

Marking Up Slides

Sometimes when showing your presentation, you may want to circle something on a slide, or underline something, or rework a diagram by hand. This is a capability that people using over-head projectors have long taken advantage of. It is also something that you can do on your computer screen, using PowerPoint.

The commands involved in marking up slides are as follows:

- To start marking up, choose Pen from the pop-up menu (shortcut: Ctrl+P). The pointer becomes pen-shaped. Drag this to draw on the slide.

- To change the pen color, choose Pointer Options, Pen Color, and then select a color from the submenu. This won't change the color of anything you've already drawn, so you can create multicolor mark-ups.

- To erase the markings already made, choose Screen, Erase Pen (keyboard shortcut: E).

- To bring up a blank black screen, which is good if you want to draw a quick chart without worrying about the background, choose Screen, Black Screen (keyboard shortcut: B). To return to the slide, choose Screen, Unblack Screen (shortcut: B).

- To bring up a blank white screen to draw on, press W. To return to the slide, press W again.

- To bring back the normal pointer, choose Arrow from the pop-up menu (shortcut: Ctrl+A).

Part
V

Ch
19

CAUTION

When you move to the next slide or the next animation on this slide, the mark-ups disappear. Unlike speaker notes, you cannot save the mark-ups as part of your presentation.

continues

continued

You also should realize that the mouse is not a good drawing tool. If you need to be able to do clearer drawings or handwriting, you may want to look into one of the many alternative input devices that are better designed for that.

Make Your Presentation Portable with the Pack And Go Wizard

A presentation can end up with much more than one file. With links to movie clips, sound effects, and narration, there may be many files involved in your presentation, and finding them all to copy around can be hard.

The Pack And Go Wizard is a part of PowerPoint that helps you take your file and put it on floppy disk so that you can transfer it to another machine, or mail copies out to people. It will gather all of the files together, compress them to make them take the least possible space, and then spread the files across as many disks as are needed. This gathering of files is also good if you're going to be e-mailing the presentation to someone.

If you're going to be sending your presentation to others, you should design it with an eye towards keeping it compact. Things like video clips and narration can take up a lot of disk space, and a lush multimedia presentation can take up many disks.

To run the Pack And Go Wizard, perform the following steps:

1. Load the presentation you want to pack into PowerPoint.
2. Choose File, Pack And Go. A Pack And Go Wizard dialog box appears.
3. Click the Next button to move to the first of four screens for selecting information needed to set up your presentation.
4. In response to the question Which presentation would you like to package?, make sure that the Active Presentation check box is checked. If you want to pack more than one presentation in, also check the Other Presentation(s) checkbox, then click the Browse button to select the other presentations.
5. Click the Next button to get to the next screen, where you'll choose between saving your files to the A:\ Drive, B:\ Drive, or Choose Destination. If you want to save your file to the hard drive for e-mailing, use the Choose Destination option; then click Browse to find a convenient directory in which to store the files.
6. The Next button takes you to a screen with two options you can (and probably should) select. Include Linked Files makes sure that all the linked-in files (including animations and narration) are packed in with the other files. Embed TrueType Fonts copies all the fonts that you use with your presentation; if you don't select this and the computer you install the files on doesn't have the same fonts, then your presentation will look different.

7. Click the Next button again to choose between Don't Include The Viewer and Viewer For Windows 95 Or NT. If you're taking your presentation to another computer that already has PowerPoint or a PowerPoint Viewer program, then you don't need a viewer. If you're sending your file somewhere that may not have the viewer, you should include it.

   The viewer is included on the installation CD-ROM. Insert the CD-ROM into the CD-ROM drive before selecting this option. (If you don't have the CD-ROM, see the next section.)

   If you're sending your presentation to someone who has Windows 3.1, the viewer won't work on his machine. Instead, click the Help button and select Help with this Feature for information on getting a viewer for older versions of Windows.

8. Click Finish. The program starts condensing the files and prompts you for new disks when needed.

N O T E The version of the viewer included on most PowerPoint and Office installation disks is the PowerPoint 95 viewer. While this will work to show the PowerPoint 97 presentations, there is a more powerful viewer available that is designed specifically for PowerPoint 97. If you download and install the 97 viewer on your machine (as described in the next section), then the Pack And Go Wizard will include the 97 version, rather than the 95 version, in your packed presentation. ▪

Whoever installs the presentation from the disks should insert the first disk and use the Windows Run command to run the program Pngsetup.exe, which prompts for the installation of the rest of the disks.

If you're e-mailing the presentation, the two files that you'll need to e-mail are Pngsetup.exe and Pres0.ppz.

N O T E If you have a large presentation, you might want to use recordable CD discs to store it. However, if you do this, don't use the Pack And Go Wizard because whoever views the presentation has to install it on his hard disk, eating up a lot of space. Instead, duplicate the file structure that contains your files on the CD-ROM and put a copy of the viewer program on the disc as well. That way, all the user needs to install on the hard disk is the viewer. ▪

Part
V

Ch
19

Using the PowerPoint Viewer

The PowerPoint 97 Viewer discussed in the previous section is available for free download from the Web. Using the viewer, someone can look at a PowerPoint slide show with all of the viewing options built into the Slide Show view (plus the ability to print pages). What it doesn't have is the ability to edit the show in any way. This way, anyone with Windows 95 can view a presentation, but only people who buy PowerPoint can make one. This viewer can view not only presentations created with PowerPoint 97, but those created with older versions of PowerPoint for Windows or Macintosh as well.

If you have PowerPoint, choose <u>H</u>elp, Microsoft On The <u>W</u>eb, <u>F</u>ree Stuff, and your Web browser will be started up and bring up the proper page including a download link. People who don't have PowerPoint should go to **http://www.microsoft.com/OfficeFreeStuff/ PowerPoint/** to download the viewer.

As of this writing, the announced viewer for older versions of Windows still is not available. Microsoft says that it will be available soon; it may well be available by the time you read this, and will be downloadable as described previously.

When someone without PowerPoint installs the viewer on their machine, they can view a presentation by selecting the presentation file (file name ending in .ppt) with the Windows Run command. You can also create a text file where each line has the file name of a different presentation on it. Give the text file the extension .lst. When someone runs that file, the Viewer shows all the listed shows in order.

The command to start the viewer directly is `ppview32`. If you start it directly, you get a file browser letting you select the presentation or list file, as well as letting you set some options about how the presentation appears. If you start the viewer with the name of a presentation (that is, `ppview32 Sales.ppt`), the viewer starts and shows the listed presentation. There are several command-line options that you can use with the ppview32 command, which are useful if you're setting up a batch file to run a presentation:

- `/A` sets the slide show to automatic (timed) advance.
- `/R3-7` shows just slides 3 through 7.
- `/L` makes the show loop continuously.
- `/K` asks for a password before showing a kiosk display.
- `/P` brings up a Print dialog box.
- `/V` asks the user whether it should disable the macros whenever a presentation containing macros is loaded. (This is a form of virus protection; it is possible to write destructive macros.)

If you don't include `/A`, `/R`, and `/L`, the show will run as indicated in the presentation's Set Up Show dialog box settings.

N O T E The viewer can also be used from within Netscape Navigator and Internet Explorer to view presentations stored on the Internet or an intranet. For more information on this, see Chapter 21, "Putting Your Slide Show on the Internet."

Setting Up a Kiosk

Sometimes, you want to be able to set up a machine to display a presentation somewhere where people can interact with it without you looking over their shoulder. You don't want them to be able to interrupt the show, add Slide Notes, mark up the slides, or, worst of all, monkey with other things on the computer. You want them just to be able to look at the presentation and point and click the interactive bits. This is good for trade show displays, for information booths, and for many other places where people can just casually walk up to the computer.

You can do this by setting up the presentation in kiosk mode. Once you start a presentation in kiosk mode, you can hide the keyboard and processor away from prying hands, just giving people access to the screen and a mouse. In kiosk mode, the right mouse button does not pop up the menu, so the user won't have access to those commands.

To set a presentation to kiosk mode, click the Slide Show menu, select Set Up Show, and then select the Browse At A Kiosk option. Also select the Loop Continuously Until ESC option.

A good trick in setting up a kiosk display is to set every slide for an automatic timed advance *except* for the first slide (that is, use the Rehearse Timings feature to set the timings, use Set Up Show to select Using Timings, and then bring up the transition for the first slide and clear the Automatically check box.) That way, if someone walks away from the presentation in the middle, the slides will keep advancing until it loops back to the first slide; then the presentation will wait there until someone interacts with it.

- If this is more than just a casual setup, you may want to consider using a non-mouse input device. A trackball is a good choice because it can be fastened into place, avoiding mischief and accidents.

- If you're willing to spend more money, look into the possibility of getting a *touch screen*, a special monitor that can detect where people are touching the screen. That way, the user just has to point to the link with his finger.

- Simplicity can be important in kiosks placed in public places, where you cannot expect everyone to be computer friendly. For situations like that, not only should you use the trackball, but you may want to avoid using a button at all. If you use Mouse Over links rather than Mouse Click links, your interactivity can be button-free. Be careful, however, that if slide A has a link to slide B, slide B doesn't have a link in the same area of the slide. Otherwise, the moment someone gets to slide B, he'll be taken away to another slide!

Part

V

Ch

19

Preparing Yourself for a Presentation

When you're standing in front of an audience showing a PowerPoint presentation, the slides (whether they be a computer display, slide projector slides, overheads, or handouts) are not the biggest factor. You are. If you cannot present information effectively, the slides won't be much good. If you can, you could probably do a fair job of conveying the information even without slides.

The following are some things to remember when getting yourself ready:

- *Rehearse.* Some people can "wing it," but unless you know you're one of them, don't count on it. Make sure that you don't skip over parts by just assuming that you'll have something to say when the time comes.

- *Use notes.* Make some notes, either handwritten notes or using the Speaker Notes feature (if you're doing a two-screen show). These should just be small things to remind you of your points.
- *Don't prepare a full script.* You'll end up staring and talking to the paper, which is not an effective way to communicate.
- *Test it with a one-person audience.* It doesn't matter whether that person is actually interested in what you're talking about; the exercise of talking will concentrate your attention.
- *Dress neatly.* Depending on the sort of audience you're facing, you might not have to dress up, but what you wear should always be clean and make you look good.

Preparing the Room and Equipment for the Presentation

Don't let the physical situation of the room and equipment catch you by surprise. Check them out ahead of time. Some things to consider are the following:

- Where's the light switch? If you're going to be using a projector, you'll want to know how to turn the lights down while leaving enough light for people to see you and to take notes.
- Close the shades ahead of time.
- See whether your controls will reach far enough so that you can stand near the screen rather than the projector. It's a better place to address the audience from, so that they won't keep turning to look at you rather than the slide.
- Test your computer or projector ahead of time. During the presentation is not the time to learn that you're missing a cable or have a burnt out bulb. (Keeping a spare projector bulb close at hand is a good safeguard.) Actually flip through the whole slide show, to find any possible problems.
- Find a good spot for the projector. It's tempting to move it far back to get a large image, but that often causes a washed-out image.
- Focus the projector ahead of time; then make sure no one moves it.
- With slide projectors, make sure that you're familiar with the remote control. Too much time gets lost during presentations because people lose control of the forward or backward movement of the slides.
- If the room is large, consider having multiple projectors set up, so that everyone can see.
- If you're using a computerized presentation, turn off your screen saver. You don't want your slide to disappear in the middle of a presentation, particularly not if it gets replaced by pictures of flying toasters. To turn off standard Windows screen savers, choose Start, Settings, Control Panel. In the Control Panel, double-click the Display icon. On the dialog box that appears, select the Screen Saver tab. Choose None as your screen saver and clear the Low-Power Standby and Shut Off Monitor options, if available.

Holding the Audience's Attention

When dealing with all the nifty features of PowerPoint, it's easy to get caught up in the little design details and lose track of the big picture. Having sleek-looking slides is not the goal of a presentation. The goal is to communicate to the audience, and in many cases to convince them. The presentation is just a tool.

People are not always eager for your presentation, and even when they are, they may be distracted or drowsy (which a darkened room for projecting does not help). To keep their attention, try the following:

- *Speak clearly.* Make sure to put a slight pause between each word, but don't exaggerate it.

- *Don't be too quiet.* Don't shout, either, but do bring the sound up from your throat instead of just shaping it with your mouth.

- *Don't stay at one speed or one volume.* If you want to excite the audience at one point, show your own excitement by picking up the speed and the volume. Get them thinking about a specific point by slowing down when you make the point and pausing after it.

- *Use humor.* An amused audience is an attentive audience. Don't go totally outside your presentation to tell a joke, but work something funny in. If you're using an example, don't just use the generic "let's say there's a guy who works for a company". Pick a specific, silly name: "let's say there's this guy Antonio Chung-O'Goldberg, who works for International Vulcanized Turkey Stuffing, Inc."

- *Look at each new slide when it comes up.* Silently read it over. Not only will this give the audience time to read the slide, but by turning your back on them, you're encouraging them to focus on the slide. Then turn back towards them and start talking, and you'll have their attention again.

- *Overhead and slide projectors can be noisy.* If you're dealing with a noisy one and have an extended point to make, you might want to turn off the projector after everyone has read the slide and turn it on before going to the next slide.

- *Make each statement directly to an audience member.* This not only helps keep the attention of the audience as a whole, but it makes it easier to keep in mind that you're conveying information to people. Don't address every statement to the same person; switch from time to time. Even if one person is in charge, everyone in the room is there for a reason, and you should try to act like they're supposed to be hearing the information as well. You can have one or two "favorites" whom you return to frequently. (Watch a good stand-up comedian for an example of how this works.)

Communicate Effectively During the Presentation

Holding the audience's attention doesn't do any good if you don't get your point across and make sure that it's understood. Tricks to make sure that your point comes across are as follows:

- *Introduce yourself.* Tell the audience who you are and what you do. Even if it's a room full of people that you know, they may not know your full connection to the topic at hand. People are more willing to trust you as a source if they know your qualifications.

- *Get to know the audience.* If the audience is a small gathering of people you don't know, get them to introduce themselves to you. This will give you context for their comments and help you gauge their sophistication.

- *Know your audience's level of understanding on the topic involved.* If you're talking about a new phone system to a bunch of engineers, you probably won't have to explain all the technical terms. If you're giving the same talk to a group of receptionists, they'll probably have a better sense of the way messages need to be routed but less understanding of the wiring concerns. Odds are that the audience will have a range of understanding; it's better to over explain a little than to confuse people.

- *Don't just read what's on the slides.* The slide content should be the basis for what you're about to say, something to build on rather than the whole content.

- *Tell them where the presentation is going.* You don't have to give the full details and conclusions in advance, but the audience should have a sense of why they're getting each piece of information that they get.

- *Use examples.* People have a much better time understanding abstract concepts (such as "successful products can kill a company") when they have a concrete example. ("The Hula Hoop craze was so big that the manufacturer built more plants to meet demand and had heavy debt when the fad faded.")

- *Don't talk down to your audience.* If you know what you're talking about, you should be able to communicate it to them. The moment you seem to skim over something you don't think they'll understand, you reduce your believability. If there isn't time to explain something, say so, or direct them to where a better explanation can be found.

- *Stop for questions.* Otherwise, if someone gets confused early on, you've lost them for the entire presentation. In a small room, you can usually pause for questions as you go. In a larger room, plan to stop for questions when you end a major subtopic of your presentation. (Having a slide that just says Questions? is a good way to keep a presentation controlled.) Even if you just have time to pick a few raised hands when you stop, the odds are good that you'll hit on some common questions that have puzzled many.

- *Keep it simple.* Don't go into long asides that don't serve your point. Don't go into thick technical detail. Don't be verbose. A few well-chosen words can work wonders.

CHAPTER 20

Collaborating via a Local Network, Intranet, or the Internet

Start a Presentation Conference

Display your presentation to other viewers' computers over a data network.

Get others connected

Have other people view the presentation conference.

Mark up slides together

Have members of your audience mark up slides along with you.

Create a conference-compatible presentation

Avoid using items that do not work in presentation conferences.

A presentation conference lets you share a presentation with people on lots of computers simultaneously. The information flows between computers over a data network, whether it's the Internet or an in-house intranet or local area network. This is a handy way to run a presentation meeting without having to drag everyone to the same location. ∎

Starting a Presentation Conference

A *presentation conference* is a presentation that is displayed simultaneously on a number of computers. These computers can be connected via a LAN, an intranet, or over the Internet. To see the presentation, everyone involved has to have PowerPoint 97 running on their computers. There is one person who is running the presentation from their machine; this person is called the *presenter*. Everyone else is considered to be the *audience*.

> **N O T E** A *local area network* (*LAN*) is a group of computers connected by a single cabling scheme
> so that they can share and exchange information.
>
> An *intranet* is a group of computers and LANs linked together, using the same communication
> protocols that the Internet uses.

To start a presentation, the audience members have to:

1. Start PowerPoint.
2. Choose Tools, Presentation Conference. A Presentation Conference Wizard dialog box appears.
3. Click Next to get to a screen offering a choice between being Presenter or Audience, as shown in Figure 20.1.

FIG. 20.1

The same command is used to start a presentation conference as a presenter or as an audience member.

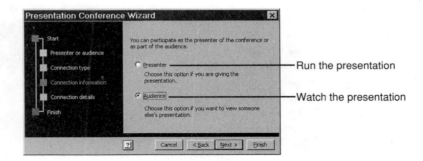

4. Choose Audience, then click the Next button.
5. A new screen appears to ask what sort of connection you are using. If you're using a LAN or an intranet, select, select Local Area Network, and skip to step 7. If you're using the Internet, choose Dial-in To Internet.
6. Click Next, and connect to the Internet now.
7. Click Next. A network address for your computer will now be displayed, as shown in Figure 20.2. If you're using the Internet, it will be listed as an IP address. Otherwise, it will be a computer name. You need to give the presenter this address before he can start the presentation.
8. Click Finish. Now you'll have to wait for the presenter to start the presentation.

FIG. 20.2

The network address uniquely identifies your computer among all the computers on the network or Internet.

Network address

Then, to show the currently active presentation with the settings on the Set Up Show dialog box, the presenter must:

1. Choose Tools, Presentation Conference. A Presentation Conference Wizard dialog box appears.

2. Click Next to get to a screen offering a choice between being Presenter or Audience, as shown in Figure 20.1.

3. Choose Presenter, then click Next.

4. Click Next twice.

5. If you need to connect to the Internet, do so now.

6. Click Next. The dialog box shown in Figure 20.3 appears.

7. For each member of the audience, enter the computer name or IP address that they gave you, then click the Add button. (If you'll be presenting again to the same list of computers in the future, you can save it using Save List, and recall it later using Open List. However, people dialing in to the Internet may get a different IP address every time, so the list will not work for such audience members.)

8. Click Finish. The Wizard will ship the presentation to all the users, and you can start running the presentation.

FIG. 20.3

The presenter of a presentation conference needs the address for all the audience's computers.

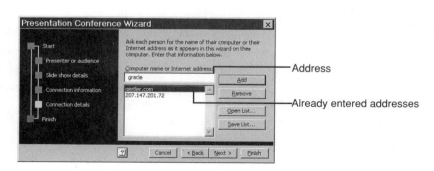

Address

Already entered addresses

Part

V

Ch

20

Participating in a Presentation Conference

After the conference is running, the presenter has access to the full set of tools, including the Meeting Minder, Speaker Notes, Slide Meter, and the full standard contents of the right-click button.

The audience does not see any of the standard tools. The only thing that they have access to is the pen for marking up the slides. Whenever anybody, whether presenter or audience, marks up a slide, the markups are visible to everyone.

Limitation of Conference Presentations

Unfortunately, if you want a presentation to work properly in a presentation conference, you can't use all PowerPoint's features. The following things will not work:

- Video clips
- Narration
- Sound clips (you can, however, use the standard sound effects built into PowerPoint)
- Organization charts
- Microsoft Graph charts
- Any item added to the presentation using the Insert, Object command

If you really need a chart in your presentation, draw it up yourself using the standard drawing tools. Alternately, you can turn it into a standard picture and add it to your slide. To do this:

1. Create the object on your slide.
2. Select it and hit Ctrl+C to copy it to the clipboard.
3. Start up Microsoft Paint. (You'll probably find it on under Start, Programs, Accessories.)
4. Choose Image, Attributes. An Attributes dialog box appears.
5. Set Width and Height to 10, then click OK.
6. Hit Ctrl+V to paste the chart image into Paint.
7. A Paint dialog box appears asking Would You Like The Bitmap Enlarged? Click Yes.
8. Choose File, Save (keyboard shortcut: Ctrl+S). When the file browser appears, pick a name and location for the item.
9. In PowerPoint, delete the original chart, then use the Insert, Picture, From File command to add the Microsoft Paint version to the slide.

▶ **See** "Getting a Picture from a File," **p. 140**

CHAPTER 21

Putting Your Slide Show on the Internet

The World Wide Web is fulfilling the promise of the personal computer, bringing the capability to reach the world into the hands of the individual. Using PowerPoint's Web features, you can take your presentation and put it where anyone with an Internet connection and a modern Web browser (running on any sort of computer) can see it. Or you can put it on your intranet, giving easy access to it to your entire organization, while keeping it out of prying eyes from outside. ■

Save a presentation in HTML

Turn your presentation into a Web-style site.

Select Web page style

Pick the design for buttons and the dimensions of the pages.

Save in a more powerful format

Store your file in a format that can be put on the Web, but which can contain more than an HTML presentation.

Use Viewer with a browser

Set up your browser to use the PowerPoint Viewer to see the more powerful Web presentations.

Put it on the Web

Put your presentation where everyone can see it.

Limitations of Web Presentations

It must be noted that the goal of PowerPoint's Web site creation features is to enable you to take presentations created for other reasons and put them on the Web.

If your main goal is to create a Web site, PowerPoint is not the tool to use. The Web sites it creates are not very Web friendly, because:

■ A standard Web page automatically fits itself to the width of the Web browser window; a PowerPoint page is a set width. If a PowerPoint page is viewed in a larger window, it looks small. If it's viewed with a smaller window, then it will have to be scrolled side-to-side.

■ A standard Web site can be displayed with the fonts and colors that the user is most comfortable with (although many sites choose to override those settings); this is not possible with the slides of a PowerPoint Web presentation.

■ A standard Web site takes 1 byte to represents each letter of text. A PowerPoint site, however, turns the slides into pictures, so even a page that just has a dozen words on it can take up tens of thousands of bytes. This makes it much slower to transfer over the Internet, so the user will have to wait longer to see what you have to say.

As such, if you want to start designing Web pages, you'd be better off using another tool. If you have Microsoft Office, then you have Microsoft Word, which is much better for designing Web pages. Better still are programs like NetscapeComposer, Microsoft FrontPage, Arachnophilia, NetObjects Fusion, or Hot Dog Pro, although each of those takes at some learning. (If you want to get serious about the Web, you should learn *Hypertext Mark-up Language*, better known as HTML. It's fairly easy to learn.)

Placing Your Presentation on the Web with PowerPoint Viewer and HTML Formats

If you have a slide presentation anyway, using the Web features of PowerPoint is a quick way to get it on the Web. There are two different formats that you can use for it on the Web, each with their own strengths and weaknesses.

■ The major downside to the PowerPoint Viewer format is that it requires the user to have the PowerPoint Viewer, and to have the viewer configured with their browser. Because the Viewer is, at this point, only available for Windows 95 and NT (and may soon be available for Windows 3.1), that means it is not at all accessible to people running other types of computers or operating systems. People using a Macintosh, a UNIX system, WebTV, or many other systems won't be able to view the presentation.

■ If you use the standard HTML format, your Web site can be viewed by anyone with a graphical browser, without the installation of any additional programs. (Even people who have browsers that don't support graphics will be able to view the text from the slides.) The standard HTML will not support video, sound (including sound effects and narration), automatic slide advances, animation, and transitions.

■ If you use the HTML with PowerPoint Animation format, you will have a mix of problems and strengths of both formats. To view the presentation, the user must be running Windows 95 or NT, must use either Netscape Navigator or Internet Explorer as his Web browser, and has to download the PowerPoint Animation Player (the browser will offer to download it automatically). With this player in place, the presentation will include sound, automatic slide advances, animation, and transitions. However, it will only include those features supported by the previous revision of PowerPoint (PowerPoint for Windows 95). This means, for example, that certain types of animation (including all chart animation) won't work, nor will some forms of interactivity. You are usually better off going with one of the other formats.

 TIP Nothing says that you have to use just one format. You can save it in multiple formats, and have a Web page where the user selects which version he wants.

Converting Your Presentation to Web Pages

To convert your presentation into standard HTML Web pages:

1. Load the presentation into PowerPoint.

2. Choose <u>F</u>ile, Save As <u>H</u>TML. A Save As HTML dialog box appears, listing 6 steps to create HTML files.

3. Click <u>N</u>ext. You'll be offered a choice between designing a new layout (choosing a size for the slides, type of buttons, and so on), and using the features of a layout you've used before (if you've saved as HTML before and saved the layout), as seen in Figure 21.1.

4. If you want to use an existing layout, choose <u>L</u>oad Existing Layout, click the name of the layout type on the layout lists, then click the square next to Layout Options at the left of the dialog box. Skip to step 11.

Otherwise, select N<u>e</u>w Layout, then click <u>N</u>ext.

FIG. 21.1
After selecting an existing layout, don't just click <u>F</u>inish. You still have to pick a file location.

Part

V

Ch

21

5. You will now be offered the choice between Standard and Browser Frames. With the Browser Frames option, the users browser screen will be broken into segments, one of which will have the slide, another of which will have a list of slides he can quickly select from. However, this Web page won't work properly on older browsers, and it does reduce the amount of space available for the slide itself. Standard is probably a better choice. Pick which you want, then click Next.

6. The next screen lets you select graphic type, the file format for the included graphics. There are three choices. GIF is a good choice if you're using solid color backgrounds and not a lot of fades, fills, or photographs. JPEG is a good choice if you are using fades, fills, and photos (if you pick JPEG, you have to pick a Compression Value between 50% and 100%; lower numbers mean lower quality graphics, but faster download times.) PowerPoint Animation format is sort of a compromise between using Standard HTML format and using Viewer format; it requires a special viewer, and is basically outmoded by the existence of the Viewer. Select the one you want, then click Next.

7. The next screen wants you to guess what size browser window your users will be using, and how much of that window you want filled with your graphics. Unless you specifically know what everyone's going to be using, it's best to go with the smallest screen setting (640 By 480); it will lose some detail, but everyone will be easily able to see the slide, and it will make for faster downloads as well. From the Width Of Graphics drop-down menu, select how much of the screen width the slide will take up; I recommend using the 3/4 Width Of Screen choice. Click Next to move on.

8. The next screen asks for information that will appear on an introduction page for the presentation. If you want, you can put in your E-Mail Address, Your Home Page, and Other Information. You can also choose to include links to Download Original Presentation (letting people get a copy of the full, non-Web version of the presentation for viewing with PowerPoint or the Viewer), or to Internet Explorer (which is basically advertising Microsoft's Web browser on your site; it really gains you nothing.) After you've made your selection, click Next.

9. This screen lets you select whether to have everything besides the slide set to your choice of color (Custom Colors), or to the color scheme that the user has set in his browser (Use Browser Colors). If you choose Custom Colors, click the Change Background (Web page background color), Change Text, Change Link (color of a text hyperlink), or Change Visited (color of a text hyperlink to a page the user has already seen) to get a color selector from which you can select the color you want. You can also choose to have Transparent Buttons. Click Next when you're done with the color scheme.

10. Select from the four types of buttons, three graphical, one just text, as shown in Figure 21.2. These buttons will be used to let the user go from slide to slide. If your presentation is aimed at an English-speaking audience, use the text buttons; not only are they easier to understand, they also download quicker. Click Next.

FIG. 21.2

The text buttons are easier to understand than the graphic buttons, and they download more quickly.

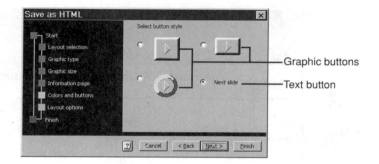

Graphic buttons

Text button

11. Select whether you want the navigation buttons above, below, or to the left or right of the slide. A check box lets you Include Slide Notes In Pages. Click Next after making your selection.

12. Click the Browse button to bring up a file navigator, letting you select a directory to store the Web site in. Click Select to leave the navigator.

13. Click Finish.

14. A dialog box appears, telling you Type A Name For These HTML Conversion Settings If You'd Like To Use Them Again Later. Either enter a name then click Save, or just click Don't Save.

15. An HTML Export In Progress dialog box appears, counting off each slide as it translates it. When it's done, the dialog box says The Presentation Was Successfully Saved As HTML. Click OK.

The HTML files will now be on your hard disk.

Viewing Your Web Presentation

To see how your Web presentation came out, open up your Web browser and use its Open File command to navigate to the directory where you stored the HTML version. There, you will find a sub-directory with the same name as your presentation. That sub-directory has all the files for the Web site. Open up the file Index.htm and you'll see a Web page similar to the one in Figure 21.3.

Start viewing the presentation by clicking where it says Click Here To Start. You will be taken to your first slide. The presentation will look something like Figure 21.4, although the exact look will depend on what options you selected.

When viewing the slide, you can use the Web page's Next link to advance to the next slide. You also have First, Previous, and Last links to move to specific slides, Index to move back to the opening slide, and Text to switch to viewing a version of the presentation that shows a text version of the slide, rather than a picture of the slide.

Part

V

Ch

21

FIG. 21.3

The opening screen of the Web presentation includes an index of slides.

Date presentation was saved as HTML

Click here to start slide show

Slide titles. PPT Slide means an untitled slide

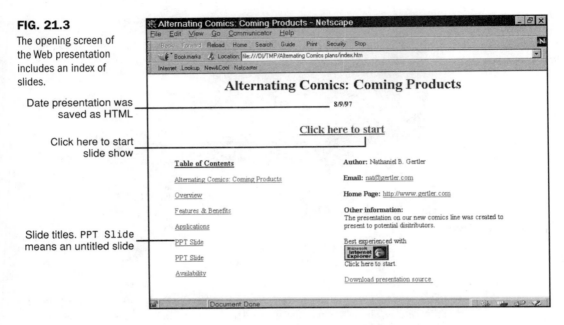

FIG. 21.4

This example of a slide Web page uses text buttons and slide notes, and does not use browser frames.

Slide

Links to other slides

Back to the index slide

View text version of slide

Speaker notes

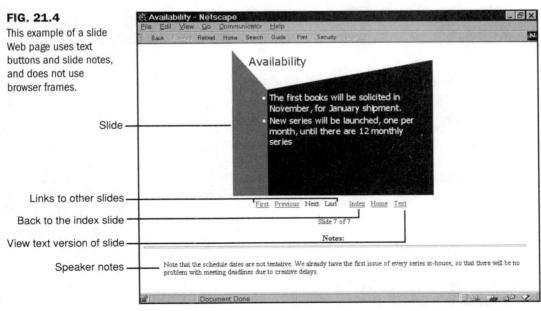

In addition, any hyperlinks on the slide to other slides or to Web pages will work. Simply click them. Hyperlinks to web pages actually work better here than they do viewing them in PowerPoint, as they don't involve switching to another program.

Publishing Your Web Presentation

All the files that you need included on the Web site will be in that one folder. Be sure to include all of those files.

The exact method of transferring your presentation to the Web depends on your Web server hardware and software, and the publishing software. See your Web administrator for details.

> **CAUTION**
>
> Before you publish your presentation on the Web, where people the whole world over can see it, you should make sure that it doesn't include sensitive corporate information. Many presentations designed for showing within a company should not be shared with the outside world.

Using the PowerPoint Viewer with the Web

If you want your full presentation to be visible to those with the PowerPoint Viewer, just take the files that make up your presentation and put them up on your Web site. Use relative links (as discussed in Chapter 18, "Using Special Effects in Your Presentation"), and make sure that all the linked-in files are installed in the same position relative to the main presentation file (the .ppt file). The easiest way to make sure that all the files keep the same relative position is to keep all the linked-in files in the same directory as the main file.

> **CAUTION**
>
> Remember also that the Web can be a slow way of transferring data. During the Web's typical busy periods, a dial-in user may only be getting about 1K of data per second. That means that a presentation that takes up 4 megabytes will take around an hour to move to his machine. To avoid this problem, you should avoid using sounds (except for the built-in sound effects), narration, and video. You should also be aware that installing the Viewer will take up about 7 megabytes of the user's hard disk space.

The exact method of configuring your browser to handle these depends on the make and revision of the browser that you're using. You will need to configure it as a handler or helper application. Your browser will need the following information about PowerPoint presentations:

- File extensions: PPT, PPS, POT, PPA, and PWZ
- MIME type: application
- MIME sub-type: vnd.ms-powerpoint
- Handler or Helper: Select the path and file name for the viewer (Ppview32.exe for the Windows 95/NT version, Ppview16.exe for the Windows 3.1 version.)

Part
V

Ch
21

You should be aware that, if you have PowerPoint on your system, the browser may have already been automatically set up to use PowerPoint itself to view such presentations. Unless you change it, when the presentation is downloaded, it will be brought up in PowerPoint in one of the standard editing views. You can then view the presentation as it's meant to be seen by choosing the Slide Show, View Show command.

Using the Web Toolbar

A recent addition to Microsoft Office is the Web toolbar, a toolbar available across the Office components (and in Internet Explorer) which lets you pull up documents from the Web, an intranet, or off of your hard disk. This is handy in an environment where you are reading many documents off of the Web, or where the documents have built-in hyperlinks to each other.

 To view the Web toolbar, click the Web Toolbar button:

The other buttons on the Web toolbar are:

Web Toolbar Buttons	
Button	**Function**
⇐	Return to the previous document.
⇒	After having gone to previous, go back ahead.
⊗	Stop trying to get current document when it's taking too long.
⟳	Reload current document, reflecting changes since last loading.
⌂	Load the document stored as your *Start Page*, a document that you've configured for quick access.
Favorites ▾	Choose document from a list of stored favorite documents, or choose Add To Favorites to include the current document on the list.
◎	Choose to open a document using a file browser, to set the start page, or to select between currently open documents.
▣	Close all toolbars except the Web toolbar.
Address	Drop the menu to select a recently-accessed document, or type a file name or URL into the field.

Advanced PowerPoint Topics

CHAPTER 22

Customizing PowerPoint

PowerPoint is designed and shipped with a generic set of toolbars containing buttons for most of the functions that people will need the majority of the time. However, a lot of people and jobs fall outside of those "mosts", so you also have the ability to pick and choose the toolbars and buttons you need, or even to add entire new commands. Most of what you learn here also applies to the other Microsoft Office programs. ■

Rearrange toolbars

Choose which toolbars are available, and where they appear on the screen.

Add and remove buttons

Have exactly the buttons you need.

Create a new toolbar

Build a toolbar for your own needs.

Change the menus

Add and remove commands to suit your needs.

Use add-ins

Expand PowerPoint's capabilities by linking in special programs with additional functions.

Arranging Toolbars

PowerPoint opens and closes toolbars as it thinks you'll need them. However, you can override its choices, getting rid of toolbars you don't need, and adding toolbars you want. Just right-click any toolbar to see a list of available toolbars. The ones with checks next to them are the ones currently visible. Choose one to switch it between being visible and being hidden.

To reposition a toolbar, drag it by the vertical lines at its left end. If you drag it over the bottom half of another toolbar, it appears below that toolbar. If you drag a toolbar over the top half of another toolbar, it is added to the right end of that toolbar (which works well if you have two short toolbars, but with long toolbars the right ends of both toolbars will end up hidden).

If you release the toolbar over the central editing area, it turns into a dialog box full of buttons. You can resize this box by dragging the right or lower edge of the box. To drag it back into standard toolbar position, drag it by its title bar back into a position toward the top or bottom of the screen.

Some menus and submenus (such as the AutoShape menu and all its submenus) can be turned into toolbars for quicker access. You can recognize these menus because they have a gray bar at the top. Drag this bar; it works just like dragging the title bar of a button window.

Customizing and Creating Toolbars

You can drag a button by holding down Alt as you drag it. You can drag it to another position on the same toolbar or to a position on a different toolbar; as you're dragging it, an insertion line appears to show you where the button would appear. If you drag it off of the toolbars entirely, the button gets deleted.

To create a new toolbar:

1. Choose Tools, Customize. A Customize dialog box appears.
2. Click the New button on the Toolbars tab. A dialog box appears asking for the Toolbar Name.
3. Type in the name, then click OK. A new toolbar appears as a button window. (It won't have any buttons yet.)
4. If the new toolbar overlaps the Customize dialog box, drag it off of there. Otherwise, when you go to work with the Customize dialog box, the toolbar will be covered.

To add a button for any menu command (or even commands not on the menus) to a toolbar follow these steps:

1. In the Customize dialog box, click the Commands tab. This tab is illustrated in Figure 22.1.
2. From the Categories list, select the category for the command you want. A list of commands in that category appears on the Commands list. (If you're not sure what a command does, select it, then click the Description button.)

3. Drag the command you want from the Commands list onto the toolbar. Commands with picture items at the left create picture buttons. Commands without pictures create buttons with the words on them.

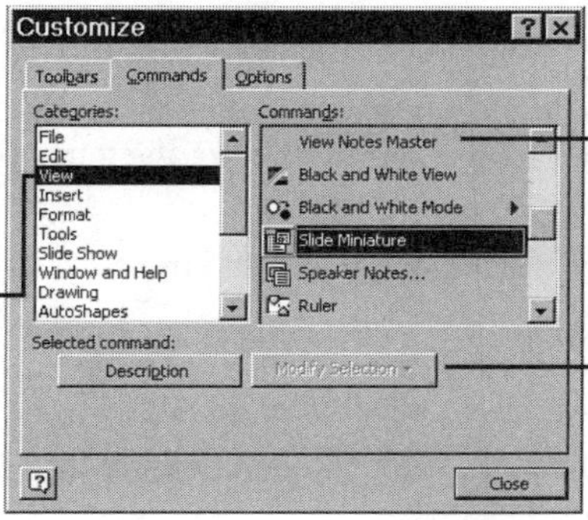

FIG. 22.1
The Customize dialog box is the center for changing your buttons, toolbars, and menus.

Command category

Commands in category

Change selected button or menu item

While the Customize dialog box is open, you can change the picture, the effect, or the ScreenTip for any button. Click the button to select it (the buttons don't perform their normal function while this dialog box is open), then click the Modify Selection button for a list of button-modifying commands. (For more information on the Modify Selection effects, see Table 22.1.)

The Options tab of this dialog box has a series of handy options. You can choose Large Icons to make your buttons larger; Show ScreenTips On Toolbars, which makes a command name appear when you position the pointer over a button for more than a second; or Show Shortcut Keys In ScreenTips, to help you learn the keyboard shortcuts. There's also a menu to select the animation that is used to make menus appear.

You can undo customizations to a toolbar by selecting the toolbar on the Toolbars tab, then clicking Reset.

Changing the Menus

The Customize dialog box is also the center for changing the menus. Menus, like buttons, will not perform their usual function while this dialog box is open. At this time, you can:

- Rearrange the menus by dragging the menu title to another position on the menu bar, or to a toolbar.
- Delete a menu by dragging the menu title into the editing area.
- Move or delete a menu item by dragging it from the menu to a new position or into the editing area.
- Add an item to the menu by dragging it from the Commands list on the Commands tab onto the menu title (so that the menu opens) and then down into position on the menu.
- Change the name of a command or the button by selecting the menu item, then clicking the Modify Selection button to get a menu of commands.

Table 22.1   Modify Selection Commands

Command	Effect
Reset	Return item to its original setting.
Delete	Remove item.
Name	Change the name of a menu item, or the ScreenTip for a button. Put an ampersand (&) before the letter you want underlined as a hot key.
Copy Button Image	Move the button image onto the clipboard.
Paste Button Image	Use image from clipboard as the button image for this item.
Reset Button Image	Return to original button image.
Edit Button Image	Opens up the editor seen in Figure 22.2 for changing the button's picture.
Change Button Image	Select a new picture for the button from 42 otherwise unused images.
Default Style	Shows button image on button, text on menus.
Text Only (Always)	Shows text on button or menu.
Text Only (In Menus)	Shows text on menu; button image, if there is one, on button.
Image And Text	Shows image and text on both buttons and menus.
Begin A Group	Put separator line above or left of this item. Choose this again to remove.

FIG. 22.2

The Button Editor is a simple but effective way to change a button's appearance.

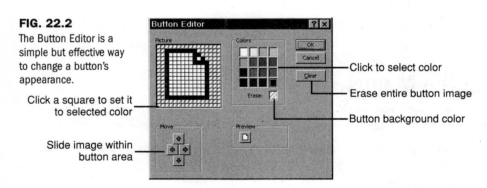

Click a square to set it to selected color

Slide image within button area

Click to select color

Erase entire button image

Button background color

Expanding PowerPoint with Add-Ins

Add-ins are programs that give PowerPoint additional features. Microsoft offers a number of free add-ins (choose Help, Microsoft On The Web, Free Stuff). Other add-ins are available elsewhere, either for free or for purchase.

Add-in files have the extension .ppa. After you have the add-in file, you have to install it so that PowerPoint knows it is there. To do this:

1. Choose Tools, Add-ins. A dialog box appears, listing all the Add-ins that PowerPoint already knows are available. The ones with an x next to them are the ones that PowerPoint loads when it starts.
2. Click the Add New button. A file browser opens up.
3. Use the browser to select the file, then click OK. The file will now be added to the list.
4. Click the Close button to leave the dialog box.

You can choose which add-ins are automatically loaded in by selecting them and clicking the Load or Unload button. If you are loading an add-in that you aren't using, you're just wasting memory and loading time.

The Remove button totally removes the selected add-in from the list. It does not, however, remove the .ppa file from your hard disk.

> **CAUTION**
>
> PowerPoint is a stable program overall, but the Add-in Manager causes problems for many users. The manager may not properly list all the installed Add-ins, or the list may appear in an odd form. The problems seem to be worsened by heavy memory usage. If this happens to you, close all open programs, reboot Windows, just start PowerPoint, and try using the Add-in Manager again.

CHAPTER 23

Integrating PowerPoint with Other Programs

One of the key advantages to computing in the modern office environment is the capability to reuse data. Information created in a word processor can easily be used in a presentation. A presentation slide can be placed on a spreadsheet as an illustration. Everything is reusable. The programs that make up Microsoft Office are designed to work tightly together. Other modern programs are also designed to allow information to be easily transported from one to the next, and can also be used with PowerPoint, although not quite as easily. ■

Understand linking and embedding

Use two different methods for including information from other programs.

Put a spreadsheet on a slide

Display a Microsoft Excel spreadsheet as part of your presentation.

Put slides in a spreadsheet

Place a presentation into an Excel spreadsheet.

Link a slide to a text document

Bring up a Word document with a click on a hyperlink.

Save PowerPoint graphics

Store graphics from PowerPoint in formats usable by other programs.

Include program objects

Link images from other programs into PowerPoint.

What Are Linking and Embedding?

There are two different general methods of including a document of one type within a document of another. These methods are as follows:

- *Linking*. When you link one document to another, a pointer to the second document is included in the first document. If, for example, you link an Excel spreadsheet into a PowerPoint presentation, then the PowerPoint file just keeps track of the file name for the Excel spreadsheet. Whenever you load the presentation, PowerPoint loads and displays the information from the spreadsheet file. That way, if you create the link on Tuesday, then change the spreadsheet on Wednesday, and load the presentation on Thursday, the presentation will load up all the changes made on Wednesday, displaying the most recent version of the spreadsheet. However, if the spreadsheet file is deleted or moved, PowerPoint will not be able to find it.

- *Embedding*. When you embed one document in another, the entire second document is copied into the first document. If, for example, you embed an Excel spreadsheet into a PowerPoint presentation, the entire spreadsheet file is copied and stored as part of the presentation file. PowerPoint never looks at the original spreadsheet file again, because it has its own copy. If you embed a spreadsheet file into a presentation on Tuesday, then change the original spreadsheet on Wednesday, and show the presentation on Thursday, the data from Tuesday will be displayed. It doesn't matter what you do to the original spreadsheet, because PowerPoint still has its own copy.

Deciding whether you want to embed or to link a document is usually a question of whether you want it changed when the original document is changed. You also have to consider disk space and ease of movement; embedding a document takes up more disk space (because you have both the original document and the embedded copy to store), but it's easier to move to another computer (because you don't have to move the original document as well).

Embedding an Excel Worksheet in a PowerPoint Slide

If you have Microsoft Excel and want to create a new Excel spreadsheet Worksheet on a slide:

1. In Slide view, click the Insert Microsoft Excel Worksheet button.
2. A grid like the one seen in Figure 23.1 appears below the button. Drag to select the number of rows and columns that you want in your table. If you just click a cell, you can select a table with up to 4 rows and 5 columns, but when you drag, the grid expands with your drag, allowing you to select up to 6 rows and as many columns as will fit on the screen . (If you need more rows or columns, you can resize the Worksheet later.)

FIG. 23.1

The maximum Worksheet width you can select is limited by the space between the button and the screen edge.

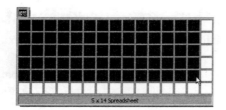

3. The spreadsheet grid appears on the slide. While the title bar still says Microsoft PowerPoint and the view is still the Slide View, Excel's menus and toolbars are displayed. Use the full Excel capabilities to design your Worksheet.

4. When done, select any item outside of the Worksheet to return to normal PowerPoint editing. The row buttons, column buttons, scrollbars, and other Excel spreadsheet items disappear, and all that is visible are the contents of the cells.

You can resume editing the Worksheet at any time by double-clicking it to reenter Excel mode. The Worksheet is considered *embedded*, meaning that the Worksheet is stored within the presentation file, and that the identity of the creating program is also stored, so that PowerPoint can call on that program to edit it later.

To use part of an existing Excel Worksheet on a PowerPoint slide:

1. Load up the Worksheet in Excel.

2. Select the range of cells that you want to base your chart on.

3. Press Ctrl+C to copy these cells to the clipboard.

4. In PowerPoint Slide view, choose Edit, Paste Special. A Paste Special dialog box appears.

5. Select Paste if you want the Worksheet in PowerPoint to always keep the data it has now.

   Select Paste Link if you want PowerPoint to check the original Worksheet every time it loads the presentation, and updates the information if it has changed.

6. Click the OK button. The selected Worksheet cells appear on the slide. (If you double-click this grid, you will go into the Excel editing mode described previously. You will also find that the entire original Worksheet has been pasted in; it's only displaying the selected range, but the rest is there if you scroll.)

For more information on using Excel, check out Que's *"Using Microsoft Excel 97,"* by Laura Monsen.

Part
VI

Ch
23

Moving Word Information into PowerPoint

To copy a portion of Word text into a PowerPoint text box, select the text, then go to step 3 of the preceding procedure.

▶ For information on turning a Word outline into a PowerPoint presentation, moving a PowerPoint outline into Word, or even sending the entire presentation to Word, **See** Chapter 9 , "Creating an Outline".

▶ For information on creating a Word table in PowerPoint, **See** Chapter 13, "Working with Tables".

Embedding a Presentation into Excel or Word

You can create a PowerPoint presentation within an Excel Worksheet or a Word document, or copy an existing presentation into those documents. This way, if you're distributing the Worksheet or document, you can include a presentation with it. To do so:

1. In Word or Excel, choose Insert, Object. An Object dialog box appears, with two tabs.

2. If you want to start a new presentation within the document, click the Create New tab. Select Microsoft PowerPoint Presentation from the Object Type list.

    If you want to put an existing presentation into the document, click the Create From File tab. There, click the Browse button, use the file browser to find the file, then click the browser's OK button. (If you want the embedded presentation updated when the original presentation is, check the Link To File check box.)

3. Click the Object dialog box's OK button. The inserted item will appear.

To view the inserted presentation, right-click it, then select Presentation Object, Show from the pop-up menu.

Linking a PowerPoint Slide to Another Office Document

You can create a link to another Office document. This method also works for a document for a non-Office program or for directly opening a program, although those items will bring up a dialog box when linked, warning that the program being run may be damaging.

You can do that by using the linking methods found in Chapter 18, "Using Special Effects in Your Presentation". To do it more quickly:

1. In Slide view, select the object or text within an object that you want to act as a link.

2. Click the Insert Hyperlink button.

3. The dialog box seen in Figure 23.2 appears. Click the Browse button to open a file browser (which defaults to listing just Office documents), or use the Link To File Or URL drop-down list to re-select a file recently visited using the Web toolbar or recently selected from this dialog box.

FIG. 23.2
The Insert Hyperlink dialog box enables you to quickly link to other Office documents.

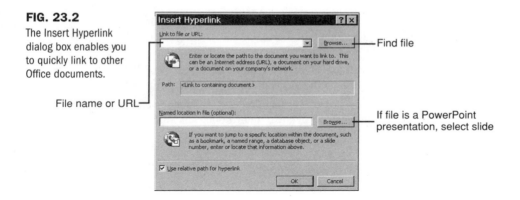

File name or URL—

Find file

If file is a PowerPoint presentation, select slide

4. Click the OK button. The link will now be in place. If you had selected a text object or text within an object, the text is underlined to indicate that it is a link.

Remember that these links will only work if the viewer's PC has the Office program that can read the documents.

Using Objects from Other Programs

More programs are constantly being created that are designed to create objects for other programs. Some of the standard Microsoft PowerPoint components, like Organization Chart and Microsoft Graph, work this way, and you can purchase additional programs for a range of special needs.

When you install one of these programs, it adds itself to a system list of available object types. PowerPoint always knows what sort of objects can be inserted. To create a new object using one of the object-creating programs installed on your computer:

1. In Slide view, choose Insert, Object. The Insert Object dialog box seen in Figure 23.3 appears.

FIG. 23.3
If you choose to Insert Object as an icon, it can only be opened up in editing, not during the slide show.

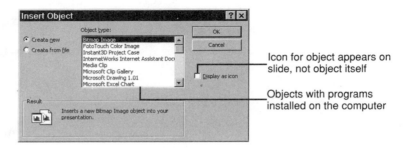

Icon for object appears on slide, not object itself

Objects with programs installed on the computer

2. When the Create New option button is selected, an Object Type list appears in the center of the dialog box, listing all the object types that have programs on this computer. Select the object type that you want.

3. Click the OK button. An editing area for the new object appears on the slide, and the buttons and menus are those of the object-creating program. Build your object.

4. When done, click outside of the object's editing area to return to standard Slide View. You can resume editing the object at any time by double-clicking the object.

To insert an object that you've already stored in a file:

1. In Slide view, choose Insert, Object. The Insert Object dialog box appears.

2. Select the Create From File option button. The list of object types is replaced by a File field.

3. Click the Browse button, and use the file browser to select the file you want.

4. If you leave the Link check box empty, the object will be embedded. If you check it, then the file is loaded each time the presentation is opened, so if you change the file, you change the presentation.

5. Click the OK button, and the object appears on the slide.

After the object is in place, you can resume editing it at any time by double-clicking it. When it is selected, there will also be a (Whatever Object Type) Object submenu on the Edit menu, which will include a Convert command. Use this command to change one object into another compatible object type, or to *activate* it with another object program, which lets you edit it after as a different object type but returns it to the original object type when done.

Saving to Other Graphic Formats

You can save your slides in standard graphic formats, letting you use the images of those slides in other ways and other programs. To do this:

1. Select File, Save As. A file browser appears.

2. From the Save As Type drop menu, select one of the graphic types that appear toward the bottom of the menu. These include Portable Network Graphics (*.PNG), GIF (*.GIF), and JPEG Interchange Format (*.JPG).

3. Use the browser's standard features to select a name and location for the files.

4. Click the OK button.

5. Another dialog box appears, asking Do You Want To Export Every Slide In The Presentation?

If you click Yes, PowerPoint turns the file name you chose into a directory, and puts one file for each slide into that directory. These files will be named Slide1, Slide2, and so on, with the appropriate extension for the graphic format you selected. When done, PowerPoint displays another dialog box to let you know that the files have been put in that directory.

If you click No, PowerPoint exports only the currently selected slide (if more than one are selected, it outputs the first). The file has the name you selected in the browser.

The Save As command can also be used to save a presentation in a format readable by earlier editions of PowerPoint. Realize, however, that you may lose some of the features of the presentation in doing so, as the earlier versions do not support of all the current PowerPoint functions. ●

CHAPTER 24

Automating Your Work with Macros

by Brian Reilly

The Visual Basic for Applications (VBA) language has been incorporated into PowerPoint 97. With this language, PowerPoint 97 gives you the ability to write your own macros to perform time-consuming, repetitive tasks with just the click of a button. If you're an advanced user, you can also develop new solutions either entirely in PowerPoint or by integrating the solution across PowerPoint, Excel, Word, or Access.

With macros, you can not only automate repetitive tasks, but you can also program decision-making within the program, based on additional input from whoever is using it in a given situation—for example, a salesperson making a presentation. If you've already written macros in Excel or Word, you'll find PowerPoint's macro language very exciting. And even if you've never written a piece of macro code before, PowerPoint's macros can increase your productivity in a variety of ways. Whether you're experienced at creating macros or not, this chapter helps you understand PowerPoint's macro environment, and shows you how to plan and create your own macros. ■

Write macros that automate tedious repetitive tasks

The macro recorder can record your actions and play them back for you at the touch of a key, so you don't need to be nervous about writing code. It writes the code for you as you go.

Modify code written by the macro recorder to perform decision making for you

As powerful as the macro recorder is, there are many things it just cannot or does not record.

Write advanced code that will let you perform some advanced operations with only a few lines of code

Code shortcuts can accomplish tasks by looping back through the same instructions until finished.

Visualize the Object Model

The Object Model is the hierarchy of the PowerPoint code. Every object has its place in the model and a relationship to other objects. The Object Model is the underlying structure of PowerPoint commands.

What Is a Macro?

If you're new to macros, the first order of business is to understand just what a macro is. In simple terms, a *macro* is a series of commands that are all executed in sequence. For example, you might describe the series of steps associated with making a cup of instant coffee as the following:

1. Go into the kitchen.
2. Find the teakettle.
3. Add water to the teakettle.
4. Put the teakettle on the burner.
5. Turn on the burner (the one with the teakettle on it).
6. Wait until the water in the teakettle boils.
7. Turn off the burner.
8. Add a teaspoonful of instant coffee to an empty coffee cup.
9. Pour the boiling water into the coffee cup.
10. Add milk or cream and sugar, if desired.

If you had a macro that could do this chore for you, you could perform all 10 steps with one command. The macro is the equivalent of saying to one's spouse, "Darling, please make me a cup of coffee."

The coffee example may seem simplistic, but it has all the necessary comparisons to a macro. It has objects (teakettle, water, coffee cup, burner, instant coffee, milk, sugar). It has methods (boil, turn on/turn off the burner, add). It has properties (empty). It has sequence. It even has decision-making (if).

There are many similar tasks in PowerPoint that might be automated in this fashion. Suppose, for example, you want to be able to turn all your drawing toolbars on or off in just one step. Your steps might be:

1. Turn on the Drawing toolbar.
2. Turn on the Picture toolbar.
3. Turn on the WordArt toolbar.
4. Turn off all other toolbars.

Or you might want to print several presentations overnight while you're in bed, and you don't want to get out of bed repeatedly to issue the File, Print command for each new copy of the file. Here, the steps would be:

1. Print the first file in this directory.
2. Print each successive file in this directory.
3. When you have finished the last file in this directory, stop.

Both of these examples have several things in common. They are repetitive tasks and they both can be executed from the keyboard. But in the first example, you have to use several keystrokes, and in the second example, you have to wait for the prior command to finish executing before the next command can be given.

Such tasks can be automated with macros, which can save you a great amount of time, especially if you frequently perform these tasks. In the second case, the printing of several long presentations to a color printer may take quite a few hours. You could not, until now, issue the command to print the second presentation until the first presentation was finished printing. Now with one keystroke, you can print them all at once, literally in your sleep.

Automating Repetitive Tasks with a Macro

What tasks can be automated? Virtually anything that can be created on the keyboard can be automated with a macro. There are two caveats here:

- The macro recorder only records what is going on in PowerPoint. If you switch to Excel during the recording of a macro, the recorder does not record the process in Excel. There are ways to activate other programs like Excel, but that has to be performed with specifically written code and not through the macro recorder.

- Some things that may be recorded may not be performed often enough to warrant the time involved in creating a macro. You need to decide if the time involved to automate a simple task outweighs the amount of time that may be necessary to do it manually whenever that situation arises.

Certainly, if you find yourself doing a specific task frequently, then you should consider automating the task with a macro. When the task is very time-consuming and subject to possible keyboard error, you should definitely consider creating a macro. If it takes substantial time to execute sequential commands before you get access back to your computer—as in the printing of the series of files to a color printer—you should definitely consider automating the process with a macro, because you will be able to do something else while the computer is doing all the work.

There are two ways to build macros. You can create them by:

- Recording steps, saving the recording, then telling PowerPoint to play them back whenever you need to
- Actually scripting the macro's code

Using the Macro Recorder

PowerPoint's macro recorder is just like a good assistant who writes down exactly what you did and can reproduce those actions any time you tell him to. Assume you have added the text to a presentation and want to start adding graphics to the pages, but you first want to have the Drawing, Picture, and WordArt toolbars on-screen. Instead of opening each of the toolbars individually (then closing them when you're finished, then reopening them later), you can record a macro to display the toolbars all in one step. Here's how to record this macro:

1. Choose Tools, Macro, Record New Macro.
2. The Record Macro dialog box appears, as shown in Figure 24.1. This dialog box gives you three options:
   - A chance to name the macro. Descriptive names can help, but PowerPoint also lists a default name such as Macro1 if you don't choose a name of your own. In this case, name your macro **Show_Graphics_Toolbars**.
   - A file location to store the macro. The active file is the default.
   - A text description to help you remember what you are doing in this particular macro; this is for documentation purposes only and has no effect on the macro. The default is the current user name and the current date. A good documentation practice is to type a description of what the macro does—for example, **Shows the Drawing toolbars**.

After filling in the dialog box in step 2, make sure that the toolbars you are trying to open through the macro are not already open, and choose OK to start recording the steps of the macro. Then just perform the operation that you want to record. In this case, the operation is displaying three toolbars. First, choose View, Toolbars and highlight the Drawing Toolbar option, and select it by clicking the mouse. The Drawing toolbar should appear on-screen. Remember that the macro records whatever you do. If you make a mistake, fix it, and then go on, the macro thinks that all of this was intentional and records it. So it's a good idea to rehearse the steps you plan to put in the macro, and perhaps even write them down so you don't trip up.

3. Display the Picture toolbar by choosing View, Toolbars. Then highlight the Picture option and select it by clicking the mouse.

4. Display the WordArt toolbar by choosing View, Toolbars, then highlight the WordArt option, and select it by clicking the mouse.

5. Now that you have finished recording the steps to your macro, click the Stop Recording button. (This icon appeared automatically on the screen when you clicked the OK button to start the recorder.)

FIG. 24.1

Recording macros is like recording on a VCR.

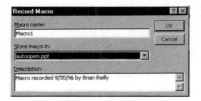

Now you are ready to test that macro. But because you have already displayed the toolbars, let's record a second macro to hide them. This new macro is handy when you no longer need the toolbars on-screen and want to hide them quickly.

Repeat the preceding steps and name the macro **Hide_Graphics Toolbars**. Note that this time, you are deselecting each of the toolbars.

You can now test the first macro, which displays the toolbars. To do this:

1. Choose Tools, Macro, Macros or press Alt+F8. The Macro dialog box appears, as shown in Figure 24.2. The dialog box contains a list of available macros.

2. Select Show_Graphics_Toolbars, then click Run. The macro runs, and the three graphics toolbars should appear on your screen.

To hide the toolbars, just repeat the preceding steps and choose the Hide_Graphics_ Toolbars macro. The macro should run, and the three toolbars should disappear.

FIG. 24.2
The Macro dialog box
lists all available
macros.

> **N O T E**   You save macros in your presentation files. This can be beneficial; if you are sharing a
> file with someone else, you can share macros as well. Remember, however, that some
> macros can actually cause trouble.

Following the creation of the Word Concept virus that was carried in an AutoOpen macro (one
that opens automatically when a Word document is opened), Microsoft and its consumers
became very wary of opening files from unknown sources because the files might contain macros
which in turn may contain viruses. New with Office 97 is a warning box that appears prior to
opening any file that contains a macro. The new warning box permits you to open the file with
macros enabled or disabled, or not to open the file at all. Figure 24.3 shows the dialog box. If
you prefer, you can disable this warning altogether.

While this warning may be irritating to some computer users, it's reassuring to those whose
systems have been infected by a virus. If you are receiving files from any outside sources, even
your coworkers on a network, it might be in your best interest to leave the warning on. However,
the warning doesn't necessarily mean that a virus is present, and it does not clean a virus if one
exists. It's just a device to allow you to disable macros if you want. ■

FIG. 24.3
Office 97 alerts you
when you open a file
that contains a macro,
because the macro
may carry a virus.

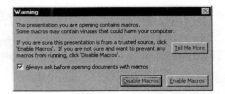

The Structure of a Macro

Now that you've created and run a simple macro, it's a good time to take a look inside it to
see what makes the macro work. The macro recorder translated your actions into VBA
code and recorded that code. While VBA code looks somewhat like English, as with any
computer code there are some very specific syntax issues that are necessary to address

for the code to run without error. Let's look at the code, then explore the structure of the macro. To view the code in the Show_Graphics_Toolbars macro, take the following steps:

1. Choose Tools, Macro, Macros.
2. Select Show_Graphics_Toolbars, then choose Edit. You see a window that looks similar to Figure 24.4. For the time being, let's focus only on the macro's code:

```
Sub Show_Graphics_Toolbars()
'
' This macro displays the Drawing, Picture, and WordArt toolbars.
'

    Application.CommandBars("Picture").Visible = True

    Application.CommandBars("Drawing").Visible = True
    Application.CommandBars("WordArt").Visible = True
    Application.CommandBars("Formatting").Visible = False

End Sub
```

FIG. 24.4
The code that the macro recorder generated for the Show_Graphics_Toolbars macro.

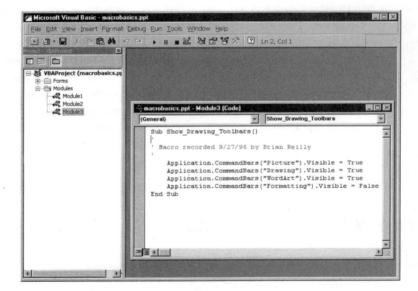

Part
VI

Ch
24

What Is the Code?

The code is everything that appears between the words Sub and End sub. It includes three critical elements:

- The first line which names the macro command. This is defined by the words Sub Command Name(). Note that the command name is restricted to just one word. The use of _ is actually a character just like any typed character and is used for making the command names easier to read.

From the code's perspective, it would also be acceptable to name the command `Sub ShowGraphicsToolbars()`. Uppercase or lowercase is also irrelevant to command names; uppercase letters are used only to make the code easier to read later. The command must always be ended by parentheses, which tell the program that this is a command name line and not part of the commands to execute.

- The group of commands which perform the task you want the macro to accomplish. These are the lines sandwiched between the first and the last lines of the macro. In the example, the first line of code to execute is `Application.CommandBars("Picture")`. `Visible=True`. The Application.CommandBars tells the application (PowerPoint) to do something with the CommandBars, which is the program's name for the toolbars. `("Picture")` isolates the Drawing toolbar. `.Visible = True` tells the program to set the property of that specific toolbar to be visible as opposed to not visible. Note that in the last line of the group, the Formatting toolbar had been visible and was turned to not visible when you recorded the macro.

- The last line, which tells the macro to stop working. This is defined by the words `End Sub()`.

N O T E There can be a fourth part of a macro that is actually not code. It serves purely to document what is happening in the macro so that you can remember what you were trying to accomplish. It is always preceded by an apostrophe because any line of code preceded by an apostrophe is ignored by the program and is for human readership only. If you have ever changed a line in a file such as your Autoexec.bat file, you may have "remarked" out a line with an apostrophe or *REM* (remark). This remark tells the code to ignore this line because it does not contain code to execute.

The Visual Basic Editor

Visual Basic 5.0 is the language used in Office 97 to write macros. It exists in a different environment than it did in previous versions of Visual Basic for Applications (VBA). The program that controls VBA code in PowerPoint, as well as the other Office applications, is the Visual Basic Editor (VBE).

The VBE is a separate program that works with all the programs that support VBA. The VBE exists separately from the main application such as PowerPoint. However, the code is kept in Project folders that are stored in specific presentations. In a sense, the VBE is similar to Microsoft Graph in that Graph creates and edits the datasheet and chart, but the chart and datasheet are stored inside of PowerPoint.

The *Project folder* is the container document for all elements of a specific project, whether it be one simple macro or a complex set of commands that develop an Office solution across several Office applications.

Several kinds of different elements can be contained in the Project folder:

- A number of modules where the code for various macros is stored.

- UserForms, which are custom-designed dialog boxes to get information from the user to use in the program. Actually, all modules are stored in a subfolder named Modules; UserForms are stored in a subfolder called Forms.

Figure 24.5 shows the VBE open and the module with the code to show/hide the Drawing toolbars open.

Part
VI

Ch
24

FIG. 24.5
All modules and UserForms are contained in the VBAProject folder.

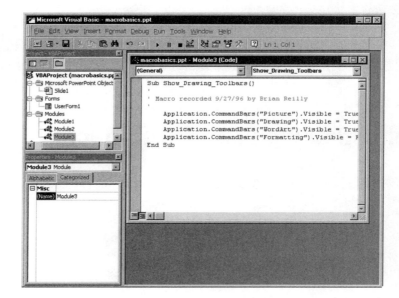

While you looked at the VBE and wrote code in the macros to show/hide Drawing toolbars, there is another way to view the Project folder and all its components. To open the VBE:

1. Open the presentation for which you want to view the Project folder, if it is not already open.

2. Choose <u>T</u>ools, <u>M</u>acro, <u>V</u>isual Basic Editor or press Alt+F11.

When you open the VBE, you are presented with three potential separate elements:

- The Project Explorer, which is docked to the VBE frame
- The Property window for Project Explorer
- A separate window for the editor

The *Project Explorer* is just like the Explorer program for showing folders and files in a tree format. You can click the + or - check boxes to expand or collapse any folder. The Project Explorer displays the Project files for any open file that has a Project file. Advanced users can use this excellent tool to copy macros from one project to another.

The *Property window* contains information about an object. For example, an object may be visible or not. It will have other characteristics depending on the object, such as a font will have a font name, font size, and font color. The information about a specific object is contained here, and if the property of that object is changeable, it can be changed here.

The third window is where one records or writes the specific code associated with a macro. You may know the term *method*; a method is the code that is assigned to an object that knows how to manipulate the object's data.

Understanding PowerPoint Macros

While using the macro recorder is a good way to record specific actions, there are many occasions when you will have to modify the code that is recorded. A good example of this is in the Show_Drawing_Toolbars macro—the recorder did not take into account the existing environment when recording the changes you wanted to make. You may need to go in and manually change the recorded code to do exactly what you want. And if you want to use decision-making in the code or if you want to activate another application such as Word or Excel, you will certainly have to write some of the code yourself.

The macros for showing and hiding toolbars really should reference all the toolbars, and might look like the following:

```
Sub Show_All_Toolbars()
'
' Displays all non-custom and one custom toolbars in PowerPoint 97
'
    Application.CommandBars("Standard").Visible = True
    Application.CommandBars("Formatting").Visible = True
    Application.CommandBars("Animation Effects").Visible = True
    Application.CommandBars("Common Tasks").Visible = True
    Application.CommandBars("Control Toolbox").Visible = True
    Application.CommandBars("Drawing").Visible = True
    Application.CommandBars("Picture").Visible = True
    Application.CommandBars("Reviewing").Visible = True
```

```
      Application.CommandBars("Visual Basic").Visible = True
      Application.CommandBars("Web").Visible = True
      Application.CommandBars("WordArt").Visible = True
End Sub
```

To be able to change the code, you need to examine the structure of the VBA Project, which is the first main level of creating macros in the VBE.

Assigning Macro Code to Objects and Toolbars

Now that you have learned how to record simple macros and modify them in the VBE, you can learn about the three different ways to run a macro as shown in Table 24.1. You can use any or all of the following methods. Note the differences between executing a macro while in Slide Edit and Slide Show modes.

Table 24.1   Assigning Macros to Objects in PowerPoint

How to Run the Macro	Works in These Modes	Comments
From the menu	Edit, Outline, Notes, Slide Master, Slide Sorter.	You may have to reference the specific page with a line such as **With Activeslide**.
From a toolbar	Edit, Outline, Notes, Slide Master, Slide Sorter. Could add custom toolbar buttons to the Web toolbar that is available under certain Slide Show view options.	
From an object on the page	Only in Slide Show view.	

Let's take each of these options separately and define the steps. You've already learned how to run a macro using the menu (Tools, Macro, Macros). Let's now learn how to assign a specific macro to a toolbar button. To do this, you need to have created a specific button on either a custom toolbar or added one to an existing toolbar. To create a new toolbar button and assign a macro command to it, perform the following steps:

1. Open the presentation that contains the macro you want to add to the toolbar, if it is not already open.

2. Choose Tools, Customize.

3. Select the Toolbars tab from the dialog box and click New.

4. Name the new toolbar and click OK.

5. Click the Commands tab in the dialog box, and select Macros from the Categories window.

6. From the Commands window, drag the macro you want to use to the new toolbar.

7. Click Close.

Assigning a macro command to a toolbar button permits you to execute the code associated with that macro anytime you click that toolbar button.

In the third case, attaching macro commands to page objects in Slide Show view permits you to perform a variety of tasks during a slide show. For example, you can launch a data collection session from a user during a self-running slide show at a trade show, or even collect data from a viewer of your Web page if you've chosen to use PowerPoint 97 to create your Web page. Or, you can use it to attach commands to simple navigation buttons such as the forward arrow for the next page and the backwards arrow to return to the most recent page.

To attach a macro command to any object on a page, choose Slide Show, Action Settings to tell it to launch a macro either when the object is clicked or when the mouse passes over the object. The following steps show specifically how to assign a macro to an object on the page:

1. Select the object you want to assign the macro to.

2. Choose Slide Show, Action Settings.

3. From the Action Settings dialog box that is presented, choose Mouse Click or Mouse Over to register the settings based on the action you want to set.

4. Click the Run Macro button and choose the macro to assign from the now available pull-down list.

5. Click OK to finish.

These steps enable you to assign a macro command so that you can execute macros when you need to.

TROUBLESHOOTING

Why doesn't my macro work now? Sometimes when you record or even write a macro, the code tests fine but it doesn't work later. The most frequent cause of this is that the macro does not run from the same location you originally tested from.

For example, Let's say you have a slide with a picture it in the top-left corner and the macro is programmed to select that picture and move it to a new location. If you run that macro from a page with no picture, you receive an error message. Placing the line of code `On Error Resume Next` in the macro tells the macro to skip over errors and continue to execute. But use this line of code with caution. It may cause the macro to ignore other errors that you may not want to ignore.

Writing Your Own Code

Now that you know about the macro recorder and the VBE, it is time to write some of your own code that cannot be written solely with the macro recorder. You may encounter several situations when you need to write your own code. Here are two examples:

Part
VI

Ch
24

- When you don't know how many times you need to perform an operation. For example, when printing of a series of files, you will likely have a varying number of files from day to day, and they will likely have different names from day to day. In a case like this, it would be handy to be able to tell the program to print all the files in the specific directory and to stop when it has printed them all.

- When you have to decide what action to take based on a condition that you cannot predict. For example, you might not be able to make a decision about what presentation design to apply until you know whether a financial statement shows a profit or a loss.

These are only two examples of how writing your own code can make the macros you write much more powerful than those written solely with the macro recorder. Let's take a look at these two examples and how each situation can be structured.

One of the first principles of writing code is to write short, easy-to-understand sets of commands. These commands can then be used over and over again by other macros that combine these commands together in order to execute what you are after.

As a good example of this, you should think of the task of printing all files in a given directory as two different tasks. The first task is to get a list of all the presentations in a directory. The second task is to print each of those presentations sequentially. If you create two macros, one for each task, you could then reuse the first macro, getting a list of all files in a specific directory, and reuse that again later if you wanted to show each of these files in sequence in a screen show instead of printing them. Then you would only have to write the code to show each file and let the new macro to show these files *call* the first macro to repeat the Get All Files list.

Calling a macro from another macro runs the called macro. This is an excellent technique for reusing code in many places. To place a call to a macro from another macro, just type the name of the macro to run without the Sub or ().

For Each...Next

Let's write the code to print all the files in a given directory. Because you have defined this procedure as having two steps, you can create two separate macros—one for the first step and one for the second:

1. List all the files in a specific directory.

2. Print each of those files.

To create the first macro, the one that lists the files in the correct directory, do the following:

1. Switch to the VBE by choosing Tools, Macro, Visual Basic Editor (or press Alt+F11).

2. Choose Insert, Module to get a blank module.

3. Type **Sub Print_All_Files()** and press Enter. Notice that the program automatically adds End Sub for you.

4. Type the following lines of code:

```
Sub Choose_Files()

Set fs = Application.FileSearch
With fs

'    Substitute your target directory here
    .LookIn = "C:\My Documents"
    .FileName = "*.ppt"
    If .Execute(SortBy:=msoSortByFileName, SortOrder:=msoSortOrderAscending)
> 0 Then
        MsgBox .FoundFiles.Count & " files(0s) found."

'    Open and print each presentation found there
        For i = 1 To .FoundFiles.Count
            Presentations.Open FileName:=.FoundFiles.Item(i),
ReadOnly:=msoFalse

'    Here's where we call the other macro:
            Print_Presentation
        Next i
    Else
        MsgBox "No files found."
    End If
```

```
        End With

        End Sub
```

 TIP I added the `MsgBox` line to provide feedback that this is performing the correct task. It is a useful technique that you can use to give yourself feedback while you are testing the code that ensures you are indeed getting the correct value to that point. You can delete it after the code is debugged and running correctly.

The important thing to realize here is that the `For Each...Next` command lets you get all instances of a circumstance when you don't know how many times that circumstance might occur. When the command finds no more values, it stops looping and proceeds with the next line of code.

For the second macro—the one to print the active file—you can just turn on the macro recorder and record your actions as you print the current file using the print settings you'd like to use for your files. You should get something like this depending on the choices you make in the Print dialog box:

```
Sub Print_Presentation()
'
' Macro recorded 9/29/96 by Brian Reilly
'
    With ActivePresentation.PrintOptions
        .RangeType = ppPrintAll
        .NumberOfCopies = 1
        .Collate = msoFalse
        .OutputType = ppPrintOutputSlides
        .PrintHiddenSlides = msoTrue
        .PrintColorType = ppPrintBlackAndWhite
        .FitToPage = msoTrue
        .FrameSlides = msoFalse
        ' Substitute the name of your printer or remove this line to use the
default printer
        .ActivePrinter = "HP LaserJet 4L"
    End With
    ActivePresentation.PrintOut

End Sub
```

To test the two new macros, choose Tools, Macro, Macros or press Alt+F8. Pick Choose_Files and click OK. Your two new macros will do all the work of locating, opening, and printing every file in the directory you entered.

Note that there are always several ways to write the code to perform the same task. Many programmers try to write the shortest amount of code possible because the macro will run somewhat faster. Others try to spend the least amount of time writing the code and let the machine take a few more seconds to execute it. It is all a matter of personal style, and as you gain experience in writing code in VBA and especially in PowerPoint, you will undoubtedly find faster ways to do things. The most important thing is to get started and write some code that helps make you more productive.

If Then...Else

The command to judge a conditional statement is extremely powerful. It can cycle through many possibilities for you and automatically execute different commands depending on the condition that is met. The following example changes the design template based on whether a range in the Excel sheet shows a profit or loss for the current period. While this is a very simple example, you can easily adapt it to change the design template for each division if you have some divisions in the black and some in the red.

The presentation will have been created with links to the spreadsheet range. The If statement is used to define whether to apply an upbeat background for a profitable period or a downbeat background for an unprofitable period.

Again, because the decision is a choice of two potential outcomes, you should create three macros:

- One to apply the upbeat design scheme
- One to apply the downbeat design scheme
- The master macro to decide what the outcome is and then call the appropriate macro to apply the correct scheme

The two following macros are very simple; they apply either template to the active presentation. Both have been created as new templates and saved as Upbeat.pot and Downbeat.pot, respectively.

```
Sub Apply_Upbeat_Design()

    ActivePresentation.ApplyTemplate
➥FileName:="C:\Office97\Templates\Presentation Designs\Upbeat.POT"
End Sub


Sub Apply_Downbeat_Design()

    ActivePresentation.ApplyTemplate
➥FileName:="C:\Office97\Templates\Presentation Designs\Downbeat.POT"
End Sub
```

The controlling macro is a bit more complicated because it needs to open a specific spreadsheet in Excel and check the value of the range named Profit_Loss to determine if that value is greater than zero (profit) or less than or equal to zero (loss). Refer to the Excel application as an object and therefore declare the variable name you will assign to the Excel application. In this case, the variable name is declared in the first line of the module so it is available to any macro that runs within this module. Then, open the Excel application and the specific file. Check the value of the range Profit_Loss. Based on the returned value, you can choose which design to apply. The code that does this is as follows:

```
Dim appxl as Object
Sub Open_Excel_Profit_Loss_file()
Set appxl = CreateObject("Excel.Application.8")   '\sets the variable
                                                  '\name to the application
Appxl.Visible = False                             '\operates invisibly
         '\next line opens the file
Appxl.Workbooks.Open "c:\Excelfiles\Profit_Loss_file.xls"
         '/checks to see if value is profit
If appxl.Range("Profit_Loss").Value > 0 Then
         '\run the Apply_Upbeat_Design macro
Apply_Upbeat_Design
ElseIf appxl.Range("Profit_Loss").Value <= Then
Apply_Downbeat_Design
'\must end all If statements with End If
End If
         '\closes Excel and does not save since file is unchanged
Appxl.Quit
End Sub
```

This application runs entirely inside of PowerPoint. It references the outside program—Excel—opens that program with the command from PowerPoint, checks the value in the Excel file, and returns that value to PowerPoint so that the PowerPoint macro can decide what option to execute. There is no need in this case to operate a macro in Excel. Similar examples can be executed with Word and Access. You can get values from any of these programs, and copy to or from any of these programs all from within PowerPoint.

Exploring the PowerPoint Object Model

In the first macro written in this chapter, Show_Drawing_Toolbars(), there are two lines that show the hierarchy of the objects relevant to that macro:

```
Application.CommandBars("Drawing").Visible = True
    Application.CommandBars("Formatting").Visible = False
```

In these particular lines, four levels of this hierarchy are shown. This hierarchy is known as the Object Model. The *Object Model* is a visualization of how every object in PowerPoint relates or does not relate to another object. By accessing the correct object through the commands, you can manipulate it with code manually.

While the Object Model may look difficult to understand at first, it is really the easiest way to conceptualize PowerPoint code. Figure 24.6 shows the relationship between the objects in the top two levels of the model. In this example, the top level is the Application—PowerPoint. The next level down is Presentations (if it is a collection of Presentations) or Presentation (if it is a single presentation you are referring to). Figure 24.7 repeats the objects in the Presentation level and shows the relationship to one type of object—Shapes, the next level down.

FIG. 24.6

This figure shows the top two levels of the Object Model for PowerPoint 97.

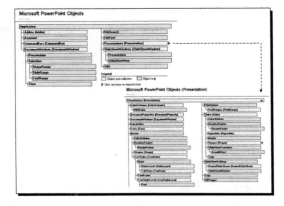

FIG. 24.7

The second and third levels of the Object Model are continued in this figure.

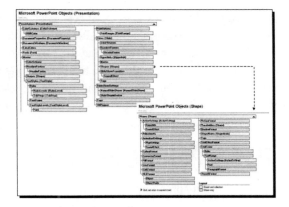

To refer to an object such as a shape and refer to its fill property, you would first have to reference the Application, then the Presentation, then the shape, then the fill property. In code, it might look like the following:

```
'This opens the presentation
Presentations.Open FileName:="D:\My Documents\Model.ppt", ReadOnly:=msoFalse
'This selects the third page in the active presentation which is Model.ppt
    ActiveWindow.View.GotoSlide Index:=3
'this actually uses the presentation in the Active Window and selects the 'Rect-
angle #8 on that page
```

```
ActiveWindow.Selection.SlideRange.Shapes("Rectangle 8").Select
' Then it sets the properties for that shape
    With ActiveWindow.Selection.ShapeRange
'the Fill is visible for this particular shape
        .Fill.Visible = msoTrue
'the fill is a solid fill instead of a patterned or shaded fill
        .Fill.Solid
'it sets the color property in RGB colors
        .Fill.ForeColor.RGB = RGB(0, 0, 255)
'the End With means you stop referring to this particular shape.
    End With
```

You can access the Object Model while in the VBE by pressing the F2 key. When you do this, you see something similar to Figure 24.8. You can select an object in the left pane of the window and see all the possible objects available to that object. To use the toolbars example, follow these steps:

1. If you are not already in the VBE, press Alt+F11.

2. Press the F2 key to bring up the Object Browser. You can use the Object Browser to find the potential relationships from any object.

3. From the choices in the scroll bar on the screen, click CommandBar.

4. If you scroll the Members of Command Bar window downward, you see the property value of Visible.

FIG. 24.8
The Object Model is available by pressing the F2 key.

Whether you are an advanced code writer or a new code writer, I advise you to pick several commands you may understand—such as File, Save—and explore the Object Browser to get a better feel for it. It will be time well spent when you need to troubleshoot some errors in the code you write.

CHAPTER 25

Building Your Own Custom Presentation

by Brian Reilly

Microsoft has finally implemented its plan to integrate a common programming language in all of the Office 97 products. Now, with the addition of Visual Basic for Applications (VBA) to PowerPoint, Word, Project, and Access, you can create very nice-looking custom presentations that use elements from all of these sources, choosing the best source for each task.

For example, while Access is the workhorse at storing and manipulating a very large database, you might prefer Excel to analyze that database. Word is still the best place to create tables and to write about the analysis done in Excel. PowerPoint, though weak in the area of analysis, is the thoroughbred of the group at assembling all of the others into easily understood and easily navigated graphic presentations.

With VBA, you can integrate all of these products and create custom presentations in seconds. ■

Create custom presentations that show or hide key information, such as a customer's name, throughout the entire presentation

You can make a simple 15-second change and have that reflected in an entire presentation immediately.

Create custom presentations that let you change the underlying data immediately during the presentation without leaving Slide Show view

Whether you need to change languages during a presentation to explain a particularly complex concept in a different language or change the categories you want to examine during a budget review, you can do this at the click of a button.

The Foundation of a Custom Presentation

Many companies give essentially the same presentation to many customers and would like to customize their presentations to each specific customer. Until now, this could have been a fairly time-consuming project. However, with PowerPoint 97, the task is much easier.

Imagine that you are presenting a market analysis of sales results to a customer. What will vary from market to market is the list of products and the list of retailers in that marketplace. However, the structure of the tables and charts will remain constant. The trick then is to manipulate the underlying data in Excel and create all your tables and charts in Excel. Then by using VBA in PowerPoint 97, you can control the manipulation of the data in Excel so that all your charts and tables are re-created from code and then instantly updated in PowerPoint.

Let's look at some specific examples of what you can do to customize your presentation.

Customizing Data in Presentations

A host of opportunities enable you to customize data in presentations. I have seen requests to hide all customer names in a chart except for the name of the particular customer being presented. There are also situations where the names of customers will vary by market—for example, when presenting to a retailer. A frequent request is for the ability to create a presentation that can be instantly switched into a different language.

Customizing Names to Hide in Charts

The ability of Excel to manipulate data is frequently a key to customizing the data in a presentation. If you want to hide all the customer names except the name of your particular audience's company, you can do that in an easy step if you prepare your tables and charts correctly in the first place. Figure 25.1 shows a worksheet in Excel with a list of customer names from Customer1 to Customer4.

FIG. 25.1

Hide customer names by using formulas for customer names.

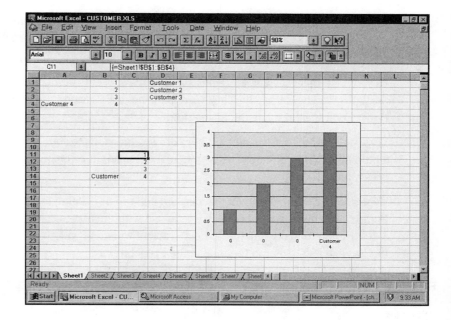

The chart shown is created from the range B10:C14. However, the customer names in B10:B14 are formulas referring to the actual text in the range A1:A4. If you were to create all your charts like this one with the customer names being formulas referring to cells A1:A4, you could just drag the customer names you want to hide into another location such as column D, and they disappear from all charts immediately.

Each chart created in Excel should then be copied and pasted into PowerPoint by choosing Edit, Paste Special, Paste Link.

Switching Languages During a Presentation

With the continuing globalization of the economy, you may find yourself presenting to audiences whose native language may be different from yours. Sometimes complex concepts are better understood when explained in the native language of a particular audience. You could carry multiple copies of the same presentation, but if you found yourself in the middle of a presentation and wanted to switch languages, it would be somewhat distracting to both the presenter and the audience to open another presentation and find your place in the new version.

Part

VI

Ch

25

You can now do this instantly with the use of VBA. If you have created your presentation by typing the text into individual cells in Excel, you could attach macro commands to change the text from one language to another instantly.

However, in this case you are going to place the contents of the Excel cells directly into the Title placeholder or the Click Here placeholder on each PowerPoint page and let the PowerPoint master apply the formatting.

Let's look at that in more detail. There are several steps to setting up this presentation and a little bit of VBA code to be written to make the language change at any point during the presentation.

Type some of the text into Excel cells and add the translation to the adjacent column. Figure 25.2 shows a section of a spreadsheet with the text for page 1. Column A is used as a description to make it easier to keep track of what text will go where. Column B contains the English text. Column C contains the French text.

FIG. 25.2
Using the first column to describe where the cell contents will go will be helpful later.

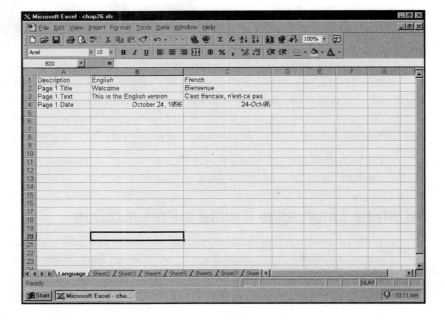

The next step is to add two option buttons to a PowerPoint page, because you will want to be able to choose only one language to show at a time.

The other choice that you might have made would be to use check boxes to get user input with a mouse click. However, check boxes are used in situations where you can make multiple selections. The Properties dialog box is a two-column table. The first column lists the description of the property and cannot be modified. The second column shows the setting of that property and this is where you modify the settings. To add the two option buttons to the PowerPoint page:

1. Switch back to the PowerPoint presentation or open a new presentation.

2. If the Control Toolbox is not visible, make it visible by choosing <u>V</u>iew, <u>T</u>oolbars and clicking in the check box next to Control Toolbox. See Figure 25.3 to view the Control Toolbox toolbar.

FIG. 25.3
The Control Toolbox is new to PowerPoint.

3. Click the option button to select that tool.

4. Drag the mouse on the page to draw the option button. This is very similar to adding a shape with one of the drawing tools. You see the option button, and if you made the button large enough, you can see the text OptionButton1 on the button face. Repeat steps 3 and 4 to add a second option button. That button is automatically named OptionButton2.

5. Size both buttons, just like a drawing object, and place them into the desired position on the page (see Figure 25.4).

FIG. 25.4
These option buttons permit you to make choices of a language during a slide show.

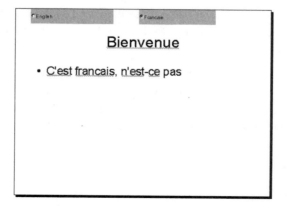

Part
VI

Ch
25

At this point, you have added the buttons to control the presentation language during the slide show. There are several options that can change the interface, and they all relate to the Properties of the OptionButtons.

Change the caption property to be more descriptive than OptionButton1 or OptionButton2. It really would not be a very user-friendly application if the descriptions on buttons contained generic text. Fortunately, you can change not only the name on the button, but also other properties of the button such as the font type, color, and size.

You can also change the color of the button. If you right-click the mouse on the option button, you see the menu shown in Figure 25.5. Click the Properties choice to access the Properties dialog box. To change the caption on the button, just type your new description in the box to the right of Caption on the Alphabetic tab in the Properties dialog box.

FIG. 25.5

Right-clicking the option button brings up these choices.

You can add pictures to the Button face so the buttons can now become a significant design element that you can use. For example, assume that in this example of choosing a different language, you had two pictures of flags that you have saved as USFLAG.BMP and Frflag.bmp. You can consider using these flag images on the buttons rather than using text. You need to assign a macro to the button later in this process, but first you can place the flag images on the two buttons.

To place a picture on the button, select the row in the Properties dialog box for Picture; initially, it says None. You are presented with a drop-down button in the right column of the row. Figure 25.6 shows much of the Properties dialog box. You can then just browse your directories to find the correct picture to insert on the button. This process is very similar to inserting a picture into a PowerPoint page, but it is done within the confines of the Properties dialog box.

FIG. 25.6
Properties are
changed in the
Properties dialog box.

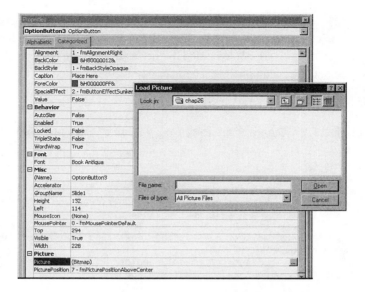

 TIP When making changes to the properties of a variety of objects, you can use the pull-down box at
the top of the Properties dialog box to switch immediately to another object and view those
properties.

You are now ready to write several different macros to handle the actual changing of text
on the slide. This process involves several steps, so the first thing you should do is to list
the steps such as the following:

1. Clear the existing text on a page by deleting the existing text in each placeholder.
2. Activate Excel and open the spreadsheet that is the container for all of the language
   versions.
3. Copy the correct range of Excel cells to the Clipboard.
4. Activate PowerPoint, select the correct text placeholder, and paste the contents of
   the Clipboard.
5. Repeat steps 3 and 4 for each range in the Excel sheet that needs to be changed.

 TIP If you are copying several bullet points from Excel, you can select the multiple cell range and copy
it to the Clipboard. When the range is pasted into a bullet placeholder, PowerPoint recognizes
each cell as a different bullet.

Listing 25.1 shows the way to accomplish each step for changing the text from English into French. Similar code would reverse the process. Note that the lines of code that begin with an apostrophe are not executed by the macro and are comments to explain what the next line of code accomplishes. The macro in Listing 25.1 clears the present text values of the Title and bullet placeholders on this slide.

Listing 25.1   Clearing Present Text Values of Title and Bullet Placeholders

```
Sub Clear_Title_and_Bullet_Placeholder_Text()
'
' Macro recorded 10/22/96 by Brian Reilly
' This selects the active slide and the Title Text placeholder
    ActiveWindow.Selection.SlideRange.Shapes("Rectangle 2").Select
' This selects all the text in the placeholder
    ActiveWindow.Selection.ShapeRange.TextFrame.TextRange.Select
    ActiveWindow.Selection.ShapeRange.TextFrame.TextRange.Characters(Start:=1,
➥Length:=0).Select
' This sets the contents of the placeholder to nothing
    With ActiveWindow.Selection.TextRange
        .Text = " "
'this With/End With section is not necessary because the master page controls
'the formatting, but if you use the macro recorder you will see this code.
        With .Font
            .Name = "Times New Roman"
            .Size = 44
            .Bold = msoFalse
            .Italic = msoFalse
            .Underline = msoFalse
            .Shadow = msoFalse
            .Emboss = msoFalse
            .BaselineOffset = 0
            .AutoRotateNumbers = msoFalse
            .Color.SchemeColor = ppTitle
        End With
'This End with closes the With from the With ActiveWindow.Selection.TextRange
'        .Text = " " line of code
    End With
'This unselects the Title Text placeholder and is not necessary
    ActiveWindow.Selection.Unselect
'This line selects ("Rectangle 5") which is the Bullet Placeholder
    ActiveWindow.Selection.SlideRange.Shapes("Rectangle 5").Select
    ActiveWindow.Selection.ShapeRange.TextFrame.TextRange.Select
'This sets the text in the bullet placeholder to nothing
    ActiveWindow.Selection.ShapeRange.TextFrame.TextRange.Characters(Start:=1,
Length:=4).Select
    ActiveWindow.Selection.TextRange.Text = " "
    ActiveWindow.Selection.Unselect
End Sub
```

The next task is to open Excel and copy the appropriate range to the Clipboard. Because you will be performing several copy and paste actions between Excel and PowerPoint, it is wise to separate these into separate tasks:

1. Open Excel and open the file containing the language translations.
2. Copy the first range to the Clipboard.
3. Use the Alt+Tab keys to switch back to PowerPoint and paste the contents of the Clipboard into the correct placeholder in PowerPoint.
4. Copy the second range to the Clipboard in Excel.
5. Paste the contents of the Clipboard into the correct placeholder in PowerPoint.
6. Close the Excel application and do not save the Excel file because no changes were made.

The macro in Listing 25.2 opens Excel and the correct file.

Listing 25.2 Opening Excel and the Correct File

```
'Option Explicit means we have to declare all variables.
Option Explicit
' Dim declares the variable xlapp as an object. It could be called anything, but
¦xlapp is 'somewhat descriptive and will help you remember that it refers to
¦the xl application.

Sub Open_xl_langfile()
'This sets the variable xlapp equal to the Excel.exe file to open Excel
Set xlapp = CreateObject("Excel.Application.8")
'The next choice is whether to run Excel visibly or invisibly
'For debugging purposes, set visible = True so you can follow the steps
'Then when all is working change Visible = True to = False and it will not show
'up on the screen
xlapp.Visible = False
'Next you open the correct file. Use the correct path name or it will not work.
Xlapp.Workbooks.Open "c:\MyDocuments\langfile.xls"

End sub
```

Now the Excel file would be open and running invisibly behind the PowerPoint screen show. The next task you want to do is copy the appropriate cells from Excel and paste them into the appropriate placeholders in PowerPoint. The macro in Listing 25.3 does just that.

Listing 25.3   Copying Excel Cells and Pasting into PowerPoint Placeholders

```
Sub Copy_Paste_Page1_French()
'If xlapp is still declared as a variable and this code is in the same module as
¦the previous code, you do not have to re-declare it.
' copies cell C2 to the clipboard
Xlapp.Range("C2").Copy

' You should probably break the following code into several more macros that
¦would be called from this point, but in this case to simplify the logic it is
¦continued in this macro.
'This selects the Title placeholder
ActiveWindow.Selection.SlideRange.Shapes("Rectangle 2").Select
    ActiveWindow.Selection.ShapeRange.TextFrame.TextRange.Select
'This selects the first character in the Title placeholder which is empty in
this case.
    ActiveWindow.Selection.ShapeRange.TextFrame.TextRange.Characters(Start:=1,
Length:=0).Select
'This pastes the contents of the Clipboard into the Placeholder
    With ActiveWindow.Selection.TextRange
        .Paste
End With

'This copies Cell C3 in Excel to Clipboard
Xlapp.Range("C3").Copy
'This selects the bullet placeholder
ActiveWindow.Selection.SlideRange.Shapes("Rectangle 5").Select
    ActiveWindow.Selection.ShapeRange.TextFrame.TextRange.Select
'This selects the first character in the bullet placeholder which is empty in
¦this case.
    ActiveWindow.Selection.ShapeRange.TextFrame.TextRange.Characters(Start:=1,
Length:=0).Select
'This pastes the contents of the Clipboard into the Placeholder
    With ActiveWindow.Selection.TextRange
        .Paste
End With
End sub
```

Now that these macros are written, it is time to combine them into one macro that calls each macro in sequence and makes the language change. That way, you can assign only one macro to the OptionButton2 for the French flag. When you write the similar code to change the contents of the placeholders to English, you can reuse some of these macros such as the one that opens the correct Excel file. To call other macros from a macro, just type the name of the macro in the correct sequence to execute, but do not include the Sub or () part of the macro name. The macro to change the language from English to French is shown in Listing 25.4.

Listing 25.4 Changing the Language from English to French

```
Sub Change_To_French()

Clear_Title_and_Bullet_Placeholder_Text
Open_xl_langfile
Copy_Paste_Page1_French
End sub
```

This macro changes the text in both placeholders on the page. Making the appropriate changes to these macros to change the presentation text back to English is now a very quick and easy task to accomplish. Because the Excel file is still running invisibly in the background, you don't need to reopen Excel. But you do have to change the macro to copy cells B2 and B3, instead of C2 and C3. Just copy the entire macro `Copy_Paste_Page1_French` and paste it into a module (see Listing 25.5). Then you only have three simple changes you have to make along with two other changes that won't affect the code. All of the changes to be made are:

1. Change the name to say `English` instead of `French`.
2. Change C2 to B2.
3. Change C3 to B3.
4. Optionally, change the comment for C2 to B2.
5. Optionally, change the comment for C3 to B3.

Part
VI

Ch
25

Listing 25.5 Copying and Pasting the Macro into a Module

```
Sub Copy_Paste_Page1_English()
'If xlapp is still declared as a variable and this code is in the same module as
¦the previous code, you do not have to re-declare it.
' copies cell B2 to the Clipboard
Xlapp.Range("B2").Copy

' You should probably break the following code into several more macros that
¦would be called from this point, but in this case to simplify the logic it is
¦continued in this macro.
'This selects the Title placeholder
ActiveWindow.Selection.SlideRange.Shapes("Rectangle 2").Select
    ActiveWindow.Selection.ShapeRange.TextFrame.TextRange.Select
'This selects the first character in the Title placeholder which is empty in
¦this case.
    ActiveWindow.Selection.ShapeRange.TextFrame.TextRange.Characters(Start:=1,
Length:=0).Select
'This pastes the contents of the Clipboard into the Placeholder
    With ActiveWindow.Selection.TextRange
        .Paste
End With
```

continues

Listing 25.5   Continued

```
'This copies Cell B3 in Excel to Clipboard
Xlapp.Range("B3").Copy
'This selects the bullet placeholder
ActiveWindow.Selection.SlideRange.Shapes("Rectangle 5").Select
    ActiveWindow.Selection.ShapeRange.TextFrame.TextRange.Select
'This selects the first character in the bullet placeholder which is empty in
¦this case.
    ActiveWindow.Selection.ShapeRange.TextFrame.TextRange.Characters(Start:=1,
Length:=0).Select
'This pastes the contents of the Clipboard into the Placeholder
    With ActiveWindow.Selection.TextRange
        .Paste
End With
End sub
```

N O T E   If you want to close Excel instead of keeping it running in the background, you need to add another macro with the following single line:

```
xlapp.Quit
```

Or, just add it as a last line when you are finished copying and pasting from Excel.

The last thing to do so that all this works is to assign the macro to change the language to the correct OptionButton on the page. This is done by calling the macro—for example,

```
Sub Change_To_French()
```

from the OptionButton2 code. Return to the PowerPoint page and right-click the OptionButton2 which should have the French flag on the button face. Choose <u>V</u>iew Code. That will show you the code for OptionButton2 which is empty at the moment. Type the command to call the `Change_To_French` macro into the second line as follows:

```
Private Sub OptionButton2_Click()
Change_To_French
End Sub
```

That's all there is to it. While this example dealt with changing languages, it could also easily have changed charts or ranges that reflect different budgets in spreadsheets or budgets that reflect different divisions. The OptionButtons that let you navigate the presentation don't have to be included on every page. You may choose to create multiple presentations such as one for each division each month. Depending on what your specific needs are, if you take some time to set up the spreadsheets carefully, you can create multiple presentations every month with the click of a few buttons instead of spending all the late nights performing these repetitive tasks. ●

Appendixes

Installing PowerPoint

Microsoft PowerPoint 97 is available by itself, or as part of a Microsoft Office 97 package. Both can only be purchased on CD-ROM. If you do not have a CD-ROM drive, you must purchase the CD-ROM version, then use the form enclosed in the box to order a free floppy disk copy. Delivery can take up to four weeks, however, and floppy installation will be cumbersome; if you've been thinking about getting a CD-ROM drive for your computer, now is the time.

The installation procedures are the same whether this is the first version of Office or PowerPoint that you have, or whether you are upgrading from pre-97 versions. ■

Microsoft offers full versions and upgrade versions of Office 97 products. The difference between the two is that to use far-cheaper upgrade versions you are required to have one of a long list of products already installed on your machine. The list contains many popular programs that provide the functions of one or more Office components. The odds are good that you have one of these, but if you don't, you should consider buying one. Some of the programs listed are cheap enough that you can buy one of them and the upgrade for less than the price of the full version.

If You Bought PowerPoint 97 Separately

Before you start trying to install PowerPoint, make sure that you have enough space on your hard disk. You'll need about 50 megabytes (M) of free space. If you don't have that much, you'll need to delete some files. Be sure to empty your Recycle Bin when you're done (by right-clicking the Recycle Bin icon and selecting Empty Recycle Bin), or else those files may still be taking up space on your disk.

1. If you're installing the CD-ROM version, put it into your CD-ROM drive. The installation program starts automatically, bringing up a selection of things you can do. Select Install Microsoft PowerPoint.

2. If you bought PowerPoint on floppy disks, put the disk marked Disk 1 into your floppy disk drive. From the Windows taskbar, choose Start, Run. In the dialog box that appears, type **a:\setup** and then click OK to start the installation program.

3. After you've started the installation process, the installation program shows a series of dialog boxes asking you questions. Answer them. (Many of the choices have default answers already filled in for you.)

4. When you get to choosing between Typical Installation and Custom Installation, click Typical Installation.

5. You'll see a list of items that you can choose whether to install. Items that you'll probably want are already checked off. The one thing that isn't checked off that you should add is Web Page Authoring (HTML). Click the box next to that if you want to use PowerPoint to create presentations for the World Wide Web.

6. Click OK to continue with the installation process. The installation program will lead you through the rest of the procedure.

If You Bought Microsoft Office 97

There are two different procedures for installing from the Microsoft Office 97 package. One is for people who have not yet installed Office 97 at all; the other is for people who installed Office 97 already on their machines, but chose not to install the PowerPoint 97 components at that time.

First-Time Office 97 Installation

Before you start trying to install PowerPoint, make sure that you have enough space on your hard disk. If you're installing the complete Standard edition Office package, you'll need about

150 megabytes (M) of free space. If you're installing the complete Professional edition of Office, you'll need about 200M. If you only want to install PowerPoint, you'll only need 50M. If you're really low on disk space, you can choose to run Office from the CD-ROM, which will only take 25M of the hard disk. However, the Office programs will run slower if you choose this option, so only do it if you're not going to use them often.

If you don't have enough space available, you'll need to delete some files. Be sure to empty your Recycle Bin when you're done (by right-clicking the Recycle Bin icon and selecting Empty Recycle <u>B</u>in), or else those files may still be taking up space on your disk.

To install Office 97, follow these steps:

1. If you're installing from CD-ROM, put the CD-ROM into your CD-ROM drive. The installation program starts automatically, bringing up a selection of things you can do.

   If you're installing from floppy disk, put the disk marked Disk 1 into your floppy disk drive. From the Windows taskbar, choose Start, <u>R</u>un. In the dialog box that appears, type **a:\setup** and then click OK. This starts the installation program.

2. Click Install Microsoft Office.

3. The installation program shows a series of dialog boxes asking you questions. Answer them. For most of the questions, the program has suggested answers already in place.

4. At one point, you'll be asked to choose between Typical Installation, Custom Installation, and (if you're doing a CD-ROM-based installation) Run Office from CD-ROM.

   If you want to run PowerPoint from CD-ROM, choose Run Office from CD-ROM. If you choose this, the Office CD-ROM must be in your computer at all times while you are using PowerPoint.

   If you want to install all of Office, choose Typical Installation. You'll see a list of items that you can choose whether you want to install. Items that you'll probably want are already checked off. The one thing that isn't checked off that you probably want to add is Web Page Authoring (HTML). Click the box next to that if you want to use PowerPoint to create presentations for the World Wide Web.

   If you just want to install PowerPoint, and don't want to install the rest of the Office programs, choose Custom Installation. You'll see a list of parts for Office. Some of them will already be checked off. Click these entries to clear the check boxes except for the ones marked Microsoft PowerPoint, Office Tools, and Converters And Filters.

5. The installation program will lead you through the rest of the process. It should be smooth sailing from there.

Adding PowerPoint to an Existing Office 97 Installation

Many people choose not to install PowerPoint 97 when they first install Office 97, because they expect they won't need the product. If you did this, and now want to install PowerPoint 97, you need about 35M of free disk space. Follow these steps:

1. Exit all Microsoft Office 97 programs.

2. From the Windows taskbar, choose Start, Settings, Control Panel. A Control Panel window opens, displaying icons for a variety of configuration programs.

3. Double-click the Add/Remove Programs icon. An Add/Remove Program Properties dialog box appears.

4. On the Install/Uninstall tab, select Microsoft Office 97 from the list of programs, then click Add/Remove.

5. You will be prompted to insert the Office 97 CD-ROM or the first floppy disk, depending on which you installed from. Do so, then click OK. (If you're installing from floppies, you may be instructed to insert further floppies.)

6. The Microsoft Office 97 Setup program starts, and displays a Microsoft Office 97 Setup dialog box. Click Add/Remove.

7. A Microsoft 97 Maintenance dialog box appears. Put a check in the check box marked Microsoft PowerPoint. (If you want to control specifically which components of PowerPoint are installed, select Microsoft PowerPoint, click the Change Option button, then select the components from the offered list and click OK.)

8. Click OK. The Setup program leads you through the remaining steps of the installation.

Converting Other Presentations to PowerPoint 97

If you've been using another presentation program, you may be able to convert presentations that you've designed to PowerPoint 97 presentations. PowerPoint comes with translation programs that lets it read files created using Lotus Freelance or Harvard Graphics.

To do this, you need to install the Presentation Translators. You can do this when you first install PowerPoint as part of the installation procedure by selecting the Custom Installation option, or you can add them later by starting up the Add/Remove Programs program as described in the previous procedure.

When you get to the point in the installation or Add/Remove procedure where you are selecting the list of options to install from Office:

1. Click the Microsoft PowerPoint option on the list of program components.

2. Click the Change Option button.

3. On the list that appears, put a check in the Presentation Translators check box.

4. Click OK to return to the list of program components.

5. Click OK to complete the installation.

If you're installing from a PowerPoint-only disk, you won't have to select Microsoft PowerPoint; you will be taken straight to the list that includes Presentation Translators.

After you have installed the Presentation Translators, you can open these presentations easily, directly from PowerPoint. Just choose File, Open, then in the file navigator, select the type of presentation you want to open from the Files Of Type drop-down list. Select the file you want to open using the navigator, and click Open. ●

Resources

by Nancy Stevenson

Several resources can help you create PowerPoint presentations, from slide bureaus that can generate your 35mm slides to companies that produce collections of clip media. ■

Microsoft Resources

What follows are just a few representative resources to get you started. They are organized by category so you can find them easily. Many have a page on the World Wide Web, and that address, as well as a phone number, is given, where available.

PowerPoint Home Page

http://www.microsoft.com/mspowerpoint/

Here you can get information on new releases of the product, add-on products from third-party software vendors, and tips on using PowerPoint.

PowerPoint 32-Bit Viewer

http://www.microsoft.com/powerpoint/Internet/Viewer/default.htm

Go to this site to download the PowerPoint 32-bit Viewer, which enables those without PowerPoint installed on their computer to view PowerPoint presentations.

PowerPoint Animation Player

http://www.microsoft.com/mspowerpoint/internet/player/default.htm

Using this player, you can create Web pages with PowerPoint and browser extensions.

Microsoft Support

http://www.microsoft.com/powerpoint/ps_ppt.htm

Send messages to Microsoft Technical Support from this page. You can also reach them through PowerPoint. Select Help, Microsoft on the Web to connect.

Slide Bureaus

Slide bureaus are used to generate 35mm slides from your PowerPoint files. They are usually set up to receive your file online with an online order form. Turnaround can take as little as a day or two, with overnight express shipping costing you extra; however, be alert to rush charges, which can be very high. Here are some slide bureaus to check into.

Genigraphics is the service bureau for which Microsoft has integrated ordering procedures in PowerPoint. For more about this company, look in PowerPoint's Help topic index under the term Genigraphics. You can contact them at 1-714-553-1101.

Here's a list of other companies:

Company	Location	Web/Internet Address	Phone Number
Konold Kreations	Columbus, OH	Slides@aol.com	1-614-866-4376
S & L Professional Imaging	Tampa, FL	http://www. allworld.com/ s-l-imaging/	1-813-980-1400
Slide Express	Boston, MA		1-800-472-7449
Slidemaker	Eureka, CA	http://www. slidemaker.com/ index.html	1-310-396-4421
Slides R Us	New York, NY		1-800-707-0681
Slides Unlimited		slidesun@ slidesunlimited.com	1-818-705-1084
RDP	Cincinnati, OH	104047.2314@ compuserve.com	1-513-621-9136

Font Collections

You may want to get additional typefaces for use in your presentations. You can buy collections of fonts on CD-ROM or online and download them as you go. Here are a couple of suggested resources.

Adobe Systems, Inc.

http://www.adobe.com

Adobe produces the Adobe Type Library, Adobe Type Manager to fine-tune your type, and Adobe Type On Call CD-ROM. The latter allows you to call a number, order, and download new typefaces as you need them.

Jerry's World

CompuServe: **74431,225**

This online store has a wide variety of typefaces, clip art, photos, and sound effects for sale.

Clip Art and Graphics

If you like PowerPoint's ability to place pictures, photographs, videos, and sound in a presentation, you might want to expand your collection of clip media by contacting some of these vendors. Remember, you can add as much media as you like to Microsoft's Clip Gallery within the various categories.

The Clip Art Connection

http://www.acy.digexnet/%7Einfomart/clipart/index.html

This is a great source for clip art collections in various styles; they're constantly adding new art, so you might want to check in frequently.

Three D Graphics

http://www.threedgraphics.com/compadre; 1-800-913-0008

Try this service for additional textures, backgrounds, and action buttons for your presentations.

desktopPublishing

http://www.desktoppublishing.com/cliplist.html

desktopPublishing handles a wide variety of clip art, as well as photos.

Jerry's World

CompuServe: **74431,225**

This online store sells clip art collections, typefaces, photos, and sound effects.

Metro Creative Graphics, New York, NY

Metro produces a popular line of clip art on CD-ROM called ClipMASTERPRO. You can contact them at 1-212-947-5100.

PrePress Solutions, East Hanover, NJ

This company sells a large selection of photo CDs and graphics hardware. You can contact them at 1-800-631-8134, ext. 2.

Publications

Publications are available that keep you up-to-date on the latest technologies for presentations, including projection hardware, clip media, animation, and sound. Graphics- and desktop publishing-oriented publications can also be useful for finding advertisements for clip media products, projection systems, or articles on page design which can be applicable to PowerPoint slides.

Inside Microsoft PowerPoint

http://www.cobb.com/ipp/free1001.htm

This monthly newsletter is published by The Cobb Group. It's full of tips and techniques for the PowerPoint user, for $39 per year. You can get a free copy of the newsletter from their World Wide Web site.

PC World Multimedia Edition Online

http://www.multimedia.com

Formerly *Multimedia World Magazine*, this helpful publication was gobbled by *PC World* and is now known by the aforementioned name. This is their online location, where you can search for articles in the category of presenting.

Software

Some products are available that can either build elements, such as animations, which can be used in PowerPoint presentations, or that work as add-on products to make PowerPoint easier to use. Here are a few you might want to explore. You might also want to check into shareware products by cruising around multimedia or graphics forums on your online service or the Internet.

N O T E The release of versions of these products that support PowerPoint 97 may lag slightly behind the release of PowerPoint itself. However, these software products have supported PowerPoint in the past and are likely to offer compatible versions in the near future. Check for availability.

AddImpact!

Gold Disk, 1-800 465-3375

This product adds a new toolbar to PowerPoint that makes it easier to add voice, animation, and sound effects.

Animation Works

Gold Disk, 1-800 465-3375

Build your own animations for use in PowerPoint presentations by using this set of tools from Gold Disk.

PointPlus Maker

Net-Scene, **http://www.net-scene.com**

PointPlus Maker allows you to view PowerPoint presentations embedded in HTML pages. Using this software, you can publish PowerPoint presentations as Web-compressed files.

WalkThrough

Virtus Corporation, 1-800 847-8871

WalkThrough is a 3-D drawing program you can use to build animations for use in PowerPoint presentations. l

Glossary

16-bit   In Windows, refers to the way memory is accessed. 16-bit applications access memory in 16-bit "chunks" (2 bytes). Most pre-Windows 95 applications are 16-bit.

32-bit   In Windows, refers to the way memory is accessed. 32-bit applications access memory in 32-bit "chunks" (4 bytes). Large portions of Windows 95 and many of its new applications are 32-bit applications, and may run faster because it has become more efficient to access chunks of memory.

A

accelerator key   A keyboard shortcut for a command. For example, Shift+Delete is an accelerator command for the Edit, Cut command.

action buttons   Predrawn button icons that can be placed on a PowerPoint slide and associated with an animation effect.

activate   To bring a window to the front and make it active.

active printer   The printer that will be used by programs.

active window   The window that is currently being used. Active windows show the "active window color" in their title bar (settable through the Control Panel). Other windows are inactive. To activate an inactive window, you must click somewhere in the inactive window or use the taskbar to select the window (see *taskbar*). On the taskbar, the active window looks like a pressed button; inactive windows are represented by unpressed buttons.

add-ins   Supplemental programs that can be loaded and used to add commands and features to a program such as PowerPoint.

address book   A list of persons, phone numbers, and other information used by various Windows 95 programs, including Microsoft Office and its various programs.

Adobe Type Manager (ATM)   An Adobe program that enables you to work with PostScript fonts in Windows 95.

airbrush   In "paint" and graphics programs, a tool that "sprays" dots in a randomized pattern around the point indicated by the user. In most programs, the output of the airbrush can be configured to modify the color, pattern, and density of the dot pattern.

alert message   A critical warning, confirmational, or informational message appearing in a dialog box.

alignment   The spatial arrangement of text or objects on your screen; elements can be aligned along the left edge of a slide, the right edge, or centered between the two.

animation   A set of images, pictures, or drawings displayed in sequence to imply movement. Computer animation files can be inserted in programs such as PowerPoint and run by the speaker or viewer.

annotate   To add notes. For example, you can add your own notes to Windows Help.

ANSI   A standard for ordering characters within a font.

anti-aliasing   A graphics technique used to hide the diagonal edges and sharp color changes (*jaggies*) in a graphic or font. Because a computer screen possesses limited resolution, such changes highlight the pixels on the screen and don't look smooth. Using anti-aliasing smoothes out the changes and makes them appear more attractive.

Anti Virus   A program included with Windows 95 that helps eradicate viruses (see *virus*) from your hard drive or floppy disks.

API   See *Application Programming Interface*.

applet   A small application unable to run by itself. When you purchase PowerPoint or another application, it may come with additional applets. For example, PowerPoint comes with applets for manipulating fonts (WordArt), drawing graphs (Microsoft Graph), and creating graphics (Microsoft Draw).

application   A computer program.

Application Programming Interface (API)   A set of interface functions available for applications.

ASCII characters   A subset of the ANSI character standard.

ASCII file   A file consisting of alphanumeric characters only. Although virtually every file can be converted to an ASCII file, all formatting (for example, bold, italic, underline, font size, and so on) will be lost in the ASCII file.

associate   Linking a document with the program that created it so that both can be opened with a single command. For example, double-clicking a Word table embedded in a PowerPoint slide opens Word for Windows and loads the selected document.

AT command set   A set of commands originally developed by Hayes for modems. Its name originates from the fact that each command starts with "AT" (attention). Today, most modems support the AT command set, enabling Microsoft to supply the Unimodem driver with Windows 95.

ATM   Asynchronous Transfer Mode: a high-speed, but expensive, networking solution. ATM networks reach speeds of 155M/s.

attribute   A property or characteristic.

auto arrange (Explorer)   In Explorer, organizes the visible icons into a regular grid pattern.

AutoClipArt   A feature that scans a PowerPoint presentation; by matching keywords with the presentation content, AutoClipArt suggests clip art images that might be appropriate to add to the slides.

AutoContent Wizard   A PowerPoint wizard that steps you through the creation of a new presentation.

AutoLayout   In PowerPoint, applied to each slide in a presentation displaying various types of placeholders used for entering slide content. Placeholders include title, bulleted lists, clip art, charts, organization charts, and multimedia clips.

AutoShape   A menu on the PowerPoint Drawing toolbar that contains a variety of common shapes (also called *AutoShapes*) which can be drawn automatically by clicking and dragging the cursor across a slide.

B

background   The colors, patterns, and gradients that fill the interior of objects or the PowerPoint slide area itself.

background operation   A job performed by a program when another program is in the active window. For example, printing or creating a backup can be performed by Windows 95 as a background operation.

Backup   A program that comes with Windows 95 and enables the user to back up the files from a hard disk to a floppy disk, tape drive, or another computer on a network.

backup set   The set of duplicate files and folders created by a backup program (see *Backup*). This set is stored on tapes, disks, or other storage media that can be removed and stored safely away from your computer. See *full system backup*.

batch program   A text file that instructs Window 95 to perform one or more tasks sequentially. Used for automating the loading or execution of programs. Batch files have a BAT or CMD extension.

Bézier curve   A mathematically constructed curve, such as the one used in drawing programs.

bidirectional printer port   Bidirectional Printer Communications sends print files to your printer and listens for a response. Windows quickly identifies a printer that is unable to accept a print file.

binary file transfer   A data transfer in which files aren't converted. Typically used with a modem to send programs or complex documents from computer to computer.

binary transfer protocol   When using a communications program to transmit binary files, it is very important to ensure that errors are not introduced into the data stream. Various binary transfer protocols check for matches between the data transmitted and the data received. The most common protocols are Xmodem, Ymodem, and Zmodem.

bitmap   A screen page in memory. Most bitmaps represent some sort of viewable graphics. You can use a "paint" program to edit graphic bitmaps and make modifications to them. However, although objects such as rectangles and circles may appear in a graphic bitmap, these objects cannot be edited as objects. You must modify these objects one bit at a time using the paint tools in the program.

bits per second (bps)   A measurement of data transmission speed, usually over a serial data link. Roughly equivalent to baud rate. A single character requires approximately 10 bits, so a transfer rate of 9,600 baud results in about 960 characters per second (cps) being transferred. This speed, however, varies depending on the make of your modem.

black and white   A setting for displaying or printing PowerPoint presentations where only black and white, and no shades of gray, are represented.

browse   To search through or examine a directory tree of files, directories, disks, workstations, workgroups, or domains. Often done via a Browse button in a dialog box.

bullet   A text symbol, often a small solid circle, used to set off the items on a list with no sequential order.

Bulletin Board System (BBS)   An electronic service that can be accessed via a modem. A BBS typically includes collections of files, notes from other computer users, and many other services. Examples of commercial BBSes include CompuServe, Prodigy, Delphi, GEnie, and America Online (AOL). Information about Windows 95 and Windows 95 applications can be found on all these BBSes.

bus network   One of various network topologies. A bus network is one in which all of the computers on the network are connected to the main wire of the network.

**App
C**

C

Calculator   A program that comes with Windows 95 and enables you to perform standard or scientific calculations.

callout   A text label placed relative to a drawing or other object to draw the reader's attention to a specific point or element.

Cardfile   A program that comes with Windows 95 and enables you to record information cards and sort through them by using their index lines.

cascade (Windows)   To arrange all the windows so that they are neatly stacked; only their title bars show behind the active window.

cascading menu   A submenu that appears (usually to the left or right of the main menu item) when a menu selection is made.

CD-ROM drive   Uses discs (not "disks") as the storage media. These discs look much like audio CDs, but can store about 600M of data on a single disc. They can only be read by a normal CD-ROM drive (hence the Read-Only Memory portion of the device's name), and take special equipment to create (write) them. CD-ROM drives are rated in multiples of the original (1x) drives that transfer data at the same rate as audio CD players (150K/s). Today, 1x drives no longer exist, and 2x drives (300-330K/s) are cheap. 3x (450K/s), 4x (600K/s) and even 6x (900K/s) drives are available. 4x drives fulfill basic requirements needed to achieve decent performance when playing animations from a CD-ROM.

CD Audio Track   A portion of a CD which can be associated with a PowerPoint presentation and played back continuously as slides display.

CD Player   A program packaged with Windows 95. CD Player lets you play audio CDs from your CD drive in the background while you are working in another application. It offers many of the controls found in stand-alone audio CD players. As a result, it looks and operates in a similar fashion. In addition, it allows you to edit your playlist. Thus, the tracks play in the order you want.

character-based   Usually used when referring to non-Windows applications. Character-based applications display information using the ASCII character set, or characters normally found on the keyboard. Also known as *text-based*.

character formatting   In word processing, this refers to formatting that is applied to individual characters. This type of formatting includes font, effects, size, and color.

chat room   A place on The Microsoft Network where you can have a live conversation with other MSN members. They see your comments immediately.

check box   A square dialog box item that takes an off or on value. Clicking in a check box adds or removes an X in the box, indicating whether the setting is on (checked) or off (unchecked).

choose   A term used in many instructions in this book. Usually means opening a menu and clicking a command. Also can refer to dialog box items, such as "Choose Basic Shapes from the drop-down list."

clear   Typically refers to turning off the X in an option or check box.

click   Quickly pressing and releasing the mouse button. Also, PowerPoint placeholders use a click to add function or contents to a presentation.

client As opposed to *server*, a workstation that connects to another computer's resources. A client also can include the server, and doesn't necessarily have to be another workstation. Basically, a client is just another application or workstation that uses resources from another process.

client application In OLE context, a program that uses an object (such as a graphic) supplied by another application (the *server* application).

client/server networking As opposed to *peer-to-peer* networking, an arrangement in which central computers called *servers* supply data and peripherals for use by *client* computers (workstations). Typically, a server contains a large, hard disk that supplies not only data, but also programs. It even executes programs. A server might also supply printers and modems for clients to use on the network. In other words, client/server refers to an architecture for distributed processing wherein subtasks can be distributed between services, CPUs, or even networked computers for more efficient execution.

App

C

clip art A collection of images you can use in your documents. Clip art is often distributed on CD-ROM in large collections (thousands of clip art pieces) organized into categories. Various clip art formats are sold, and the most popular are CGM, WMF, BMP, and GIF format files. PowerPoint comes with a set of clip art contained in the Clip Gallery 3.0.

Clipboard A temporary storage area in all versions of Windows used for storing various types of data (for example, text, graphics, sound, and video). The Clipboard can hold one piece of information at a time for use in a program or to pass information between programs.

Clipboard Viewer A Windows 95 program enabling you to store and save more than the single item that the Clipboard can hold.

clock An area at the far right edge of the taskbar that displays the time (and date if you leave the mouse pointer over the time). You can configure the taskbar to show or hide the clock.

close button A button in the upper-right corner of a window with an X in it. When clicked, it closes the program running in the current window.

Collapse A function of PowerPoint's Outline view that allows you to temporarily hide all text except for slide titles. See *Expand*.

collapse folders To hide additional directory (folder) levels below the selected directory (folder) levels. In Explorer, you can collapse the view of a folder to hide the folders stored within by double-clicking the folder in the left pane (tree view) of Explorer. When a folder contains no additional folders, a minus sign (–) appears next to the folder.

color palette   A display consisting of various color blocks; you can select a color fill to add to an object or slide from a color palette.

color pattern   A color selection made up of two other colors.

color rendering intent   Provides the best ICM settings for three of the major uses of color printing—for example, presentations, photographs, and true color screen display printing.

color scheme   A selection of colors that PowerPoint uses for screen display of applications, dialog boxes, and so forth. The color scheme is set from the template on which a presentation is based.

COM   Refers to the serial port, usually to attach a mouse or a modem to the computer. Most computers have two serial ports, labeled COM1 and COM2. The serial port transmits data in a single-bit stream. This serial transmission of bits gives the port its name.

command   Usually an option from an application's menus. Also refers to commands typed in from a command-prompt session or from the Run dialog box from the Start menu. In essence, it's a way of telling an application or Windows 95 to perform a major chore, such as running an application or utility program.

command button   A dialog box item that causes an action when clicked.

comment   While viewing a PowerPoint presentation, notes objects called *comments* can be added directly to slides and are contained in *comment* boxes.

complex document   See *compound document*.

component   A portion of a program. When installing PowerPoint, you have the option of installing (or not) various components. For example, you might choose to not install certain graphic translators. Later, you can go back and add/remove components using the original install disks or CD-ROM.

compound document   A document (created using OLE) that includes multiple types of data. For example, a PowerPoint document that includes a Paint picture and a WordArt object is a compound document.

conference   A PowerPoint presentation with several users connected over a network or online service such as the Internet. See also *presentation conference*.

connection (HyperTerminal)   In HyperTerminal, a connection sets and saves all the configuration parameters for one party you want to contact.

connection (network) A communication session established between a server and a workstation.

connector A category of AutoShape object used to connect two or more objects. Connectors typically have arrowheads at one or both ends to indicate flow or direction.

container object An object that contains another object or several objects. For example, a PowerPoint presentation might be the container object that holds the Excel object. See also *compound document*.

control menu A menu that exists in every window and enables you to modify its parameters or take global actions, such as closing or moving the window.

Control Panel A program that comes with Windows 95 that enables you to make settings for many Windows 95 actions, such as changing network, keyboard, printer, and regional settings. Some programs (including many video card drivers) may add sections to the control panel for you to use to configure that program.

conventional memory Memory located in the first 640K.

cross-linked file A disk error (which can be found using ScanDisk) in which at least two files are linked to data in the same cluster.

current directory The directory that activates if you log onto the drive at the command prompt by typing the drive letter and pressing Enter. When you switch drives, the operating system remembers the directory that was current when you switched away. It will still be the active/current directory when you switch back; it becomes the default directory. Applications will store or look for files on that drive if they're not specifically told which directory to use. This concept also works in Explorer—when you switch back to a drive, the last active directory (or folder) is still the active one.

current window The window that you are using. It appears in front of all other open windows. See also *active window*.

cursor The representation of the mouse on-screen. It may take many different shapes.

Custom Animation A feature in PowerPoint that allows you to set special effects and the sequence of slides in an on-screen presentation.

Custom Shows A feature in PowerPoint that allows you to save different subsets of slides in a presentation to create different versions of the show from the same set of slides.

App

C

D

dash style   A line style using broken segments in various patterns.

data bits   The number of bits used to transmit a piece of information, usually 7 or 8.

database   A file or group of related files that are designed to hold recurring data types as if the files were lists.

DCI   Drive Control Interface; a display driver interface that allows fast, direct access to the video frame buffer in Windows. Also, it allows games and video to take advantage of special hardware support in video devices, which improves the performance and quality of video.

DDE   See *Dynamic Data Exchange*.

DEC printer utility   Adds features to the standard Windows 95 print window and updated printer drivers. The utility includes a very detailed help file for configuring both local and network printers. Additionally, it creates an enhanced set of property menus for configuring DEC printers.

default button   The command button in a dialog box that activates when you press the Enter key. This button is indicated by a dark border.

default printer   The printer, which is established using the Printer settings, to which documents will be sent if the user doesn't specify another printer.

deferred printing   Enables people with laptop computers to print even though their laptops are not in docking stations. Once connected in a docking station, it will automatically print. Also refers to computers whose only printer access is to a network printer, and the computer is temporarily disconnected from the network. When the network connection is reestablished, the print job starts.

density   A brightness control that lightens or darkens a printout to more closely reflect its screen appearance and to compensate for deficiencies in toner or paper quality.

design   The visual elements of a slide. When changing presentation templates in PowerPoint, the Apply Design command is used. A template contains various design elements for slides such as graphic objects and a color scheme.

desktop   The screen area on which the windows are displayed.

desktop pattern   A bitmap decorating your desktop. You can select one of Windows 95's patterns or create one of your own.

destination document   The document into which a linked or embedded document is placed.

device driver   A program that provides the operating system with the information it needs to work with a specific device, such as a printer.

Dial-up Networking   Dialing into a network from a remote site by using a modem.

dialog box   An on-screen message box that conveys or requests information from the user.

distribute   To arrange elements on a slide relative to each other horizontally (from left to right) or vertically (top to bottom).

dither pattern   A pattern of dots used to simulate an unavailable color or grayscale in a printout or graphic. Most frequently used when specifying a printout of a color graphic on a monochrome printer or simulating more colors in a graphic than are available in the current graphics mode.

docking station   For a portable computer, an external device that provides additional resources such as speakers, CD-ROM, keyboard, empty card slots, and so on. A docking station is typically plugged into a portable computer using the port replicator connection.

document   A file created using an application. For example, you might create a text document using a word processing application (such as WordPad) or a presentation document using a graphic application (such as PowerPoint).

document formatting   In word processing, refers to formatting that is applied to a whole document. Document formatting includes margins, headers and footers, and paper size.

document window   The window in which a document appears.

DOS   A term used to refer to any variation of the Disk Operating System (for example, MS-DOS and PC-DOS).

double buffering   The process of displaying the screen currently in the frame buffer while painting the next screen in another portion of RAM. Then the new screen is quickly copied to the frame buffer. This makes video playback and animation appear much smoother.

App
C

double-click   To press the mouse button twice in rapid succession while keeping the mouse pointer motionless between clicks.

download   Retrieving a file from a remote computer or BBS (see *upload*).

drag   To move an object on the screen from one place to another by clicking it with the mouse, holding the mouse button down, and pulling it to where you want it to be.

drag and drop   A particular action you can make with the mouse. Click an object such as a folder, then hold down the mouse button as you drag the object to a new location. You drop the object by releasing the mouse button.

drop-down list   A dialog box item showing only one entry until its drop-down arrow is clicked.

Dynamic Data Exchange (DDE)   A feature of Windows 95 that allows programs to communicate and actively pass information and commands.

E

editable fax   A file transfer between computers, with the additional option of a cover page. Once received, the editable fax can be edited in the application that created it—or another application capable of reading that file type. For example, if you send a document created in Microsoft PowerPoint for Windows, the recipient can open it in PowerPoint, PowerPoint Viewer, or Lotus Freelance, using import filters if necessary.

ellipsis   Three dots (…). An ellipsis after a menu item or button text indicates that selecting the menu or clicking the button will display an additional dialog box or window from which you can choose options or enter data.

e-mail   Electronic mail; a message file that can be sent electronically through a phone line using a modem and either a network or online service, such as the Internet.

embedded object   Data stored in a document that originated from another application. Differing from a linked object, this type of object doesn't have its own file on the disk. However, it runs its source application for editing when you double-click it. For example, a Word table embedded in a PowerPoint presentation.

embossed   A shadow effect that can be applied to text to make the letters appear raised from the background.

Encapsulated PostScript (EPS) file   A file format for storing PostScript-style images that allow a PostScript printer or program capable of importing such files to print a file in the highest resolution equipped by the printer.

engraved   A shadow effect that can be applied to text to make it appear to be carved into the background.

Enhanced Meta File (EMF)   The process of converting generic spooling print instructions to the instruction set "understood" best by a particular printer. This conversion has the capability to create faster printouts of better quality.

escape codes   A set of codes that appear in a text string on a terminal. Although these escape codes (which provide formatting information) aren't visible in terminal emulation, they will show up as non-text characters if you capture the text to the screen or printer. In fact, some escape codes may cause the printed output to skip pages, switch into bold mode, and other undesirable effects because the codes may conflict with printer command codes.

exit   When you are finished running Windows applications and Windows, you must not turn off the computer until you correctly exit Windows. Windows stores some data in memory and does not write it to your hard disk until you choose the Exit command. If you turn off the computer without correctly exiting, this data may be lost.

Expand   A function in Outline view of PowerPoint that allows you to open up all the lines of an outline to display all the detail points. See *Collapse*.

expand folders   Views the structure of folders that are stored inside other folders. In Explorer, you can expand the view of a folder that has a plus sign (+) next to it to see the folders stored within by double-clicking the folder in the left pane (tree view) of Explorer. When a folder does not contain any additional folders, a minus sign (–) appears next to the folder.

expanded memory   Memory that conforms to the LIM 4.0 standard for memory access. Windows 95 has the capability of converting extended memory (see *extended memory*) to expanded memory (using Emm386.exe) for programs that require it. However, most modern programs no longer use expanded memory.

Explorer   A program in Windows 95 that helps you view and manage your files.

export   To send a copy of a file from one program to another program. You can export a PowerPoint outline to Microsoft Word, for example.

extended memory   Memory that can be accessed by Windows 95 beyond the first megabyte of memory in your system.

F

file allocation table (FAT)   The native DOS file system that uses a table, called the file allocation table, to store information about the sizes, locations, and properties of files stored on the disk.

file converter   Takes the file format and transforms it to a format that the application can read. During a file conversion, text enhancements, font selections, and other elements are usually preserved. Sometimes, however, these elements are converted to a similar format, and then converted to ASCII format.

file name   The name that a file system or operating system gives to a file when it's stored on disk. File names in Windows 95's file system can be 256 characters long. Additionally, Windows 95 assigns a file name compatible with older DOS (eight characters with a three-character extension) naming conventions.

file name extension   The three-character extension that you can add to a file name—either the standard eight characters of DOS and Windows 3.1, or the long file names of Windows 95. The file name extension is only visible in Explorer if you enable the appropriate option. Otherwise, the extension is hidden. Nevertheless, the extension is still part of the file name, even when you can't see it—it is this extension that Windows 95 (as well as earlier Windows) uses to associate a document with the application that created it.

file utility   A program that can directly manipulate the information available on the disk that defines where files are found, sized, and other attributes. It is important to not use file utilities that were designed for earlier versions of Windows, as Windows 95 stores some file information in different places—and earlier file utilities could scramble the file information, destroying the file.

fixed-space font   Fonts that have a fixed amount of space between the characters in the font.

folder   Represents directories on your drives. Folders can contain files, programs, and even other folders.

folder window   A window in Explorer that displays the contents of a folder.

font   A description of how to display a set of characters. The description includes the shape of the characters, spacing between characters, effects (for example, bold, italic, and underline), and the size of the characters.

foreground operation   The program in the active window.

format   To apply certain characteristics to text or an object, such as size or color.

forum   On The Microsoft Network, a folder with a collection of related documents and subfolders.

frame   Using a drawn object such as a square as a border around another object on a slide.

freeform   A drawing style and drawing object type that provides no preset definition to the object. Freeform drawing is similar to drawing on paper with a pencil and no ruler or guides to direct the line.

free rotate   A PowerPoint function that allows you to turn an object in any direction, 360 degrees.

full system backup   A backup set (see *backup set*) that contains all the files on your hard drive, including Windows 95 system files, the Registry, and all other files necessary to completely restore your system configuration on a new hard drive.

App

C

G

GIF   The Graphics Interchange Format (a graphics file format).

Genigraphics   A slide service bureau for which PowerPoint provides a built-in preparation wizard.

gradient   A subtle shading from lighter to darker in a background of one or two colors giving the effect of a light source from the selected direction.

graphic   A visual element which can be added to a slide, such as a line drawing, shape, or picture.

graphic format   The protocol used to save a graphic file, such as EMF, GIF, or EPS.

grid   A background pattern that defines regular intervals — for example, a 1/4-inch grid displays dots in the background every quarter inch in a rectangular pattern. Many graphics programs make a grid available. Even when turned on, a grid won't print. When you "snap to grid," your graphic endpoints are constrained to fall on a grid point.

group   To associate two or more objects so that any action—formatting, moving, copying or resizing, for example—is applied to all the objects as if they were one object.

guide   A set of two movable, intersecting lines that can be displayed on PowerPoint slides to enable you to place objects precisely.

H

handouts   Printed output of PowerPoint presentations containing miniature versions of two, three, or six slides. Audience handouts are intended to be distributed to presentation viewers to help them follow a presentation.

header information   Data sent to a printer to define aspects of the printout and prepare the printer prior to printing. PostScript documents include header information.

Help   A program that gives you information about how to run Windows 95 and its programs, including how to use the Help program.

hidden file   A characteristic of a file that indicates that the file is not visible in Explorer under normal circumstances. However, by selecting the View option to view all files, hidden files will still be visible.

hidden object   Slide or element on slide that temporarily doesn't appear on-screen and is not included in printed output of a PowerPoint presentation.

hierarchical   A way of displaying text or graphics in a structure. In a hierarchical structure, items closer to the top of the structure are considered *parents* of items connected to them, but which are lower down in the structure. The tree structure of PowerPoint's Outline view is an example of a hierarchical structure.

home page   A document on the World Wide Web dedicated to a particular subject. From a home page, you can use hyperlinks to jump to other home pages to gain more information.

HP JetAdmin   A tool that can be used to install and configure networked Hewlett-Packard printers using the HP JetDirect network interface. The HP JetAdmin utility appears as a substitute for the Windows standard Printer window. This utility can also be used to interface printers connected to a NetWare LAN.

HTTP   Hypertext Transport Protocol; used to designate a site on the World Wide Web. PowerPoint presentations can be opened at HTTP sites.

hue   The numerical representation of the colors of a color wheel. It is almost always seen with saturation and brightness.

hyperlink   A link in a document that, when activated (often by clicking it), links—or jumps to—another document or graphic.

HyperTerminal   A program included with Windows 95 that enables you to easily connect to a remote computer, a bulletin board, or an online service. It replaces Terminal from Windows 3.1.

Hypertext Markup Language (HTML) A hypertext language used to create the hypertext documents that make up the World Wide Web.

I

I-beam The shape the cursor takes in the area of a window where text can be entered.

icon A small graphic symbol used to represent a folder, program, shortcut, resource, or document.

Image Color Matching (ICM) A technology developed by Kodak that creates an image environment that treats color from the screen to the printed page. Microsoft licensed ICM from Kodak to be able to repeatedly and consistently reproduce color matched images from source to destination.

import An OLE term. In Object Packager, you can import a file into a package and later embed it into a destination document.

inactive An open window that is not currently in use. On the taskbar, the active window looks like a pressed button; inactive windows are represented by unpressed buttons.

Inbox Holds incoming and outgoing messages and faxes that are sent or received over Microsoft Outlook.

indent In the PowerPoint outline structure, to demote or make a line of text subservient to another line.

Industry Standard Architecture (ISA) The design of the 8/16-bit AT bus (sometimes called the *classic bus*) developed by IBM in the original IBM PC.

in-place editing A feature of OLE 2. With in-place editing, you may edit an embedded or linked object without that object being placed into an additional window (the way it was in OLE 1.0). Instead of creating an additional window, the tools for the object you want to edit appear in the toolbar for the container object (see *container object*). Also, the menus for the object you want to edit replace the menus of the container object. In-place editing is less disruptive; it is much simpler to ensure that the changes you make to an embedded or linked object are updated to the original complex document.

insertion point A flashing, vertical line showing where text will be inserted.

Integrated Services Digital Network (ISDN) A special phone line that supports modem speeds up to 64Kbps. However, these phone lines can be quite expensive to acquire. Many ISDN adapters support two-channel access.

App
C

IntelliMouse   A Microsoft pointing device.

interactive   A PowerPoint or other multimedia presentation is interactive when the viewer is able to make selections as to how the presentation runs or what is displayed, in effect interacting with the presentation itself.

interface   The visible layer enabling a user to communicate with a computer. In DOS, the interface consists largely of typed commands and character-based feedback. Windows 95 is an entirely graphical interface, using a mouse, menus, windows, and icons to allow the user to communicate his or her instructions and requirements to the computer.

interframe compression   A technique that achieves compression of a video file by eliminating redundant data between successive compressed frames.

Internet   A "network of networks;" a global linkage of millions of computers, containing vast amounts of information, much of it available for free to anyone with a modem and the right software. The Internet is an aggregation of high-speed networks, supported by the NSF (National Science Foundation) and almost 6,000 federal, state, and local systems, as well as university and commercial networks. There are links to networks in Canada, South America, Europe, Australia, and Asia, and more than 30 million users.

Internet Assistant   A programmed series of steps a PowerPoint user can invoke to create a folder of presentation files to be moved to an Internet server.

Internet Explorer   A Web browser bundled with the Windows 95 Plus! kit. It takes advantage of features in Windows 95, such as shortcuts and long file names.

Internet Protocol (IP)   A network protocol that provides routing services across multiple LANs and WANs that is used in the TCP/IP protocol stack. IP packet format is used to address packets of data from ultimate source and destination nodes (host) located on any LAN or WAN networked with TCP/IP protocol. IP provides routing services in conjunction with IP routers, which are incorporated into many computer systems and most versions of UNIX. IP Packet format is supported in NetWare 3.11 and 4.0 operating systems, and is used throughout the Department of Defense Internet—a network of thousands of computers internetworked worldwide.

interoperability   Compatibility, or the capability for equipment to work together. Industry standards are agreed upon or used by vendors to make their equipment work with other vendors' equipment.

interrupt request line (IRQ)   A line (conductor) on the internal bus of the computer (typically on the motherboard) over which a device such as a port, disk controller, or modem can get the attention of the CPU to process some data.

intraframe compression A technique that compresses the video by removing redundancy from individual video images.

I/O address Input/Output address. Many I/O devices, such as COM ports, network cards, printer ports, and modem cards, are mapped to an I/O address. This address allows the computer and operating system to locate the device, and thus send and receive data. Such I/O addresses don't tie up system memory RAM space. However, there are a limited number of I/O addresses. You can access an I/O port in one of two ways: Either map it into the 64K I/O address space, or map it as a memory-mapped device in the system's RAM space.

IPX Internetwork Packet Exchange; a network protocol developed by Novell to address packets of data from ultimate source and destination nodes located on any LAN networked with NetWare. IPX also provides routing services in conjunction NetWare and third-party routers. An IPX packet has information fields that identify the network address, node address, and socket address of both the source and destination, and provides the same functionality of the OSI Network layer in the OSI model.

App
C

J

Journal A Microsoft Outlook feature that tracks documents created in Office programs, such as PowerPoint.

JPEG Joint Photographic Experts Group graphics file format.

K

keyboard buffer Memory set aside to store keystrokes as they're entered from the keyboard. Once it's stored, the keystroke data waits for the CPU to pick up the data and respond accordingly.

keyboard equivalent See *keyboard shortcut*.

keyboard shortcut A combination of keystrokes that initiates a menu command without dropping the menu down, or activates a button in a dialog box without clicking the button.

kiosk A booth or display area where an on-screen computer presentation may be set up for use by those visiting the area. An example of a kiosk would be an information counter in a shopping mall or booth at a trade show.

L

landscape   The orientation of a print page of output with the longer side of the page running across the top of the document.

layering   In PowerPoint, the process of placing objects one on top of another on your slide to give the appearance of a stack of objects. Objects can be brought forward to appear to be placed at the top of the stack, or sent back to any of the layers behind the first object.

layout   In PowerPoint, layouts (also called AutoLayouts) are applied to each slide in a presentation displaying various types of placeholders used for entering slide content. Placeholders include title, bulleted lists, clip art, charts, organization charts, and multimedia clips.

license   Refers to the agreement you are assumed to have acceded to when you purchased Windows 95. As with much other computer software, you don't own your copy of Windows 95, but instead just license the use of it. As such, there is a long list of legalese-type things you supposedly agree to when you open the envelope containing your copy of PowerPoint. These legal agreements are part of the license.

line style   A choice of predesigned formatting effects that can be applied to selected line objects.

linked object   In OLE terminology, data stored in a document that originated from another application. Unlike an embedded object, this type of object has its own file on the disk. The source application is run for editing when you double-click it—for example, a Paint drawing linked to a PowerPoint presentation. Linking saves space over embedding when a particular object must be included in more than one other document, because the data does not have to be stored multiple times. Additionally, you can directly edit a linked file, and all the documents that link to the file update automatically.

list box   A dialog box item that shows all available options.

local area network (LAN)   A limited-distance, multipoint physical connectivity medium consisting of network interface cards, media, and repeating devices designed to transport frames of data between host computers at high speeds with low error rates. A LAN is a subsystem that is part of a network.

local printer   A printer connected directly to your computer.

local reboot   The ability of Windows 95 to close down a single misbehaving application. When you use the Alt+Ctrl+Delete key sequence, Windows 95 queries you for the application to shut down. In this way, you can close down only the application you want, without affecting other running applications.

logical drive   A drive that isn't a physical drive, as in the floppy drive A or B. Instead, a logical drive is a drive created on a subpartition of an extended partition and given an arbitrary letter such as C, D, or E.

long file name   A reference to Windows 95's ability to use file names up to 256 characters long.

looping   To set up a PowerPoint presentation to repeat until stopped. Looped presentations are useful when a speaker is not present, such as at a trade show booth.

LPT   The parallel port used for printing. Most computers have a single parallel port (labeled LPT1), but some may have two. The parallel port transmits data one byte (8 bits) at a time. This parallel transmission of all 8 bits gives the port its name.

luminosity   When working with colors, indicates the brightness of the color.

M

macro   A sequence of keyboard strokes and mouse actions that can be recorded so that their playback can be activated by a single keystroke, keystroke combination, or mouse click. Unlike Windows 3.1 and Windows for Workgroups, Windows 95 does not come with a macro recorder. In PowerPoint, macros can be attached to toolbar buttons.

mailing list (Internet)   An e-mail discussion group focused on one or more topics. The mailing list is made up of members who subscribe to that mailing list.

manual timing   Determining the timing of slide transitions with the click of a mouse or keystroke, rather than assigning preset time increments.

master   A feature in PowerPoint that contains certain formatting settings. Additional formatting or objects placed in these views automatically appear in every corresponding location. There are four types of masters in PowerPoint: Title, Slide, Handout, and Notes.

maximize button   A button in the upper-right corner of a window with a square in it. When clicked, it enlarges the window to its maximum size. When the window is already at its maximum size, the maximize button switches to the restore button, which returns the window to its previous size.

App C

media control interface (MCI) A standard interface for all multimedia devices, devised by the MPC counsel, that allows multimedia applications to control any number of MPC-compliant devices, from sound cards to MIDI-based lighting controllers.

Meeting Minder A PowerPoint feature used to coordinate the running of a presentation conference and take meeting minutes.

Meeting Minutes The feature in PowerPoint which allows you to keep a record of discussion topics which come up during the presentation and record action items.

menu A list of available command options.

menu bar Located under the title bar, displays the names of all available menu lists.

menu command A word or phrase in a menu that, when selected, enables you to view all the commands.

metafile A Windows graphics file format.

microprocessor A miniaturized processor. Previous processors were built in integrated circuit boards with many large components. Most processors today use high-tech, silicon-based technology that improves performance, reduces heat generation, and increases efficiency.

Microsoft Client for NetWare Networks Allows users to connect to new or existing NetWare servers. It permits you to browse and queue print jobs using either the Windows 95 network user interface or existing Novell NetWare utilities. The Microsoft Client for NetWare interfaces equally well with both NetWare 3.x and 4.x servers.

Microsoft Fax A program included with Windows 95 that enables you to send and receive faxes directly within Powerpoint.

Microsoft Network, The (MSN) An online service run by Microsoft. With The Microsoft Network, you can exchange messages with people around the world; read the latest news, sports, weather, and financial information; find answers to your technical questions; download from thousands of useful programs; and connect to the Internet.

Microsoft on the Web A feature of the PowerPoint Help system that allows you to access Microsoft's home page, Web tutorial, product news, and technical support from the Help menu.

MIDI   Musical Instrument Digital Interface; originally a means of connecting electronic instruments (synthesizers) and letting them communicate with one another. Computers then came into the MIDI landscape and were used to control the synthesizers. PowerPoint can play MIDI files.

minimize button   The button in the upper-right corner of the window that has a line in it. When clicked, it reduces the window to display the taskbar only.

mirror image   An exact duplication of an object, flipped 180 degrees.

mission-critical application   An application program considered indispensable to the operation of a business, government, or other operation. Often, these applications are transaction-based, such as for point-of-sale, reservations, or real-time stock, security, or money trading.

modem   A device, usually attached to a computer through a serial port or present as an internal card. A modem makes it possible to use ordinary phone lines to transfer computer data. In addition to a modem, a communications program is required. *Modem* is short for *modulator/demodulator*—the processes whereby a digital stream of data is converted to sound for transmission through a phone system originally designed only for sound (modulator) and the conversion of received sound signals back into digital data (demodulator).

motion JPEG   Developed by the Joint Photographic Experts Group, a compression/decompression scheme (codec) for video files. It is a variation on JPEG, this group's codec for compressing still pictures. It uses only intraframe lossy compression (see *intraframe compression*), but offers a tradeoff between compression ratio and quality.

mouse pointer   The symbol that displays where your next mouse click will occur. The mouse pointer symbol changes according to the context of the window or the dialog box in which it appears.

MPEG   Created by the Motion Picture Experts Group, a specification for compressing and decompressing animation or "movie" files, which are typically very large. Although extremely efficient at reducing the size of such a file, MPEG is also very processor-intensive.

MS-DOS-based application   An application that normally runs on a DOS machine and doesn't require Windows 95. Many MS-DOS-based applications will run in Windows 95's DOS box, but some will not.

App
C

multimedia   A combination of various types of media, including (but not necessarily limited to) sound, animation, and graphics. Due to the generally large size of "multimedia" files, a CD-ROM is usually necessary to store files. Of course, a sound card and speakers are also necessary.

multitasking   The capability of an operating system to handle multiple processing tasks, apparently, at the same time.

My Computer   An icon present on the Windows 95 desktop that enables you to view drives, folders, and files.

N

narration   A recorded verbal description that can be saved with a PowerPoint presentation and played back in sync with the slides as they are displayed.

NetWare   A trademarked brand name for the networking operating systems and other networking products developed and sold by Novell.

network   A group of computers connected by a communications link that enables any device to interact with any other on the network. The word *network* is derived from the term "network architecture," which describes an entire system of hosts, workstations, terminals, and other devices.

Network Interface card (NIC)   Also called a network adapter, an interface card placed in the bus of a computer (or other LAN device) to interface to a LAN. Each NIC represents a node, which is a source and destination for LAN frames, which in turn carry data between the NICs on the LAN.

non-Windows program   A program not designed to be used specifically in Windows. Most non-Windows applications or programs are character-based in nature (for example, DOS programs).

Note   Also called Notes Pages. This feature allows you to add comments to individual PowerPoint slides to assist a speaker in making a presentation. A comment with background information or reminders that can be added to each slide in a PowerPoint presentation to aid a speaker in making the presentation.

Notepad   A program that comes with Windows 95 and enables you to view and edit text files.

nudge   To move a drawing object on a slide by a very small, preset increment.

O

object   Any item that is or can be linked into another Windows application, such as a sound, graphics, piece of text, or portion of a spreadsheet. Must be from an application that supports object linking and embedding (OLE).

object linking and embedding   See *OLE*.

OEM fonts   Provided to support older installed products. The term OEM refers to Original Equipment Manufacturers. This font family includes a character set designed to be compatible with older equipment and software applications.

Office Art   A collection of media clips including clip art, animation, and sound, that comes with all Microsoft Office products.

Office Assistant   A Help system feature that allows you to enter questions about an Office product in a natural language format (such as by typing a simple English sentence, rather than a keyword).

offline   A device that is not ready to accept input. For example, if your printer is offline, it will not accept data from the computer, and attempting to print will generate an error.

offset shadows   A shadow effect that is set slightly apart from the object assumed to be casting the shadow. An offset shadow effect can seem to add depth to an object.

OLE   Object linking and embedding; a data-sharing scheme that allows dissimilar applications to create single, complex documents by cooperating in the creation of the document. The documents consist of material that a single application couldn't have created on its own. In OLE, version 1, double-clicking an embedded or linked object (see *embedded object* and *linked object*) launches the application that created the object in a separate window. In OLE version 2, double-clicking an embedded or linked object makes the menus and tools of the creating application available in the middle of the parent document. The destination document (contains the linked or embedded object) must be created by an application that is an OLE client, and the linked or embedded object must be created in an application that is an OLE server.

OLE Automation   Refers to the capability of a server application to make available (known as *exposing*) its own objects for use in another application's macro language.

online   Indicates that a system is working and connected. For example, if your printer is online, it is ready to accept information to turn into a printed output.

option button   A dialog box item that enables you to choose only one of a group of coices.

App
C

Organization chart   A chart object that can be placed in a PowerPoint presentation representing the hierarchical structure of an organization, such as a corporation.

orientation   For printer paper, indicates whether the document is to be printed normally (for example, in Portrait mode) or sideways (in Landscape moe).

Outline view   The view in PowerPoint where you can enter presentation content and reorganize it according to a standard outline hierarchy.

overlapping objects   Elements on a slide which appear to be stacked so that one is "behind" the other.

P

Pack and Go Wizard   A wizard used to prepare a PowerPoint file for presentation at a remote location.

Paint   A program that comes with Windows 95 and enables you to view and edit various formats of bitmaps.

palette   A collection of tools. For example, in PowerPoint, there is a color palette that displays the 48 colors available for use in creating a graphic.

pane   Some windows, such as the window for Explorer, show two or more distinct *areas* (Explorer's window shows two such areas). These areas are referred to as *panes*.

Panose   A Windows internal description that represents a font by assigning each font a PANOSE ID number. Windows uses several internal descriptions to categorize fonts. The PANOSE information registers a font class and determines similarity between fonts.

paragraph formatting   In a word processing program, formatting that can be applied to an entire paragraph, including alignment (left, center, right), indentation, and spacing before and after the paragraph.

parallel port   A port (usually used for printing) that transmits data 8 bits at a time. This parallel transmission of 8 bits at a time gives the port its name.

partition   A portion of a physical hard drive that behaves as a separate disk (logical drive), even though it isn't.

path   The location of a file in the directory tree.

pattern   An arrangement of lines or dots that can be used to fill the internal area of an object, such as a drawing.

PC Cards   Formerly called PCMCIA cards, small (usually only slightly larger than a credit card) cards that plug into special slots provided in notebook computers. PC Cards can provide functionality for additional memory, modems, sound, networking, hard drives, and so on. PC Cards normally identify themselves to the computer, making configuring them quite simple.

PCMCIA   The old name for PC Cards (see *PC Cards*).

pen   While showing a PowerPoint on-screen presentation, you can draw on the slides themselves with an electronic pen. Pen colors can be determined while setting up the presentation.

personal information store   Outlook's term for the file that contains the structure of folders that make up your Inbox, Outbox, sent files, deleted files, and any other personal folders you may choose to create.

Phone Dialer   A program that is included with Windows 95 that enables you to place telephone calls from your computer by using a modem or another Windows telephony device. You can store a list of phone numbers you use frequently, and dial the number quickly from your computer.

picon   Small, bitmapped images of the first frame of your video clip. They can be used to represent the in and out source of your video segments.

PICT   A Macintosh picture file format.

PIF   A file that provides Windows 95 with the information it needs to know in order to run a non-Windows program. Unlike earlier versions of Windows, there is no PIF editor in Windows 95. Instead, you set up a PIF file from the properties for the file. Access the file properties by right-clicking the file from My Computer.

placeholder   Part of a PowerPoint layout that provides a shortcut to entering presentation content by allowing the user to enter various types of information into a presentation with a one-click interface.

play list   In CD Player, a list of tracks from an audio CD that you want to play.

Plug and Play   An industry-wide specification supported by Windows 95 that makes it easy to install new hardware. Plug and Play enables the computer to correctly identify hardware components (including plug-in cards) and ensures that different cards don't conflict in their requirements for IRQs, I/O addresses, DMA channels, and memory addresses. In order to fully implement Plug and Play, you need an operating system that supports it (as stated, Windows 95 does), a BIOS that supports it (most computers manufactured since early 1995 do), and cards that identify themselves to the system (information from these cards is stored in the Windows Registry). If you have hardware, such as

App

C

modems that aren't Plug and Play (so-called *legacy hardware*), then Windows 95 will prompt you for the information necessary for setup, and store such information in the Registry.

point size   The unit used to measure the size of a font in increments of 1/72 of an inch.

pointer   The on-screen symbol controlled by the mouse. As you move the mouse on the desk, the pointer moves on-screen. The pointer changes shape to indicate the current status and the type of functions and selections available.

polygon   A multisided shape, in which each side is a straight line.

port   A connection or socket for connecting devices to a computer (see *I/O address*).

port replicator   On portable computers, a bus connection that makes all bus lines available externally. The port replicator can be used to plug in devices which, in a desktop computer, would be handled as cards. Port replicators are also the connection used to connect a portable computer to its docking station.

portrait   An output orientation that places the top of a document along the shorter side of the paper.

postproduction editing   The steps of adding special effects, animated overlays, and more to a "production" video.

PostScript   A special description language, invented by Adobe. This language is used to accurately describe fonts and graphics. Printers that can directly read this language and print the results are termed *PostScript printers*.

PowerPoint Animation Player   An add-in program that works with a Web browser to play animated PowerPoint presentations on the Internet.

PowerPoint Central   An online magazine with articles and advice on using PowerPoint. *PowerPoint Central* also contains links to the Office 97 ValuPack and various Internet sites for downloading additional media clips.

PowerPoint Viewer   A program that allows someone to view a PowerPoint presentation on a computer without having PowerPoint itself loaded.

presentation   A term for a set of PowerPoint slides. A PowerPoint presentation can be a stand-alone unit with recorded narration and interactive capabilities, or used in conjunction with a live speaker.

presentation conference   The ability to have several people at different locations view a PowerPoint presentation over a network or the Internet.

printer driver   A Windows 95 program that tells programs how to format data for a particular type of printer.

printer fonts   Fonts stored in the printer's ROM.

printer settings   A window that displays all the printers for which there are drivers present. You can select the default printer from the installed printers, as well as configure each printer using the shortcut menu and the Options dialog box.

printer window   For each installed printer, you can view the printer window. The printer window displays the status of each print job in the queue, and enables you to pause, restart, and delete the print job.

processor   The controlling device in a computer that interprets and executes instructions and performs computations, and otherwise controls the major functions of the computer. This book discusses Intel 80x86-series processors, which are miniaturized single-chip "microprocessors" containing thousands to millions of transistors in a silicon-based, multilayered, integrated circuit design.

program file   A program that runs an application directly (not via an association) when you click it.

program window   A window that contains a program and its documents.

promote   In PowerPoint outlines, to place a line of text at a higher level of detail in the outline hierarchy.

property sheet   A dialog box that displays (and sometimes enables you to change) the properties of an object in Windows 95. To access a property sheet, right-click the object to view the shortcut menu, and select Properties from the shortcut menu. Property sheets vary considerably between different objects.

proportional   To keep the relative relationships between the measurements of elements in an object. Objects can be resized proportionally, retaining their original relative proportions (a square stays a square), or disproportionally (a square becomes a rectangle).

proportional-spaced fonts   Adjust the intercharacter space based on the shape of the individual characters. An example of a proportional-spaced font is Arial. The width of a character is varied based on its shape. Adjusting intercharacter spacing is really a function of kerning, which is similar but not exactly the same. For instance, the letter A and the letter V are typically stored in each font as a kerning pair, which means they will be spaced differently when appearing next to each other. In a monospace font versus a proportional font, you will see a difference in the width of the letter i.

App
C

protocol   Rules of communication. In networks, several layers of protocols exist. Each layer of protocol only needs to physically hand off or receive data from the immediate layer above and beneath it, whereas virtual communications occur with the corresponding layer on another host computer.

Q

queue   Documents lined up and waiting to be printed, or commands lined up and waiting to be serviced. Use the Printer window to view the print queue for a printer.

Quick View   A program included with Windows 95 that enables you to view files stored in 30 different file formats without needing to open the application that created the file. Quick View is available from the File menu of Explorer if a viewer is available for the selected file type.

QuickTime   Developed by Apple, a compression and decompression (codec) scheme for animation files. It is unique in that versions are available for both Windows and Macintosh, enabling software designers to provide their data in a format compatible for both platforms.

R

RAM   Random Access Memory; physical memory chips located in the computer. Typically, Windows 95 machines have 16 million bytes (16M) of RAM or more. However, Windows 95 will run on machines with 8M of RAM.

raster font   A font in which characters are stored as pixels.

read-only   Characteristic of a file indicating that the file can be read from, but not written to, by an application. Note however, that a "read-only" file can be deleted in Explorer, although you will get a warning (beyond the normal "are you sure" you normally get when you try to delete a file) if the file is read-only.

Recycle Bin   An icon that appears on the Windows 95 desktop. To discard a file, you drag the file from Explorer, My Computer, or any other file handler to the Recycle Bin. This action hides the file—but doesn't actually erase it from the disk. You can "undelete" the file by dragging it from the Recycle Bin back to a folder. To actually delete the file, select the Recycle Bin menu selection to empty the Recycle Bin.

registering a program The act of linking a document with the program that created it so that both can be opened with a single command. For example, double-clicking a DOC file opens Word for Windows and loads the selected document.

Registry A database of configuration information central to Windows 95 operations. This file contains program settings, associations between file types and the applications that created them, as well as information about the types of OLE objects a program can create and hardware detail information.

Registry Editor Ships with Windows 95 and enables you to fine-tune Windows 95 performance by adjusting or adding settings to key system information. Because Windows 95 has placed WIN.INI and SYSTEM.INI file settings in the Registry, the ability to remotely edit these parameters is an extremely powerful tool. Warning: You can totally destroy a workstation using this tool!

rehearse To run through the slides of a PowerPoint presentation while recording the time that each slide remains on-screen.

resize button A button located in the lower-left corner of a non-maximized window. When the mouse pointer is over this button, it turns into a two-headed arrow. You can click and drag to resize the window horizontally and vertically.

restore button A button in the upper-right corner of a window that has two squares in it. When clicked, it returns the window to its previous size. When the window is at its previous size, the restore button switches to the maximize button, which returns the window to its maximum size.

restore files Copies one or more files from your backup set to the hard disk or to another floppy.

revision tracking A feature of Microsoft Office products used to keep a record of any changes made to a document.

rich text format (RTF) Compatible with several word processors and includes fonts, tabs, and character formatting.

ROM (Read-Only Memory) A type of chip capable of permanently storing data without the aid of an electric current source to maintain it, as in RAM. The data in ROM chips is sometimes called *firmware*. Without special equipment, it is not possible to alter the contents of read-only memory chips—thus the name. ROMs are found in many types of computer add-in boards, as well as on motherboards. CPUs often have an internal section of ROM as well.

App
C

rotate   To move an object to any point in a 360-degree range.

ruler   A horizontal or vertical measuring device that can be displayed on the PowerPoint screen in Slide view to assist in positioning objects precisely on a slide.

S

saturation   When working with colors, indicates the purity of a color; lower values of saturation have more gray in them.

scaling   A method of reducing or enlarging an object by entering horizontal and vertical measurements, or a percentage increase or decrease.

ScanDisk   A program used to check for, diagnose, and repair damage on a hard disk. Part of your routine, hard disk maintenance (along with defragmenting your hard disk) should include a periodic run of ScanDisk to keep your hard disk in good repair. In its standard test, ScanDisk checks the files and folders on a disk for *logical errors*, and if you ask it to, automatically corrects any errors it finds. ScanDisk checks for *crosslinked files*, which occur when two or more files have data stored in the same *cluster* (a storage unit on a disk). The data in the cluster is likely to be correct for only one of the files, and may not be correct for any of them. ScanDisk also checks for *lost file fragments*, which are pieces of data that have become disassociated with their files.

scanned art   Any artwork that has been placed in a file in electronic format using a digital scanner.

screen fonts   Font files used to show type styles on the screen. These are different from the files used by Windows to print the fonts. The screen fonts must match the printer fonts in order for Windows to give an accurate screen portrayal of the final printed output.

screen resolution   The number of picture elements (or *pixels*) that can be displayed on the screen. Screen resolution is a function of the monitor and graphics card. Higher resolutions display more information at a smaller size, and also may slow screen performance. Screen resolution is expressed in the number of pixels across the screen by the number of pixels down the screen. Standard VGA has a resolution of 640 × 480, although most modern monitors can display 1024 × 768, and even higher (larger monitors can usually display a higher resolution than smaller ones).

screen saver   A varying pattern or graphic that appears on the screen when the mouse and keyboard have been idle for a user-definable period of time. Originally used to prevent a static background from being "burned into" the screen phosphors, this is rarely a problem with modern monitors. Many screen savers (including those that come with Windows

95) can be used with a password—you must enter the correct password to turn off the screen saver and return to the screen. However, someone could simply reboot the machine, so a screen saver password is not very sophisticated protection.

Scribble tool   A freeform drawing tool.

scroll arrow   Located at each end of a scroll bar, can be clicked to scroll up or down (vertical scroll bar) or left or right (horizontal scroll bar). Clicking the scroll arrow will move your window in that direction.

scroll bar   Allows you to select a value within a range, such as what part of a document to see, or what value to set the Red, Green, and Blue components of a color to.

scroll box   A small box located in the scroll bar that shows where the visible window is located in relation to the entire document, menu, or list. You can click and drag the scroll box to make other portions of the document, menu, or list visible.

select   To specify a section of text or graphics for initiating an action. To select also can mean to choose an option in a dialog box.

selection handles   Small, black boxes indicating that a graphic object has been selected. With some Windows applications, you can click and drag a selection handle to resize the selected object.

serif fonts   Serif fonts have projections (serifs) that extend the upper and lower strokes of the set's characters beyond their normal boundaries—for example, Courier. Sans-serif fonts do not have these projections; an example is Arial.

server   A centrally administered network computer, which contains resources that are shared with "client" machines on the network.

server application   In OLE terminology, an application that supplies an object (such as a drawing) to a client application (such as a word processing program) for inclusion in a complex document.

service bureau   A company that takes computer files and generates 35mm slides.

shading   Using a fill color in an object.

shadow   A perspective effect that makes it appear as though an object is casting a shadow; this adds depth to the object.

shareware   A method of distributing software, often including downloading the software from a BBS or The Microsoft Network. With shareware, you get to use the software before deciding to pay for it. By paying for the software and registering it, you usually receive a manual, perhaps the most up-to-date version (which may include additional functionality). Shareware versions of software often include intrusive reminders to register—the registered versions do not include these reminders.

shortcut A pointer to a file, document, or printer in Windows 95. A shortcut is represented by an icon in Explorer, on the desktop, or as an entry in the Start menu. Selecting the program shortcut icon or menu entry runs the program to which the shortcut "points." Selecting a document shortcut runs the application that created the document (provided the document type is associated with a program). Dragging and dropping a document onto a printer shortcut prints the document. Note that a shortcut does *not* create a copy of the program or document itself.

shortcut keys A keystroke or key combination that enables you to activate a command without having to enter a menu or click a button.

shortcut menu A pop-up menu that appears when you right-click an object for which a menu is appropriate. The shortcut menu displays only those options which make sense for the object you select and current conditions.

slide The term for the working desktop area in Slide view of PowerPoint, as well as for each page of output of a PowerPoint presentation.

slide show A term for a PowerPoint presentation.

Slide Sorter A view in PowerPoint that shows miniatures of all slides in a presentation.

Small Computer System Interface (SCSI) An ANSI standard bus design. SCSI host adapters are used to adapt an ISA, EISA, MCI, PCI, or VLB (VESA Local Bus) bus to a SCSI bus so that SCSI devices (such as disk drives, CD-ROMs, tape backups, and other devices) can be interfaced. A SCSI bus accommodates up to eight devices; however, the bus adapter is considered one device, thereby enabling seven usable devices to be interfaced to each SCSI adapter. SCSI devices are intelligent devices. SCSI disk drives have embedded controllers and interface to a SCSI bus adapter. A SCSI interface card is therefore a "bus adapter," not a "controller."

snap To control the location of objects on a PowerPoint slide by pulling them to an invisible measurement—for example, snapping them to a grid or the location of another object.

soft fonts Depending on your printing hardware, may be downloaded to your printer. Downloading fonts reduces the time taken by the printer to process printouts. Although downloading soft fonts is done only once (per session), benefits are realized through subsequent printing.

Soundblaster   An extremely popular family of sound boards, developed and marketed by Creative Labs. Because of the popularity and large marketshare of this product family, most sound boards advertise themselves as "Soundblaster-compatible," meaning that drivers provided in Windows, Windows 95, and programs such as games will work with these boards. However, some boards' compatibility is not perfect.

source document   In OLE, the document that contains the information you want to link into (to appear in) another document (the destination document).

splitting   A method of breaking up text on slides with too much information on them into a series of slides.

spool   A temporary holding area for the data you want to print. When printing a document, it can take some time (depending on the length of the document and the speed of your printer) for the document to come off your printer. By spooling the data, you may continue using your computer while the document is printing, because the computer "feeds" the spool contents to the printer as fast as the printer can handle it. When the print job is completed, the spool file is automatically deleted.

Start menu   A menu located at the left end of the taskbar. Clicking the button marked "Start" opens a pop-up menu that makes Help, the Run command, settings, find, shutdown, a list of programs (actually, program shortcuts), and a list of recently accessed documents available for you to run with a single click. For some items (such as the Documents item), a submenu opens to the side of the main item to display the list of choices. You can configure the Start menu to specify which programs are available to run from it.

Startup folder   A folder that contains any programs that you want Windows 95 to run whenever you start up. You can drag and drop program shortcuts into the Startup folder to add them to the list of programs to run.

static object   In OLE, where some objects have a "hot link" to their original application, static objects are simply pasted into a destination document using the Clipboard. These objects are not updated if the original object is updated. This is the simple "pasting" that most Windows users use on a daily basis.

stroke font   A font that can have its size greatly altered without distortion.

Style Checker   A feature of PowerPoint that checks for consistency in grammar and style in the text of slides.

submenu   A related set of options that appear when you select a menu item (see *cascading menu*).

subtitle   A secondary heading on a slide.

App
C

summary slide   A slide that can be automatically generated containing the title text from each slide in a PowerPoint presentation.

system disk   The disk containing the operating system, or at least enough of it to start the system and then look on another disk for the support files.

system fonts   Used by Windows to draw menus and controls, and operate specialized control text in Windows. System fonts are proportional fonts that can be sized and manipulated quickly.

T

tab (dialog boxes)   In dialog boxes, there may be multiple panels of information. Each panel has an extension at the top that names the panel. This small extension is called a *tab*.

TAPI   Telephony Applications Programming Interface; provides a method for programs to work with modems, independent of dealing directly with the modem hardware. All the information you give Windows during the modem configuration is used for TAPI to set up its interface. Communications programs that are written specifically for Windows 95 will talk to TAPI, which will then issue appropriate commands to the modem. This is called *device independence.*

task list   A list of currently running applications. You can switch tasks by clicking an item in the task list. The task list is accessed by pressing Alt+Tab on the keyboard.

taskbar   An area that runs across the bottom of the Windows 95 desktop. The Start button (see *Start menu*) is at the left end of the taskbar, and the clock can be displayed at the right end of the taskbar. Running applications are represented as buttons on the taskbar, the current window is shown as a depressed button, and all other applications are displayed as raised buttons. Clicking the button for an inactive application activates that application and displays its window as the current window.

template   A file containing certain graphic elements, text, or formatting styles that can be applied to any document.

text-based   See *character-based.*

text box   A drawing object that allows you to enter text within it.

text file   A file containing only text characters.

text object An object consisting of letters and numbers, as opposed to graphic elements.

textured background A background design that emulates a texture such as wood or marble.

thumbnail A miniature rendition of a graphic file. A thumbnail gives an idea of what the full-size graphic looks like, and is usually used as a gateway to view the full-size graphic.

TIFF Tagged Image File Format.

tile To reduce and move windows so that they can all be seen at once.

time-out A time period after which a device or driver might signal the operating system and cease trying to perform its duty. If a printer is turned off, for example, when you try to print, the driver waits for a predetermined period of time, then issues an error message. In computer terminology, the driver has *timed out*.

timing The automatic settings applied to an on-screen slide show that control how long each slide is displayed.

title bar The bar at the top of a program or document window that shows you what its title is. The control menu, maximize, minimize, restore, and taskbar buttons can be accessed in the title bar.

toolbar A collection of buttons that typically make the more common tools for an application easily accessible. Although often grouped in a line under the menus, a toolbar can be located on the left or right side of the working area—or even be relocated to any area of the screen the user wants. In some applications (for example, MS Office applications such as Word), the toolbar is user-configurable—the user can display different toolbars, and add or remove tool buttons from the bar.

transition The change from one slide to another in a slide show; transition effects can make the new slide appear to fly in from the side of the screen or rain down from the top of the screen, for example.

transparency A clear film printed with images and text and used with an overhead projector to display a presentation.

transparent background A background effect that allows any objects behind the transparent object to show through.

TrueType fonts A font technology developed by Microsoft in response to Adobe's success in the scalable font business with its own Type 1 and Type 3 PostScript fonts. Used as a simple means for all Windows applications to have access to a wide selection of fonts for screen and printer output. TrueType fonts greatly simplify using fonts on a Windows

App
C

computer. The same fonts can be used on Windows 3.1, Windows NT, Windows 95, and other Windows products, such as Windows for Workgroups. Consisting of two files (one for screen and one for printer), hundreds of TrueType fonts are available from a variety of manufacturers. Depending on your printer, the TrueType font manager internal to Windows, in conjunction with the printer driver, generates either bitmapped or downloadable soft fonts.

U

ungrouping   The act of disassociating objects which have been grouped together to function as a single object.

unimodem driver   A universal modem driver supplied by Microsoft as part of Windows 95. The modem driver assumes that the modem supports the Hayes AT command set (most do).

uninstalling applications   When you install an application in Windows 95, places the necessary files in many different places on your hard drive. You can't remove all of a program by simply erasing the contents of its main subdirectory. To uninstall the application—and remove all the files it placed on your hard drive—you must run a special program that should have been included with the application. Many applications do not include the uninstaller program; although, to be certified under Windows 95, the uninstaller program must be included.

unprintable area   The area, usually around the extreme edges of the paper, in which the printer is incapable of printing. For example, a laser printer cannot print in the 1/4 inch at the left and right edges of the paper. It is important to know the unprintable area, since graphics or text you place in this area will be cut off when printed.

upload   The act of sending a file to a remote computer (see *download*).

URL   Uniform Resource Locator; a string that identifies a specific location on the Internet.

V

ValuPack   A set of multimedia files and applications that come with Microsoft Office programs and can be run from the program CD.

vector fonts   A set of lines that connect points to form characters.

vertical alignment   The relative measurement of an object from elements above and beneath it.

video clip   A file containing a video sequence.

video for windows   A set of utilities and protocols for implementing full-motion video in Windows 95.

view   Different displays in PowerPoint that allow you to see the information in your presentation from different perspectives and use different tools and menu commands.

virtual memory   The use of permanent media (for example, a hard drive) to simulate additional RAM. This allows large applications to run in less physical RAM than they normally would require. When RAM runs low, the operating system uses a virtual memory manager program to temporarily store data on the hard disk like it was in RAM, which makes RAM free for data manipulation. When needed, the data is read back from the disk and reloaded into RAM.

virus   A computer program written to interrupt or destroy your work. A virus may do something as innocuous as display a message, or something as destructive as reformatting your hard drive—or almost anything in between. Your computer can *catch* a virus from a floppy disk, or even from a file downloaded from a remote source, such as a BBS. Once your computer has become *infected*, the virus may spread via connections on a network or floppy disks you share with others. A variety of virus-detecting software exists, (including one packaged with Windows 95).

volume   Disk partition(s) formatted and available for use by the operating system.

volume label   The identifier for a volume (see *volume*) or disk. This is specified when formatting the volume or disk.

App
C

W

wallpaper   A backdrop for the Windows desktop, made up of a graphics files. The graphics can be either *centered*, appearing only once in the center of the desktop, or *tiled*, repeating as many times as the graphic will fit.

WAV files   Named for the three-character extension WAV (for sound wave), a file containing a digitized sound. Depending on the sampling rate and resolution, the sound recorded in the WAV file seems realistic (provided you have the sound card and speakers to hear it). These files can be quite large, running into the multi-megabyte range for high-quality recordings.

Web browser   A software program that enables you to view home pages and retrieve information from the Internet.

wizard   Microsoft's name for a step-by-step set of instructions that guide you through a particular task. For example, there are many wizards included with Windows 95 for installing new hardware, configuring the Start menu, and changing other aspects of the environment.

word wrap   In word processing, this refers to words that cannot be completed on one line automatically "wrapping" to the beginning of the next line. Most word processors use word wrap automatically—an exception is Notepad, where you must turn on word wrap.

WordArt   An applet that comes with PowerPoint which allows you to create text enhancement effects.

WordPad   A program included with Windows 95 that enables you to do basic word processing and save the results in plain text format, Word 6 format, or rich text format.

workgroup   A collection of networked PCs grouped to facilitate work that users of the computers tend to do together. The machines are not necessarily in the same room or office.

World Wide Web   The fastest growing part of the Internet, the Web or WWW is a collection of hypertext documents. It provides access to images and sounds from thousands of different Web sites, via a special programming language called HyperText Markup Language, or HTML. This language is used to create "hypertext" documents, which include embedded commands.

WYSIWYG   Short for "What you see is what you get," this term refers to the ability of an application to display an accurate representation of the printed output on the screen.

X

x coordinate   The position of an item relative to the left side of the screen. Values increase as you move to the right.

Xmodem   An error-correction protocol (see *binary transfer protocol*) used by the DOS application XMODEM and many other communications programs. Xmodem uses CRC (cyclical redundancy check), a means of detecting errors in transmissions between modems or across wired serial links.

Y

y coordinate   The position of an item relative to the bottom of the screen. Values increase as you move down the screen.

Ymodem   Another form of Xmodem that allows batch transfers of files and (in Ymodem G) hardware error control.

Z

Zmodem   A fully functional streaming protocol where Xmodem is a send and acknowledge protocol that causes delays in the transfer equal to twice the modem lag on a connection. Zmodem is the preferred way of exchanging data because it is reliable, quick, and relatively easy to implement.

zooming   A feature used to change the size of the display on your screen by percentages.

Index

Check out Que® Books on the World Wide Web
http://www.quecorp.com

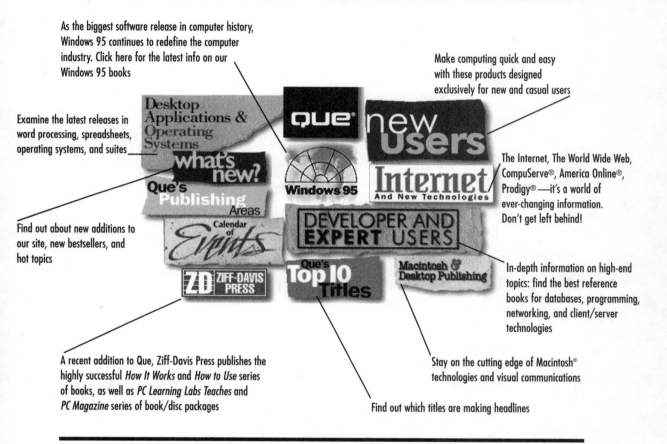

As the biggest software release in computer history, Windows 95 continues to redefine the computer industry. Click here for the latest info on our Windows 95 books

Make computing quick and easy with these products designed exclusively for new and casual users

Examine the latest releases in word processing, spreadsheets, operating systems, and suites

The Internet, The World Wide Web, CompuServe®, America Online®, Prodigy® —it's a world of ever-changing information. Don't get left behind!

Find out about new additions to our site, new bestsellers, and hot topics

In-depth information on high-end topics: find the best reference books for databases, programming, networking, and client/server technologies

A recent addition to Que, Ziff-Davis Press publishes the highly successful *How It Works* and *How to Use* series of books, as well as *PC Learning Labs Teaches* and *PC Magazine* series of book/disc packages

Stay on the cutting edge of Macintosh® technologies and visual communications

Find out which titles are making headlines

With six separate publishing groups, Que develops products for many specific market segments and areas of computer technology. Explore our Web site and you'll find information on best-selling titles, newly published titles, upcoming products, authors, and much more.

- Stay informed on the latest industry trends and products available
- Visit our online bookstore for the latest information and editions
- Download software from Que's library of the best shareware and freeware

Complete and Return This Card for a *FREE* Computer Book Catalog

Thank you for purchasing this book! You have purchased a superior computer book written expressly for your needs. To continue to provide the kind of up-to-date, pertinent coverage you've come to expect from us, we need to hear from you. Please take a minute to complete and return this self-addressed, postage-paid form. In return, we'll send you a free catalog of all our computer books on topics ranging from word processing to programming and the Internet.

Mr. ☐   Mrs. ☐   Ms. ☐   Dr. ☐

Name (first) [ ] (M.I.) ☐   (last) [ ]

Address [ ]
[ ]

City [ ]   State [ ]   Zip [ ] [ ]

Phone [ ] [ ]   Fax [ ] [ ]

Company Name [ ]

E-mail address [ ]

1. Please check at least three (3) influencing factors for purchasing this book.

Front or back cover information on book .... ☐
Special approach to the content .... ☐
Completeness of content .... ☐
Author's reputation .... ☐
Publisher's reputation .... ☐
Book cover design or layout .... ☐
Index or table of contents of book .... ☐
Price of book .... ☐
Special effects, graphics, illustrations .... ☐
Other (Please specify): _____ ☐

2. How did you first learn about this book?

Saw in Macmillan Computer Publishing catalog .... ☐
Recommended by store personnel .... ☐
Saw the book on bookshelf at store .... ☐
Recommended by a friend .... ☐
Received advertisement in the mail .... ☐
Saw an advertisement in: _____ ☐
Read book review in: _____ ☐
Other (Please specify): _____ ☐

3. How many computer books have you purchased in the last six months?

This book only .... ☐   3 to 5 books .... ☐
2 books .... ☐   More than 5 .... ☐

4. Where did you purchase this book?

Bookstore .... ☐
Computer Store .... ☐
Consumer Electronics Store .... ☐
Department Store .... ☐
Office Club .... ☐
Warehouse Club .... ☐
Mail Order .... ☐
Direct from Publisher .... ☐
Internet site .... ☐
Other (Please specify): _____ ☐

5. How long have you been using a computer?

☐ Less than 6 months   ☐ 6 months to a year
☐ 1 to 3 years   ☐ More than 3 years

6. What is your level of experience with personal computers and with the subject of this book?

	With PCs	With subject of book
New	☐	☐
Casual	☐	☐
Accomplished	☐	☐
Expert	☐	☐

Source Code ISBN: 0-7897-1438-8

7. Which of the following best describes your job title?

Administrative Assistant .... ☐
Coordinator .... ☐
Manager/Supervisor .... ☐
Director .... ☐
Vice President .... ☐
President/CEO/COO .... ☐
Lawyer/Doctor/Medical Professional .... ☐
Teacher/Educator/Trainer .... ☐
Engineer/Technician .... ☐
Consultant .... ☐
Not employed/Student/Retired .... ☐
Other (Please specify): _____ ☐

8. Which of the following best describes the area of the company your job title falls under?

Accounting .... ☐
Engineering .... ☐
Manufacturing .... ☐
Operations .... ☐
Marketing .... ☐
Sales .... ☐
Other (Please specify): _____ ☐

9. What is your age?

Under 20 .... ☐
21-29 .... ☐
30-39 .... ☐
40-49 .... ☐
50-59 .... ☐
60-over .... ☐

10. Are you:

Male .... ☐
Female .... ☐

11. Which computer publications do you read regularly? (Please list)

_____
_____
_____
_____
_____
_____
_____
_____
_____

Comments: _____
_____
_____

Fold here and scotch-tape to mail